Re-Imagining
Imprisonment in Europe

JCFJ jesuit centre
for faith & justice

About the Jesuit Centre for Faith and Justice

The Jesuit Centre for Faith and Justice was established in 1978 to promote social justice by fostering an understanding of public issues through social analysis, theological reflection and advocacy. A registered charity and an agency of the Irish Jesuit Province, it aims to influence government policy and practice and to raise awareness of difficult social issues. At the heart of the Centre's work is the belief that every human being deserves dignity and respect.

The Jesuit Centre for Faith and Justice conducts independent analysis and research in such areas as penal policy, housing and homelessness, health policy, environmental justice and economic development. Its journal, *Working Notes*, published three times a year, contains analysis of social and economic issues and their impact on society. Other publications include *The Irish Housing System: Vision, Values, Reality* (2010) and *The Irish Prison System: Vision, Values, Reality* (2012). In September 2012 the Centre hosted the international conference 'Re-imagining Imprisonment in Europe: Common Challenges, Diverse Policies and Practice'.

For further information on the Centre and its work please go to www.jcfj.ie.

Re-Imagining Imprisonment in Europe

Effects, Failures and the Future

Edited by

Eoin Carroll and Kevin Warner

The Liffey Press

Published by
The Liffey Press Ltd
Raheny Shopping Centre, Second Floor
Raheny, Dublin 5, Ireland
www.theliffeypress.com

A catalogue record of this book is
available from the British Library.

ISBN 978-1-908308-56-6

Printed in Spain by GraphyCems.

Contents

Acknowledgements

The publication of this book has been made possible by funding and support from the Jesuit Scribani Network and the Jesuit Centre for Faith and Justice. The chapters of this publication stem from the conference 'Re-imagining Imprisonment in Europe: Common Challenges Diverse Policies and Practice', hosted by the Jesuit Centre for Faith and Justice in Trinity College Dublin, September 5–7, 2012.

The Jesuit Centre for Faith and Justice is grateful to Dr Kevin Warner and Eoin Carroll for editing this book.

The views expressed in this book are those of the authors and do not necessarily reflect the views of either the Scribani Network or the Jesuit Centre for Faith and Justice.

The editors wish to acknowledge the dedicated efforts and co-operation of the many authors who have contributed to the book.

The editors would also like to thank David Givens, Publisher of The Liffey Press, for his practical and calm approach to producing this book, and Barbara Segaert, co-ordinator of the Scribani Network.

Finally, the editors are very grateful to Lena Jacobs for her patient and good humoured assistance with all things bibliographical.

About the Contributors

Aline Bauwens, PhD, is a lecturer in the Department of Criminology at Vrije Universiteit Brussel. Her particular areas of interest are reintegration, reintegration models, offender supervision and comparative penology. She is currently undertaking an analysis of one-to-one offender supervision meetings in the probation service of Belgium.

Hugh Campbell is a senior lecturer in restorative practices at the University of Ulster. He has been heavily involved in developing the University's undergraduate and postgraduate programmes in restorative practices. This has included work with key statutory and voluntary agencies in Northern Ireland. Currently he is working with the Northern Ireland Prison Service to establish a university award in Custody Prison Officer Practice. Along with colleagues, he is also working on two European research projects, one into multi-cultural conflicts and the other into the role of the judiciary in developing restorative justice.

Eoin Carroll, MSc (LSE), is co-ordinator of social policy and communications in the Jesuit Centre for Faith and Justice. He was Conference Director of 'Re-imagining Imprisonment in Europe: Common Challenges, Diverse Policies and Practice', the papers of which form this book. He has a broad area of interest including: prisons, housing need and understanding the process behind governments' development of policy. In 2013 he led an in-house research team's investigation: *Making Progress?: Examining the first year of the Irish Prison Service's Three Year Strategic Plan 2012 – 2015.*

Tim Chapman, LLB, CQSW, MSc, lecturers in restorative practices at the University of Ulster. He teaches on the Masters of Restorative Practices and conducts research in this subject. Chapman is author of '"That's how the light gets in": Facilitating restorative conferences' and co-author (with Zinsstag, E.) of 'Conferencing: European perspective' (2012) in Zinsstag, E. and Vanfraechem, I. (eds.) *Conferencing and Restorative Justice* (Oxford: Oxford University Press).

Jean Corston, Rt Hon. Baroness, is a member of the British House of Lords. From 1992 to 2005 she was a Member of Parliament for Bristol East when she was appointed chair of the Parliamentary Labour Party. She is a leading advocacy for the needs of women in prison and author of *The Corston Report: A Review of Women with Particular Vulnerabilities in the Criminal Justice System* (2007).

Anne Costelloe, PhD, has worked as an educator in Mountjoy Prison for over 20 years. She is the Editor of the Practitioner Section of the *Journal of Prison Education and Re-entry*, and a former Chairperson of the European Prison Education Association. Costelloe has published widely on prisoner education and contributed to the European Commission reports *Prison education and training in Europe – a review and commentary of existing literature, analysis and evaluation* (2011) and *Survey on prison education and training in Europe – Final Report* (2012).

Andrew Coyle, CMG, PhD, is Emeritus Professor of Prison Studies at the University of London and Visiting Professor in the Human Rights Centre, University of Essex. He was founding Director of the International Centre for Prison Studies and is a Fellow of King's College London. Coyle worked for 25 years at senior level in the United Kingdom prison services. He is a prisons adviser to the United Nations and the Council of Europe. Coyle was a principal drafter of the *European Prison Rules* (2006) and also drafted the *Council of Europe Code of Ethics for Prison Staff* (2012).

Jonathan Cummins, BA, MFA, is a filmmaker, and lecturer in the Belfast School of Art and Design, University of Ulster. He worked with the National College of Art and Design Prison Art Programme for many years. His particular interest is in who gets to speak in society, who is heard, who listens and where such conversations might take place. His films have explored themes such as the impact of prison on prisoners, their families and society.

Manuela P. da Cunha, PhD, is a senior researcher in the CRIA, Portugal, which is a centre for research in anthropology. Her areas of study are prisons and imprisonment, penal and social management of vulnerability, drug markets, and intersections of gender, crime and ethnicity. She has a forthcoming publication, 'The ethnography of prisons and penal confinement', *Annual Review of Anthropology*, Vol. 43.

Rafaela Granja is studying for a PhD and is a researcher in the Institute of Social Science in the University of Minho, Portugal. Her areas of interest include the study of prison, sociology of family and gender and parenting studies. She has a forthcoming article (co-written with Cunha, M. I. and Machado, H.), 'Mothering from prison and ideologies of intensive parenting: Enacting vulnerable resistance', *Journal of Family Issues*.

Tapio Lappi-Seppälä, PhD, is Director of the Finnish National Research Institute of Legal Policy. He has contributed to the development of criminal justice policy with the Scandinavian Research Council for Criminology, the Council of Europe and the International Penal and Penitentiary Foundation. His research interests are in criminology, comparative penal policy, sentencing and the system of sanctions. He contributed the chapter 'Imprisonment and Penal demands: Exploring the dimensions and drivers of systemic and attitudinal punitivity' in: Body-Gendrot, S., Hough, M., Kerezsi, K., Lévy, R. and Snacken, S. (eds.) *The Routledge Handbook of European Criminology* (2013).

Juliet Lyon, CBE, MA, is Director of Prison Reform Trust (PRT). PRT is an independent United Kingdom charity working to create a just, humane and effective penal system. PRT does this by inquiring into the workings of the political and criminal justice system; informing prisoners, staff and the wider public; and by influencing Parliament, government and officials towards reform. Among the various PRT publications are the 'Bromley Briefings Prison Factfiles' which provide detailed facts and figures on imprisonment in the United Kingdom.

Helena Machado, PhD, is FCT Investigator in the Centre for Social Studies, University of Coimbra and Associate Professor, Institute for Social Science, University of Minho, Portugal. Her area of interest is exploring the intersections between science, technology and the justice system with a focus on the societal, regulatory and ethical impacts in using DNA in criminal investigations as well as the use of forensic genetics in governance, social control and risk management. A recent publication which she co-wrote (with Prainsack, B.) is *Tracing Technologies: Prisoners' Views in the Era of CSI* (2012) (Surrey: Ashgate).

Rudy Machiels, PhD, is a researcher in the Department of Criminology at Vrije Universiteit Brussel. His areas of interest include ex-prisoners, prisoners, re-integration, narrative identity work, positioning and figured worlds. He is currently working on: '*Silence, We Are Filming!': Competing Discourses in a Prison Art Figured World*.

Shadd Maruna, PhD, is a professor and the Director of the Institute of Criminology and Criminal Justice, School of Law, Queen's University Belfast. Currently his primary area of research is on desistance from crime and offender rehabilitation policy. He has received a number of awards including the inaugural Howard League Research Medal in 2011. A recent book by him (co-edited with Hayward, K. and Mooney, J.) is *Fifty Key Thinkers in Criminology* (New York: Routledge).

Peter McVerry, SJ, is a Jesuit priest, a team member of the Jesuit Centre for Faith and Justice and a Director of the Peter McVerry Trust. He was given the Freedom of the City of Dublin in 2014 for his work in challenging injustice in society. In 1979 he opened a hostel for young people who were homeless, and has since opened twelve more hostels, three drug treatment centres and ninety apartments. He is a prolific writer and vocal campaigner on social issues in the national media, at public presentations as well as in books and articles.

Bronwyn Naylor, LLM, PhD, is an associate professor in the Faculty of Law, Monash University, Melbourne, Australia. Her primary areas of research and teaching are criminal law and criminal justice. Previously she was on the Law Reform Commission of Victoria and practiced as a solicitor. She has a forthcoming publication (co-edited with Debeljak, J. and MacKay, A.), *Law in Context: Special Issue - Implementing Human Rights in Closed Environments (2014).*

Mike Nellis, PhD (Cantab), is Emeritus Professor of Criminal and Community Justice in the School of Law, University of Strathclyde. He was formerly a social worker with young offenders in London and Kent and also involved in training probation officers at the University of Birmingham. He is a Quaker, with long-standing interests in penal reform and surveillance. He has written widely on the probation service, alternatives to imprisonment and particularly the electronic monitoring of offenders. His most recent book (co-edited by Beyens, K. and Kaminski, D.) is *Electronically Monitored Punishment: International and Critical Perspectives* (2012) (London: Routledge).

Aislinn O'Donnell, MA, PhD, is a lecturer in Philosophy of Education at Mary Immaculate College (University of Limerick). Over the last ten years she has developed a series of pedagogical projects which draw upon both philosophy and contemporary art practices. These take place in a variety of settings from the primary school to the prison. She has two forthcoming publications, *A Review of NCAD's Art Programme in Portlaoise Prison*, and (co-written with Tyson, S. and Hall, J.) *Cartesian Meditations? Voice, body, mind and the prison. Philosophy Imprisoned* (Lexington Books).

Dragan Petrovec, LLD, is Professor and Research Counsellor at the Institute of Criminology at the Faculty of Law Ljubljana, Slovenia. He previously worked in the Ministry of Justice as Warden of the only women's prison. His primary areas of study are penology and criminology. He has written extensively on the Slovenian prison system.

Mojca M. Plesničar, LLD, is an assistant professor and Research Fellow at the Institute of Criminology at the Faculty of Law Ljubljana, Slovenia. The Institute is the oldest institution in Europe dedicated to research in the fields of criminology, criminal justice and criminal law. Her areas of teaching and research are in the fields of sentencing, punishment, criminology and criminal law.

Patrick Riordan, SJ, PhD, is a lecturer in Philosophy at Heythrop College, University of London. His primary areas of research and teaching are political philosophy and social ethics. He has a forthcoming book, *Global Ethics and Global Common Goods* (Bloomsbury).

Kevin Warner, PhD, was Co-ordinator of Education in the Irish prison system for nearly 30 years until 2009. He chaired the Select Committee that formulated the Council of Europe recommendations on education in prison (1990). He was a Fulbright Scholar at California State University San Bernardino in 1995, and in 2009 received a PhD for research into penal policy in Nordic countries. He is now an adjunct lecturer in the School of Applied Social Science at University College Dublin and a board member of the Irish Penal Reform Trust.

Foreword

This book is an important contribution to how prison can be re-imagined. It is a collection of reflective, comprehensive and objective analyses of imprisonment throughout Europe and will appeal to the academic and novice reader in exploring contemporary issues.

Reading this book, many of us who advocate or support reform will be struck by accounts of how difficult it is to bring about meaningful change in penal systems, and to sustain progress. For me, this is one of the most consistent messages emanating from this collection and it confirms my own experience during my years working in the Irish Prison Service. It was all too often a case of one step forward, two steps back.

Even initiatives that proved to be effective and successful were often dogged by frustration. Baroness Jean Corston, author of 'The Corston Report' on the imprisonment of women in England and Wales, who is a contributor to the book, summarised her experiences as follows:

> I would like to report that the modest progress I have described has been maintained, but it is not the case. Some of the good progress in implementing recommendations has been lost.... The concept of a Champion [for women in prison] and clear leadership on the agenda have been 'lost' and the infrastructures put in place to secure the integrated approach across government for women offenders and those at risk of offending ... have now been dismantled.

She continues:

> Furthermore, there is now no written, joined-up, cross-government strategy to reduce the numbers of women in custody, and no reporting to Parliament, so it is difficult to see how momentum on progress can be maintained and evidenced.

Unfortunately, such experience is not confined to Britain. In his contribution, Andrew Coyle highlights a number of European countries where much good progress was made in the 1990s, with the result that the numbers in prison dropped significantly. He cites the Polish and the Czech systems in particular. However, in both countries the numbers in prison have dramatically increased over the past decade, almost doubling in the case of the Czech Republic. Andrew attributes this regression to the fact that both countries have adopted the Western European model of 'managing offenders'.

The Slovenia experience, as written about by Dragan Petrovec and Mojca Plesničar, shows that since the country gained its independence in 1991 the rate of imprisonment has greatly increased, having had a much lower rate when it was part of Yugoslavia. Once again, the root cause of this backward step seems to be Western European influence. Dragan and Mojca state:

> Basic criminological and sociological truths keep being ignored by establishments across the world, such as groundbreaking research on equality and its detrimental impact on society.... The clear links between poverty and our reactions to crime seem irrelevant, what works is not even the important question anymore; it is what looks good and what seems to appeal to the public that gets ahead.

All in all, then, a very depressing picture from a reformist perspective.

Consequently, many of the most progressive reforms achieved over decades have been lost or seriously scaled down and prisons in most Western European countries have become more and more places of secure containment. Retrograde change has occurred without any strong public or political reaction. An example of this here in Ireland is the increased reliance by the Irish Prison Service on 'doubling up' in its response to accommodating people in prisons. Single cell occupancy was established and became sacrosanct in England and Ireland as far back as the early nineteenth century. This principle was in place when Mountjoy Prison was opened in Dublin in 1850. However, over the past 30 years or so, this basic principle has been abandoned. Nowadays, not alone are hundreds of prisoners forced to share single cells but all new cell blocks and new prisons are designed to facilitate 'doubling up'. 'Doubling up' is now being physically structured into the Irish prison system with the inevitable result that it will be in use in Ireland for the foreseeable future. In my opinion, single cell occupancy is a very basic human right and is without doubt the most pressing issue facing prison reform activists and campaigners.

The current political position is that single cell occupancy is the 'ideal' but in the meantime, and mainly due to the economic recession, standards have to be lowered. Irish society in general, most of the media and many statutory and human rights organisations seem to accept this argument and very little opposition has been raised against what should be regarded as a totally unacceptable development. A few honourable exceptions are the Irish Penal Reform Trust and The Jesuit Centre for Faith and Justice, along with a small number of individuals who have voiced their concerns.

It is not possible here to deal adequately with the many problems and potential dangers that 'doubling up' causes. Suffice to say that bullying, sexual and physical abuse along with drug misuse are all facilitated in such an environment. In the days of single occupancy, the dangers of sexual abuse were greatly reduced. Likewise with bullying, which is widespread in most prison systems. Bullying in prisons is very difficult to eradicate, mainly due to the culture where reporting a fellow prisoner is seriously frowned upon amongst prisoners. 'Doubling up' certainly facilitates bullying and vulnerable prisoners are soft targets. Illegal drug misuse is also facilitated by cell-sharing.

In addition to the physical dangers, there are also psychological and mental health issues connected with 'doubling up'. A prisoner sharing a cell will never have the opportunity to be alone, to have his/her own space or to have a moment of privacy, and many prisoners are terrified of sharing a cell with an unknown individual. In too many cases this fear is well grounded. This causes stress, depression and anxiety. The whole issue of 'doubling up' and its negative consequences for prisoners must be the number one priority for all individuals, groups and human rights activists who support and campaign for prison reform.

Another issue that requires close monitoring is the construction of additional cell blocks and other buildings in the open spaces within secure prisons. Today, Mountjoy Prison has been described as a 'concrete jungle', with every square inch of open space built on. For example, in 1975 the Training Unit was built on an open space at the canal end of the prison. In the early 1990s, the Medical Care Unit was built in the outdoor exercise yard at the back of the D wing, removing the last open space. The end product was a mass of buildings all cramped on top of each other with no open space.

Over the years, all the other large prisons in Ireland have suffered the same fate as Mountjoy. Wheatfield/Cloverhill, which had a large amount of open space deliberately designed in the original plans, has little now as a result of new cell blocks and other facilities being built. The very same thing has happened in the Midlands/Portlaoise Prison complex, with the result that the whole site is dominated by concrete buildings with very little open space. The outdoor exercise yards are tiny and very claustrophobic. With so little open space, all our main prisons are consequently very bland environments. By contrast, the Dóchas Centre is evidence that, with a bit of innovation and creativity, a very restricted site can be developed to create a bright, open, very normal and positive environment for women in prison, while at the same time meeting all security requirements.

One final observation on prison buildings. Approximately 80 per cent of our male prisoner population is made up of people serving sentences of two years or less, yet all new cell blocks are designed and operated to provide the upper scale of security. There seems to be a 'one size fits all' approach. However, most of these prisoners do not require such levels of security, and could, for example, be accommodated in open centres. Incidentally, in Ireland only 5 per cent of our prison population is located in an open prison, this should be greatly increased and I believe that a reasonable target would be 20 per cent. Open centres are much cheaper to operate, they provide prisoners with a far more normal and positive living environment, they are less likely to cause institutionalisation and prisoners are more likely to engage in education and training programmes. Finally, relationships between staff and prisoners tend to be much more positive and engaging in open prisons.

I find two observations in the chapter by Juliet Lyon, Director of the Prison Reform Trust in Britain, to be very profound. She says:

> The punishment of imprisonment is the loss of liberty. It is not meant to be a loss of identity, or the loss of a future. Yet only a quarter of people leave prison with a job or any kind of training course to go to. Far too many are released homeless, jobless, isolated and in debt. It shouldn't surprise us that reconviction rates are so high – criminologists have written about this time and again.... Brodeur commented: 'Punishment is the one policy that is never discredited by its failure to achieve its stated objectives. If it fails to meet its goals, the only reason is that there is not enough of it.' The only response to punishment it seems is more punishment.

While I have never been a great advocate of punishment, I must admit that I never thought about it in this way – the more punishment fails, the more we increase it.

The other observation that Juliet makes is to quote a prison governor who was in charge of resettlement: 'Prisons should not be about turning out good prisoners, but about turning prisoners into good citizens.' My experience was that too many 'good prisoners' just played along with the system and never genuinely showed their true selves while in prison and seldom changed their behaviour after their release. Prison authorities and staff generally love 'good prisoners', but I agree with Juliet that prisons should be helping and supporting prisoners to become good citizens. This will require prisoners to be encouraged to be their real selves, warts and all.

Just recently, it appears that the male population in Irish prisons is showing signs of levelling off and perhaps even reducing. What is particularly encouraging is the significant reduction in the number of juveniles in custody. I believe that the main reason for this goes back to the introduction of the Children Act of 2001. This was a most progressive piece of legislation, putting huge emphasis on early intervention and family support. So, despite the fact that it has never been adequately resourced, the Children Act has contributed to ensuring that the detention of young people is nowadays very much a last resort.

Unfortunately, the decline in the male numbers is not replicated in the case of the female prison population. The number of women being committed to prison has increased sharply in recent years, with the result that 'doubling up' was introduced in the Dóchas Centre in 2009, ten years after it was opened. I have already highlighted the most damaging consequences of 'doubling up' and it is sad that this most backward step has now contaminated the very positive and progressive regime of the Dóchas Centre. Again, a case of one step forward, two steps back. When the Dóchas Centre was opened in September 1999, it introduced the principle of single room occupancy for all women in prison in Mountjoy for the first time in many years. This element of the Dóchas regime was regarded by the women as the most positive feature of the Centre. Alas, due entirely to overcrowding, it is no longer possible for the authorities at the Dóchas Centre to provide single room occupancy for all the women in custody there. The big challenge for the criminal justice system is to stop this undesirable trend of more and more women being committed to prison. Again, I would urge people to read the Corston Report to get an insight into who are the women who end up in prison.

When focussing on 'Re-imagining Imprisonment', I believe it is crucial to look at the way the children of the imprisoned are treated when they visit their parents in prison. I have always felt that this is an area that has never really received the attention that it deserves. Over the years, beginning in Mountjoy Prison in the early 1990s, external visitors' facilities have been developed in Irish prisons and nowadays the visiting centres provide facilities for families and their children while they are awaiting their prison visit. In most centres child care professionals are available to care for the children. Unfortunately, once children enter the prison proper, by and large, they are treated exactly like adults with little or no special facilities or arrangements in place for them. It is very frightening and traumatic for any child to have to go through the security procedures that are in place in prisons. In addition to the physical searching, including requiring the parent or guardian to replace nappies on small babies, they are scared when sniffed by drug dogs. When they eventually arrive in the visiting box, there are no child-friendly facilities, in many prisons nothing but a big wooden bench to sit on. Physical contact is prohibited in most prisons with the result that children are never allowed to hug or even physically touch their parents. This does not apply in places like the open prisons or the Dóchas Centre. Any re-imagining of prison systems must focus on this aspect of prison and surely a much more humane, civilised and child-friendly approach is possible.

Prison systems can justify almost any restriction on visitors to prisons, including children, on the basis of security; indeed, some prisons are excessively burdened with security. But security should always be balanced against the principle of treating people with humanity. In the case of children this requires that special child and family friendly procedures and facilities must be put in place. For example, family visiting rooms with facilities for parents to have a cup of tea, safe carpeted floors, easy chairs and child care staff to supervise the children while the parents have quality time to talk would be a massive improvement. Such a facility was in place in Mountjoy a number of years ago for long term prisoners and the feedback from prisoners and their families was very positive. Prisoners serving long sentence or life imprisonment should be enabled to have quality time with their children. I believe that the searching regime applicable to small children must be changed in the best interest of children, but this is unlikely to happen unless there is a strong public campaign.

The whole point of 'Re-imagining Imprisonment' must be to offer an alternative life for those who commit crime. However, at the very heart of this approach must be the individual who has committed the crime. Whatever new approaches are put in place, no matter how progressive or revolutionary, they will require individuals to take responsibility for their actions and to be involved directly in planning their own futures. I fully accept that personal circumstances and local cultures play a huge role in the lives of most people who end up in prison, and I accept that many prisoners and their families are often more sinned against than sinful, but I also hold the view that ultimately it is down to the individual to decide his or her future. Supporting and encouraging the individual to accept full responsibility for their own lives into the future must be the starting point. I believe that, if the necessary supports were in place, many prisoners would opt to move away from crime and prisons. Actually, most do as they mature. The problem is that it takes years for many prisoners to realise this, and as a result they spend most of their late teen years and all of their twenties in prison before they grasp the fact that prison is a waste of time.

In conclusion, I quote again from Juliet Lyon:

> We will not solve the problems of imprisonment by looking within prisons. Solutions do not lie behind prison walls; instead they lie largely within communities, within housing, within education, within work, within families. If we are to re-imagine imprisonment, we must reintegrate prison back into communities. We must make prison smaller – smaller in our minds, and smaller in number and capacity.

John Lonergan
Former Governor of
Mountjoy Prison, Dublin
April 2014

Introduction

Kevin Warner and Eoin Carroll

Today there are over 1.68 million people in prisons within the
47 countries of the Council of Europe (Walmsley, 2013). While
there have been considerable variations in penal policy and practice across European countries (Snacken and Dormortier, 2012;
Ugelvik and Dullum, 2012) including a reduction in the prison
populations in Russia and former Soviet Union states (Wamsley,
1999, 2013), there has been a significant tendency in other places
towards greater use of imprisonment and longer sentences. Yet
these trends do not reflect increasing crime levels (Coyle, 2006).
Coyle, as General Rapporteur of a conference of European direc-
tors of prison administration, noted that 'the most immediate consequence of the increasing use of imprisonment has been significant levels of overcrowding in many countries' (2006: 21), which
affects the health of prisoners in particular.

Certainly in English-speaking societies, and in varying degrees
in some other European countries, there has been a steep rise in
punitiveness in recent decades (Garland, 2001; Pratt et al., 2005).
While there has been criticism (see Matthews, 2005) in defining
punitiveness on a state's propensity to imprison, imprisonment
is the most severe punishment that the majority of countries can
impose. Others have broadened the punitive debate by including
other forms of confinement in the gambit of social control (see

O'Sullivan and O'Donnell, 2012). This book places a lense over our European prison landscape. Where it has occurred, growth in punitiveness can be seen most dramatically in three critical and inter-related developments in prison systems: (i) a rise in the number of people incarcerated; (ii) a worsening in prison conditions and in the way men and women held in prison are treated – in other words, a worsening in the *depth* of imprisonment; (iii) more negative stereotyping of those held in prison, whereby they are represented and perceived more as demonised *others*, and less as 'valued members of society'.[1]

The chapters[2] that follow all address one or more of these three punitive features, either by tracing such developments or explaining how they can be changed. The overall message of the book is that we can re-imagine imprisonment as a measure to be used far less and genuinely 'as a measure of last resort'; that where it is used, it should be in a far more humane and constructive way; and, that we can re-imagine also those people who fall foul of the law, recognising them as fellow members of our society, and seeing them more holistically and humanely.

At the root of the plea that prison be used 'as a last resort' is the recognition that, given the way it damages people, it is not a particularly sensible way of addressing many of society's problems. As Andrew Coyle (Chapter 1) says, quoting Vaclav Havel, we need 'a better way of coming to terms with certain things'. Coyle looks to the day when 'other disposals' will be the norm and prison the rare 'alternative'. He also envisages a different kind of prison: smaller, with strong links to the local community and where prisoners in-

---

[1] For example, in Ireland, a policy document issued by the Department of Justice in 1994 referred to prisoners as 'valued members of society'. Later policy statements suggested prisoners could only aspire to be 'valued members of society' (see Warner, 2011).

[2] The chapters of this book developed from the Scribani Conference 'Re-imagining Imprisonment in Europe: Common Challenges Diverse Policies and Practice' organised by the Jesuit Centre for Faith and Justice in Trinity College Dublin, September 5–7, 2012.

teract with that community and prepare for release. Juliet Lyon (Chapter 2) also, in examining the escalation of imprisonment in England and Wales, criticises 'needless imprisonment', and likewise argues that imprisonment should be 'at the far end of any justice system as a punishment of absolute last resort'. She points out that 'custody throws a long shadow', stigmatising the person long after a sentence is finished. She asks: 'at what point are they no longer a former prisoner? At what point do they lose that identity?'

Lyon says: 'At the heart of prison reform lies the recognition that people behind bars are still people'. The sense that 'prisoners are people' pervades Peter McVerry's contribution too (Chapter 3). He notes that the prison system in Ireland is 'an enormous waste of money', and argues that, instead, resources be put into restorative justice.

Tapio Lappi-Seppälä (Chapter 4) describes how – in contrast to trends in Britain, Ireland and elsewhere – Finland has shown how a country can radically reduce its prison population by means of 'a conscious, long-term and systematic criminal policy'. What is striking is that this target was achieved by a whole range of strategies, including greater use of suspended sentences, greater use of parole, increased use of fines, the eschewing of preventive detention, diverting young adults from custody and generally approaching criminal policy as part of wider social policy.

Looking only at incarceration rates, Slovenia sits with Finland and other Nordic countries, being among the most restrained in Europe in its use of imprisonment. However, as Dragan Petrovec and Mojca Plesničar point out (Chapter 5), the impressive statistic of 63 per 100,000 is deceptive in two ways. Firstly, the prison population has actually increased significantly from an even lower base since Slovenia gained independence in 1991. Secondly, regimes in Slovenian prisons have clearly deteriorated in recent years due to overcrowding and the abandonment of progressive approaches, based on socio-therapy and focused on reintegration, that had been very successful in the previous period.

Petrovec and Plesničar's description of the open, humane and supportive institutions, which operated in Slovenia from the mid-1970s to the early 1990s, find several echoes in Shadd Maruna's exploration of how the criminal justice system could promote desistance from crime (Chapter 6). Maruna notes how justice systems can be too focused on 'deficits' in prisoners and will actively inhibit change or 'recovery' by what it does to people in prison: 'stigmatising, labelling, brutalising, institutionalising, excluding'. However, he argues, 'the dynamics of desistance are not all that distant from these dynamics of stigma and that advocates of rehabilitation can learn crucial lessons for effective reform by better understanding its polar opposite.' So, he speaks of 'redemption rituals' and 'de-labelling ceremonies' which affirm the positive character of the person. Maruna stresses: 'not only must a person accept conventional society in order to go straight, but conventional society must accept that this person has changed as well.'

Jean Corston's argument that women in prison need a different approach (Chapter 7) is another challenge to stereotyping. She says that imprisoned women are 'shoe-horned into a system designed for and largely run by men.' Thus their needs, their relationships (such as with their children) and their abilities are not recognised. The strengths and personalities of imprisoned women, as well as their concerns and the pain of separation, come across strongly in their own voices in Rafaela Granja, Manuela da Cunha and Helena Machado's description of the social and economic costs of female imprisonment in Portugal (Chapter 8). This chapter brings out with great clarity the extent of the 'collateral' damage of their incarceration on their families.

Patrick Riordan (Chapter 9) examines the concept of restorative justice philosophically and argues that, contrary to how it is often seen, it is compatible with the idea of retribution. Retribution is important, he argues, not as a means to vengeance, but in terms of restoring the self-image of the victim and 'respect for the shared moral order.'

The voices of those held in Belgian prisons also come through strongly in Rudy Machiels and Aline Bauwens's research (Chapter 10). Men recount their prison experiences and their navigation of bureaucratic release procedures. In particular, the various and changing identities they adopt is well brought out, revealing complex personalities and situations which once again challenge the negative stereotypes of people in prison. This chapter also examines the release procedure from the point-of-view of probation officers, and their perspectives on the supervision and support they are expected to offer those released from prison. In requiring probation officers to exercise control as well as offering help, their task can be seen to exhibit the classic tension between care and control experienced by many who work in penal systems.

The need to move from a passive controlling role to one that is more focused on support is also at the heart of Tim Chapman and Hugh Campbell's work (Chapter 11). They are especially concerned with changing and enhancing the role of the prison officer in the Northern Ireland Prison Service as it emerges from the 'Troubles' of recent decades. They see more engaged prison officers as critical to developing regimes that cease to be ones which 'actually reinforce criminality' and become ones 'in which strong pro-social relationships, responsibility and respect can be generated within the prison as a means of preparing prisoners to have a good life and live safely in the community.' Restorative justice is seen by them to have a key role in a more effective Prison Service.

Indeed, restorative justice is explicitly advocated by several contributors to this book (Juliet Lyon, Peter McVerry, Patrick Riordan, Tim Chapman and Hugh Campbell) and closely-related ideas can be found in other chapters (such as those by Andrew Coyle, Dragan Petrovec and Mojca Plesničar, and Shadd Maruna).

There follow three chapters, each of which take a European-wide view of particular issues in penal systems: mental health, electronic monitoring and the role of education within prisons. Bronwyn Naylor (Chapter 12) addresses, from a human rights perspective, the scandal of imprisoning so many with mental illness. Referring to a report by the World Health Organization she tells us that at least 400,000 of Europe's two million prisoners 'suffer from a significant mental disorder, and more suffer from common mental health problems such as depression and anxiety.' Clearly, prison is in general an inappropriate place in which to seek to help people with such problems, and, indeed, prison frequently exacerbates them. She suggests 'three possible drivers for change': human rights litigation, especially through the European Court of Human Rights; mental-health focused reforms; and monitoring by independent bodies.

Mike Nellis (Chapter 13) surveys the use of electronic monitoring (EM) across Europe and the way in which it is now an established feature of the 'penal imaginary'. Nellis traces its origins and its introduction to Europe, and he discusses its potential – both how it might be used as a less punitive alternative to custody, and its possibilities as 'part of an ever more pervasive electronic infrastructure'. The care/control tension remerges here in a new setting: can EM be developed while retaining humanistic values that were, for example, traditionally associated with probation; or will it become just an impersonal and cheap form of large-scale surveillance and control? Will it become a better alternative to prison, or one more intrusive 'add-on' to the controlling apparatus of a punitive society?

Anne Costelloe and Kevin Warner's review of the state of education in prisons in Europe (Chapter 14) also illustrates tensions between 'liberal' or supportive approaches, and those concerned with control and behaviour modification. Costelloe and Warner explain the policies in relation to prison education that are set out by both the Council of Europe and the European Union. In both cases, these policies are derived from the tradition of adult education and are based on seeing the individual in prison as a citizen and as 'a whole person'. However, some countries pursue a narrower view of prison education, seeing those to whom it is offered as 'offenders' whose behaviour must be changed, or seeing them in demonised terms, or merely as people who must be made to work.

The final chapter by Aislinn O'Donnell and Jonathan Cummins (Chapter 15) likewise asserts the transformative possibilities of adult education within prisons. It shows deep awareness of both the destructive nature of imprisonment, and the extraordinary resilience and potential there can be within people who are incarcerated even for very long periods. The insights of O'Donnell and Cummins come from their experience of teaching philosophy and film-making respectively in a high-security prison in Ireland. A central concept in this paper is *parrhesia*, 'speaking truth to power'. That truth is evident in the written and spoken words of prisoners that, fittingly, permeate this final chapter.

It is our view that, collectively, these various chapters, from a range of authors in different parts of Europe, will challenge and offer alternatives to failed and punitive approaches to imprisonment. We hope that, taken together, they will point the way to better penal policy and practice in all three dimensions identified above: in the scale of imprisonment, in its 'depth', and in the perception of the person held in prison.

Society's response to crime must, however, take a broad view and see (as the Finns have done) criminal policy as but a part of good social policy. Perhaps we need to widen our vision even further, as Andrew Coyle advocates, and see the problems in the criminal justice system as part of a twenty-first century jig-saw where many large issues must be addressed together: 'the wasteful and unsustainable use of world resources by the few, debilitating poverty for the many, population expansion, habitat loss, species extinction, and particularly the problem of climate change'. We need to see, he says, 'that there are not many problems but one problem, linked by cause and effect'. and that we would 'be wise to look upon ourselves as a species and devise more realistic and pragmatic approaches to our problems as a whole.'

Bibliography

Coyle, A. (2006) 'Conclusion by the General Rapporteur'. *Penological Information Bulletin*, 26: 18-21.

Garland, D. (2001) *The Culture of Control: Crime and Social Order in Contemporary Society.* Oxford: University Press.

Matthews, R. (2005) 'The Myth of Punitiveness'. *Theoretical Criminology*, 9(2): 175-201.

O'Sullivan, E. and O'Donnell, I. (2012) *Coercive Confinement in Ireland.* Manchester: Manchester University Press.

Pratt, J., Brown, D., Brown, M., Hallsworth, S. and Morrison, W. (2005) *The New Punitiveness: Trends, theories, perspectives.* Cullompton: Willan Publishing.

Snacken, S. and Dumortier, E. (2012) *Resisting Punitiveness in Europe? Welfare, human rights and democracy.* London: Routledge.

Ugelvik, T. and Dullum, J. (2012) *Penal Exceptionalism? Nordic Prison Policy and Practice.* London: Routledge.

Walmsley, R. (1999) *Research Findings No. 88 World Prison Population List January 1999.* Available at: http://www.apcca.org/uploads/1st_Edition_1999.pdf (Accessed 10 April 2014)

Walmsley, R. (2013) *World Prison Population List (sixth edition).* Available at: http://www.prisonstudies.org/sites/prisonstudies.org/files/resources/downloads/world-prison-population-list-2005.pdf (Accessed 10 April 2014)

Warner, K. (2011) 'Valued members of society? Social inclusiveness in the characterisation of prisoners in Ireland, Denmark, Finland and Norway'. *Administration*, 59(1): 87-109.

The Future of Imprisonment in a Modern Democratic Society

Andrew Coyle

Introduction

This chapter is written within a threefold context: the influence of Christianity on the way that prisons have developed, particularly in the Western world; the work of the Scribani Network; and the current use of imprisonment in Ireland. The conference which provided the springboard for the chapters in this publication was sponsored by the Jesuit Centre for Faith and Justice, which by definition is an institution which operates within a Christian ethos. For that reason it is worth noting the influence which Christian principles have had on the development of imprisonment as a major feature of criminal justice, first in Europe and North America and later in other regions of the world.

Until the eighteenth century prisons were generally places where men and women were detained while awaiting some sort of legal process, which might be trial, or execution or transportation, or until a debt was paid, or occasionally simply at a ruler's pleasure. They were often places of filth, hunger and depravity.

> A small country town had for its residence for prisoners a vile thatched room, perhaps fourteen feet long, dark, filthy, and fireless, and in winter perishingly cold, where for months untried prisoners waited till the circuit court opened to hear

their case; while for security they were sometimes loaded with chains and fastened to an iron bar or bedstead (Graham, 1909: 504).

Many of the world's prisons have been constructed in accordance with the model of imprisonment which had its genesis in North America and Western Europe and which developed largely because of the efforts of Christians, many of them non-conformists, who decided that something had to be done about what John Howard (1777) had called 'the state of the prisons'. The Christian activists who became involved in prison reform at the end of the eighteenth century started with a pragmatic determination that prison conditions should be more decent and humane but within a short time they turned their attention to the concept of the prison itself. They began to see it as much more than a place of punishment and of internal exile and to see it as a place of potential personal change and reformation. This attitude was very much in keeping with the Christian theology of sin, admission of guilt, penance and redemption. More recently articulated by Pope John Paul II in 2000 when he wrote, 'Prison should not be a corrupting experience, a place of idleness and even vice, but instead a place of redemption' (Pope John Paul II, 2000: 10). In the world of prisons these principles are no longer expressed in directly religious terms but there is a clear read across in secular terms to the sequence which begins with the commission of a crime and moves on through detection, conviction by a court and punishment by imprisonment, leading ultimately to personal reformation and rehabilitation.

The Christian concepts which underpinned the development of prisons were reflected in the very architecture of the new prisons which were built in the nineteenth century. Prisoners were no longer to be held in large common rooms, with no segregation according to legal status, age, or sometimes even gender, left to their own devices by day and by night. Instead they were to be detained in serried rows of individual rooms called cells, layered on top of each other in massive accommodation blocks. Very often the cell blocks were grouped around the largest building in the prison, which was the chapel. The parallel with the monastery was immediately visual.

One can trace a further link between the Christian roots of imprisonment and modern penal philosophy by drawing a parallel between the nineteenth century notion of personal reformation through religion which saw prisoners confined to their cells with only a bible for company and subject to a daily visit from the chaplain, and the modern secular variation which sees prisoners required to undertake 'offending behaviour programmes' overseen by psychologists, who have often overtaken the priests and religious ministers of former times in the prison hierarchy.

So, even a cursory glance at the history of the modern prison can leave us in no doubt that Christianity bears a heavy burden of responsibility for the development of the prison as we know it today and that is a powerful argument that its adherents today should be at the forefront of attempts to bring about change in prison systems.

My second contextual comment continues this religious theme, but from a more optimistic perspective. The conference which led to this publication was the fifth of a series organised by the Scribani Network, named after Carolus Scribani, first Dean of the Jesuit University of Antwerp at the beginning of the seventeenth century. Since their foundation in 1540 members of the Society of Jesus have been at the forefront of Catholic religious thinking and have sought to create a bridge between personal spirituality and social and cultural reform. The network which is named after Scribani continues this tradition within a European context. The first in this modern series of conferences was held in Antwerp in 2004 on the theme of migration and enlargement in Europe, a theme again explored in the fourth conference in 2010 in Madrid. In between there have been conferences on cooperation between Africa and Europe and on the role of religion in the integration of

Europe. Given the mission of the Scribani Network, which is to nourish policy debate and to pursue concrete social action on issues of strategic importance, including the reform of social justice systems, it was timely that the conference in 2012 should focus on 're-imagining imprisonment in Europe'. Just as in the eighteenth and nineteenth centuries Christian activists in Europe and North America strove to improve the shocking state of prisons in their era, so the time has come for an informed debate about how to construct a prison system which is appropriate for the twenty-first century.

My third set of contextual comments relate to the fact that the conference was held in Dublin. In 2009 the Irish Penal Reform Trust organised a conference in the same city on the theme 'Re-imagining the Role of Prison in Irish Society', not so different from the theme of the conference in 2012. The Chairperson of the Irish Prison Reform Trust opened the 2009 conference by commenting that Ireland was at what she called 'a watershed moment' in respect of the way that it made use of prisons and that the conference presented an opportunity to chart a positive way forward rather than a negative one which predicated 'more of the same'. In my presentation at that conference I suggested that Ireland had to choose between two doors which lay ahead. One would take the country down the road which at that point was being followed in England and Wales with an ever increasing use of imprisonment. That road would take Ireland from a prison rate of 81 per 100,000 of the population, with a total in the year 2009 of just over 3,500 prisoners, to a rate of 153, with a total of around 7,000 prisoners. The other door would lead to a different model and in my speech I charted where that road might lead (Irish Prison Reform Trust, 2009).

In the three years between the two conferences prison numbers in Ireland continued to rise and in late 2012 were pushing towards 4,500, giving a rate which, while still well below that in England and Wales, was moving gradually towards it. From an external perspective it looked as though Ireland still had its hand on the doorknob

4

of the road which would lead to an ever increasing use of imprisonment. Yet, there was an obvious reluctance to commit wholeheartedly to that path. It may be that the hesitation was purely pragmatic since the plans which the government had for expanding prison places were simply not sustainable in the existing economic climate. It may also be that there was a more fundamental, rational reason for the hesitation and that warning signs were being heeded. In March 2012 the Jesuit Centre for Faith and Justice (2012) published a highly critical report on the state of prisons in Ireland and called on the government to adopt a radically different approach to imprisonment, rather than passively accepting a continual rise in the prison population and in the aftermath it appeared that the government was listening. Speaking a few months later as he introduced the annual report of the Prison Service for 2011, the Justice Minister acknowledged that the greatest challenge facing the Prison Service continued to be the increasing number of prisoners being committed to custody. At the same time he took comfort from the fact that the increase was beginning to slow down year on year and he expressed the hope that this might signal an end to ever increasing numbers (Irish Prison Service, 2012).

Lessons from elsewhere

For a quarter of a century I worked in prisons, attempting to make them decent and humane places and trying to help prisoners onto the path of reformation. This ambition has gone under many headings over the decades, most of them for some reason beginning with the letter 'r': reform, rehabilitation, resettlement, re-entry. The most recent description has been 'reducing re-offending'. It may be indicative of the uncertain times in which we live that this latest articulation is couched in terms of trying to reduce negative aspects of behaviour rather than of enhancing potential in a positive manner.

In the course of the last two centuries many countries can point to a roll call of inquiries and investigations into prisons and how to improve them. In the United Kingdom these can be traced back to the early nineteenth century. Penal historians would probably point to the Report from the Departmental Committee on Prisons (Prisons Committee, 1895), usually referred to as the Gladstone Report, as the first of the modern era. This was the report which famously prescribed 'that prison treatment should have as its primary and concurrent objects deterrence and reformation' (para. 25). Some commentators have since argued that it was this assertion which sparked subsequent schizophrenia about the purpose of imprisonment and whether this should be punitive or positive, or could attempt to be both at the same time.

In recent years reports and inquiries about a wide variety of aspects of imprisonment, both governmental and non-governmental, have been published with increasing frequency. The majority of them have identified specific failings in the system and have recommended steps that might be taken to make improvements. Few of them have had much if anything to say about the system of imprisonment *per se*. It is worth noting in passing that one of the better reports was produced in Ireland almost thirty years ago (Whitaker Report, 1985). However, most of them have taken the existing system of imprisonment for granted and findings have been restricted broadly to a variety of proposals for tweaking the current systems in the hope of improving them. Successive governments have concluded that the answer to the failure of prisons to rehabilitate those who are sent there is to send more people to prison and to send them there for longer periods, while at the same time berating those who work in prisons for not doing more to ensure that those who leave prison do not break the law again after they return to the community. That is rather like blaming the surgeon who mends a skier's broken leg for the fact that the person later returns to the slopes and breaks his or her leg again.

As I have travelled around the world I have seen numerous examples of prisons which are well managed and which provide a positive atmosphere to encourage people to improve themselves and to learn skills which might benefit them on release. Often these examples are to be found in unexpected places. I think, for example, of what is currently happening in the Dominican Republic where prisons are now run by a charismatic man who was previously rector of one of the country's leading universities and who has turned prisons which were previously hotbeds of violence and corruption into places of learning and hope. I think also of the village prisons in India where people who are serving life sentences can live with their families and go out to work to support them.

When I turn closer to home the picture is not so positive. For over 20 years I have been involved in prison reform initiatives in the wider European region which encompasses countries which are members of the Council of Europe. The Council of Europe has much to be proud of in terms of its prison reform initiatives. I think of the work of the Committee for the Prevention of Torture, the European Prison Rules (Council of Europe, 2006) and most recently the Code of Ethics for Prison Staff (Council of Europe, 2012). However, while individual initiatives have often been sound, one is entitled to question the strategy about the use and nature of imprisonment, which has been based mainly on the model which has existed for decades in Western Europe.

At the beginning of the 1990s the Polish prison system shone for a short period as a model of how a decent and humane prison system might operate, an example not only for the countries to its east but also for those in Western Europe (Coyle, 2002). Sadly, as Poland was drawn more into the orbit of Western Europe, the prison system began to take on many of the less attractive characteristics of its Western European counterparts. Successive governments accepted the advice of Western experts that the prison could be a place of individual change and could play a major role in both security and social reform. At the beginning of this reform period the use of imprisonment dropped dramatically, in 1998 the prison population stood at 54,000. However, the advice that followed led to the adoption of an expansionist model where the number of men and women in Polish prisons reached 87,776 in 2007 – reducing to around 80,000 in 2012 (Polish Prison Service, 2013).

The Czech Republic provides another example where early progressive changes have been undermined by the introduction of Western models of 'managing offenders' both in prisons and in the community. Prison numbers rose from 14,000 in 1992 to over 23,000 in 2012, due largely to a combination of factors including an increasing tendency of courts to send those who had committed minor offences to prison, combined with an increase in the average sentence length. In an attempt to deal with the problem of overcrowding the government proposed to release prisoners to house arrest at the halfway point of their sentence. In the event, the number of people in prisons was reduced dramatically by the amnesty declared by the former President of the Czech Republic shortly before he retired from office in early 2013 (Czech Prison Service, 2012/2014).

My sense of how little prisons have moved in reality in the last forty or so years was confirmed in late 2012 when I returned to a prison for young people where I worked 35 years ago. At that time it was known as a Borstal institution and was a reformatory for young men between the ages of 17 and 21, who spent an average of 10 or 12 months in custody. While the daily practicalities for the 250 young men held there was quite unremitting, the environment was designed in a positive manner. There was no perimeter wall or fence, staff wore civilian clothes. The 'boys' or 'lads', as they were known, were accommodated in 'houses' which each held an average of 100 and they attended a full day of education, work or training. The weakness of the system was that the life which the young men led during their time in the borstal bore little relationship to the communities from which they had come and to which they would return on release.

The first indication of the changed environment was obvious on my visit in late 2012 as I followed the signs marked to 'HM

Prison' and came upon the 17 feet high perimeter wall. The institution now has accommodation for up to 830 young men, held in recently built traditional cell blocks, the largest of which has space for 360 prisoners. The average length of sentence has increased and is now between two and four years. Staff were welcoming and friendly but now wear standard prison uniforms. In managerial terms the prison is probably run more efficiently than it ever was as a borstal. It is much cleaner and tidier than I remember. Yet listening to how the young men spent their days one was still struck by the dissonance between the experience in this youth prison and anything that they were likely to encounter in their communities. The hopelessness of it all was summed up as I left and made my way through the sad line of women, partners, parents and siblings, queuing to visit their young men. It is one of the abiding pictures which symbolises the futility of prisons the world over.

The future of prisons

The unavoidable reality is that the prison systems which we have in most of our countries are not amenable to reform. Well-meaning people, many of them with extensive professional experience, have been trying without success to reform prison systems for generations without any real success. That is not to say that the professional lives of these individuals, among whom I would include myself, have been a failure or that they should not have embarked on such an enterprise. For as long as prisons exist it is incumbent on all of us to do our best to reform them and, for sure, we can signal significant improvements in matters of detail. But that is different from reforming the system itself. If we wish to do that, we will have to look beyond current structures which are based on a premise from centuries past, a premise which suggests that by taking individuals out of their communities and placing them together in their hundreds, and increasingly nowadays in their thousands, in large abnormal institutions we can simultaneously punish them for the wrong they personally have done and also try to inoculate them against repeating that wrong once they return to those same communities.

So, what is to be written about the future of the prison? As the twenty-first century unfolds, will societies continue to lock up large numbers of men, women and children in confined spaces behind high walls, cut off for all practical purposes from their families and contact with the normal world? Will the numbers of people in prison continue to rise as they have in recent years? Or will the thoughts of a former Minister of State for Internal Affairs in Uganda be realised? Speaking about prisons at a conference in Kampala in 1995, William Omaria said:

> One day in the distant future, people will probably look back on what happens in most countries today and will wonder how we could do that to our fellow human beings in the name of justice (Omaria, 1997: 89).

Very few human institutions last forever. Many of the methods of judicial punishment which existed when prisons first came into use have long since ceased to be acceptable. They include the stocks, corporal punishment, transportation to another country and capital punishment. As things stand at present, it seems inconceivable in the foreseeable future that prisons should go the way of the stocks, branding and whipping and cease to exist. However, despite the current enthusiasm for imprisonment and the growth in its use in many countries, it may be that the time has come for a radical review of the use of imprisonment as a sentence of the court, for a discussion about the extent to which it benefits society, satisfies victims and is the best way of dealing with those who break the criminal law.

When he was himself a prisoner, Vaclav Havel, who was later to become President of the Czech Republic, wrote to his wife:

> I never feel sorry for myself, as one might expect, but only for the other prisoners and altogether, for the fact that prisons must exist and that they are as they are, and that

10

mankind has not so far invented a better way of coming to terms with certain things (Havel, 1990: 270).

At some point in the future we may indeed invent 'a better way of coming to terms with certain things'. For the foreseeable future there will still be a need for prisons. However, we need to be honest about its purposes and its limitations; we need to recognise that the prison can never in itself be a place of reform. Prisons are expensive resources where people are sent as punishment for the harm they have done, with the aspiration that somehow they may benefit from that experience. If we acknowledge this limited set of objectives, we can go on to identify the essential features of the prison of the future:

- It will be used as a place of last resort, as an alternative to other disposals which will become the norm

- It will hold a small number of people

- Its staff will be recruited locally and trained according to local needs

- It will have strong links to the community in which it is based

- Throughout their sentences prisoners will be given access to local resources and facilities which they can continue to use after release.

If this vision is to be realised, we will have to look beyond the narrow parameters of the criminal justice system; we must engage with a whole range of new and perhaps unexpected collaborators. I began to understand what this might involve recently when I visited an exhibition, which has been touring the world, called 'Hard Rain: Whole Earth' (Hard Rain Project, 2013). The issues highlighted in this powerful exhibition are the wasteful and unsustainable use of world resources by the few, debilitating poverty for the many, population expansion, habitat loss, species extinction, and particularly the problem of climate change. The main lesson of the exhibition is that these are pieces of a jigsaw puzzle that illustrate the twenty-first century. If we put the puzzle together we see that there are not many problems but one problem, linked by cause and effect. While each of these issues is understood by decision-makers, they are typically addressed as if they were separate problems. We will be wise to look upon ourselves as a species and devise more realistic and pragmatic approaches to all our problems as a whole.

As I thought about this exhibition and its message, it occurred to me that we should begin to consider the problems of imprisonment in particular and of criminal justice in general as yet another part of that jigsaw puzzle, only capable of solution when viewed within this wider context. If we are to do that we will have to take our discussions in this book on to another level. Those of us who are schooled in pursuing these matters within a narrow criminal justice context will find this a difficult undertaking. That brings me full circle to my earlier comments about the Scribani Network. Those who are involved in the network are well accustomed to considering the links between the individual and society and also between the major issues of our age. If they are so minded, they are well placed to assist those of us who are steeped in a criminal justice view of the world to find, in the words of Vaclav Havel, 'a better way of coming to terms with certain things'.

Bibliography

Council of Europe (2006) *Recommendation CM/Rec (2006)2 of the Committee of Ministers to member states on the European Prison Rules.* Strasbourg: Council of Europe.

Council of Europe (2012) *Recommendation CM/Rec (2012)5 of the Committee of Ministers to member states on the European Code of Ethics for Prison Staff.* Strasbourg: Council of Europe.

Coyle, A. (2002) *Managing prisons in a time of change.* London: International Centre for Prison Studies.

Czech Prison Service (2012/2014) Czech Prison Service. Available at http://www.vscr.cz/ (Accessed 23 January 2014).

Graham, H.G. (1909) *The Social Life of Scotland in the Eighteenth Century*. London: Adam and Charles Black.

Hard Rain Project (2006/2014) Hard Rain Project. Available at http://www.hardrainproject.com/ (Accessed 23 January 2014).

Havel, V. (1990) *Letters to Olga*. London: Faber and Faber.

Howard, J. (1777) *The State of the Prisons in England & Wales*. New Jersey: Paterson Smith.

Irish Prison Reform Trust (2009) *Re-imagining the Role of Prison in Irish Society*. Available at: http://www.iprt.ie/contents/1306 (Accessed 23 January 2014).

Irish Prison Service (2012) *Press release on publication of 2011 Annual Report*. Available at: http://www.irishprisons.ie/index.php/information-centre/press-releases-and-speeches/2012-speech-and-press-release/81-info/181 (Accessed 23 January 2014).

Jesuit Centre for Faith and Justice (2012) *The Irish Prison System: Vision, Values, Reality*. Dublin: Jesuit Centre for Faith and Justice.

Omaria, W. (1997) *Report of a Pan-African Seminar, Kampala, Uganda 19-21 September 1996*. London: Penal Reform International.

Polish Prison Service (2010) *Statistics*. Available at http://www.sw.gov.pl/pl/o-sluzbie-wieziennej/statystyka/ (Accessed 23 January 2014).

Pope John Paul II (2000) *Message for the Jubilee in Prisons*. Rome: Vatican Press.

Prisons Committee (1895) *Report from the Departmental Committee on Prisons*. London: HMSO.

Whitaker Report (1985) *Report of the Committee of Inquiry into the Penal System*. Dublin: The Stationery Office.

2

Re-Imagining Imprisonment:
Punishment Enough

Juliet Lyon

Introduction

Loss of liberty is the most serious punishment that can be levied by the UK Courts. Notwithstanding any improvements that can be effected in prison treatment and conditions, we should never underestimate the impact of that loss of liberty. It is a punishment and felt as a punishment.

Imprisonment defines our society. In 1910, when he was Home Secretary, Winston Churchill said:

> The mood and temper of the public in regard to the treatment of crime and criminals is one of the most unfailing tests of the civilisation of any country. A calm and dispassionate recognition of the rights of the accused against the state, and even those of convicted criminals against the state, a constant heart-searching by all charged with the duty of punishment, a desire and eagerness to rehabilitate in the world of industry all those who have paid their dues in the hard coinage of punishment, tireless efforts towards the discovery of curative and regenerating processes, and an unfaltering faith that there is a treasure, if you can only find it, in the heart of every man – these are the symbols which in the treatment of crime and criminals mark and measure the stored-up strength of a nation and are the sign and proof of the living virtue in it.

These are familiar words to many penal reformers, but what Churchill said later in the same speech in Parliament may be slightly less familiar, and I'll return to that at the end of this chapter.

A place of last resort

When we talk about 're-imagining imprisonment', we have to re-imagine it within some sort of bounds. Globally there has been huge inflation in sentencing. Prison populations have swelled, fuelled by pre-trial detention, the imposition of short custodial sentences where a fine or community sentence would previously have been passed and a marked increase in overall sentence lengths. The facts and figures – for the UK, for Ireland – are readily available from government sources and civil society organisations. One of the ways that we need to re-imagine imprisonment is that imprisonment – actual loss of liberty – should be restricted to the comparatively few whose offending is so serious that no other punishment can be justified.

Rather than 'alternatives to custody', if we could re-imagine prison as the alternative, used only when everything else has failed that would be a good start. More effective measures to reduce offending can be employed in many cases including public health solutions – we shouldn't restrict ourselves to measures within the justice system. We need to think about enabling people to break away from addictions through treatment. We need to think about public health solutions such as social care for people with learning disabilities, and the mental health treatment that should be available as a matter of course to those who need it.

Community sentencing – which in England and Wales is beginning to outperform prison sentences by a factor of almost 10 per cent – is a cheaper, more effective measure, and is clearly the direction in which to go. However, the question remains: 'why is prison always our focus, the abiding image to which we return, rather than other options that work to enable people to get away from offending, and to cut crime?'

The chair of the Prison Reform Trust, Lord Woolf, who investigated the disturbances at Strangeways in 1990, has a telling phrase about imprisonment: he says we should focus on reducing prison numbers to an 'unavoidable minimum'. This begs the question, what is an unavoidable minimum? Is there a number? His answer, for England and Wales, is that it's probably the same as the number in custody when he undertook that investigation – about 45,000. Today the prison population in England and Wales is nearer 85,000.

Reform of our system rests largely on reducing imprisonment – shrinking the justice net, and putting prison where it belongs – as an important place of absolute last resort. This is not meant to be a criticism of those who work in prisons – some of the best penal reformers are those who work day in day out to reform prison from within. They often work in appalling conditions, under great difficulty – but they are trying to change things, trying to bring some humanity and respect into what is often a very difficult situation. Despite this, at the heart of prison reform is the need to reduce the use of imprisonment. That's the most positive way of re-imagining imprisonment.

This view was endorsed strongly by the former governor of Britain's only therapeutic prison, HMP Grendon, when he gave the Swarthmore lecture:

> Despite the enthusiasm for working at the small steps of improvement in conditions and the development of caring relationships I have always maintained that prisons should be places of last resort – that they should not be seen or promoted as places for transformation and change even though I know they can become that for many (Newell, 2000).

There is always an expectation of organisations like Prison Reform Trust and Penal Reform International that we should focus entirely on improving treatment and conditions. However, there can be unintended consequences of improving treatment and conditions, unless you first establish that principle of last resort.

It can be attractive to the courts to send a person to prison because they need a detox, and the sentencers know that they can get it almost immediately in custody. The same can be said of mental health assessments since the NHS has taken over prison health – although the World Health Organisation has roundly criticised countries where prison is commonly misused as a convenient place to dump people who are mentally ill. Education standards have been improved in British prisons, so second-chance education for young people might be available – I say might, because most of us know that prisons are overcrowded, and few will actually benefit from education reform.

Piecemeal improvements – all of which have been hard fought for and hard won – create the risk of an environment which is seen as essentially rehabilitative, a capacious social service, in which we will then happily incarcerate more people.

Inflation in sentencing

It's not just that we are imprisoning more people; we're locking them up for considerably longer. Research published by the Pew Centre in the United States shows that people who were released in 2009, compared to people convicted of similar crimes released ten years before that, have served on average about nine months longer – a thirty-six per cent longer sentence than they would have served in 1999. This trend in increasing the length of prison time is also seen in many European countries.

Anecdotally, from visiting prisons regularly in my work for the Prison Reform Trust, it did not seem to be that long ago when a sentence of more than four years was considered a long sentence and remarked upon by prison staff. Four years now seems commonplace. The number of people serving a life-sentence has also expanded massively. Ten years ago just 9 per cent of the prison population in England and Wales were serving life or an indeterminate sentence. Today it's 19 per cent.

When it comes to remand and short sentences, needless imprisonment can be reduced. Pre-trial detention is a global issue, and although the UK does not hold people for as long as many countries do, we do hold too many people for too little reason. An important development is the new remand clause within the Legal Aid, Sentencing and Punishment of Offenders (LASPO) Act, which states that if a person is awaiting trial for an offence that carries no real prospect of imprisonment, then they should not be held on custodial remand. Magistrates now have to apply this 'no real prospect test', thereby reducing those held unnecessarily on remand. In 2012 there has been a 12 per cent reduction in the number of people on custodial remand in England and Wales.

Our most fearful experiment in sentencing has been called to a halt by the then Secretary of State for Justice Ken Clarke. This was the ill-drafted and rushed 'indeterminate sentence for public protection' – the IPP sentence. Nobody anticipated the effect it would have. Hilary Benn MP, who was then Prisons Minister for England and Wales, was asked in Parliament how many people would receive a sentence of this kind, and he said – in the House of Commons– that he didn't know, but that it could be as many as 600 people. Today there are 6,500 people who have been given that sentence – 3,500 of whom are already held beyond tariff. Although this sentence has recently been abolished, there is now a serious residual problem that has yet to be resolved. Not surprisingly this Kafkaesque sentence has left many prisoners institutionalised and angry and their families in despair. It is a terrible way to learn that it is simply unjust to lock someone up, not for what they have done, but for something they might do in the future (Hough and Jacobson, 2010).

The fair way would be to reverse the burden of proof, and place that burden on the State. The State, through prison governor's and staff assessments and reports as well as the Parole Board, must then justify the continued detention of these people. Within those 6,500 people, there will be a handful who are extremely dangerous, and who will need to be detained in one way or another. The vast majority, however, will have been given that sentence because they were not able to present themselves well in court or where dangerousness was sensed but not properly defined or fully proven. There's a preponderance of mental health need within the population that have been given an IPP sentence. About 80 per cent of the women who are serving an IPP sentence are there for arson, or an arson-related offence, which usually has links to mental health need.

The IPP sentence is iconic. It sheds light on the way we see imprisonment – the notion that if we could sentence people for longer, if we could eradicate all risk, then we would have fewer victims and somehow improve society by simply locking people away behind metal doors.

An inconvenient truth: Victims behind bars

The line between victim and offender isn't as clear cut as many would like to believe. Many of the people who end up within the prison system are themselves victims. If you look at women within the prison system you see a group of women – most of whom have committed petty, albeit persistent offences – who are victims themselves of violent crimes, of domestic violence, of sexual abuse or rape. This is not a group of people who are happy and healthy who suddenly turn to crime for no reason.

The Prison Reform Trust commissioned a study of children in prison where we looked at over 6,000 children who went into some form of custody over the six months from July to December in 2008. The study, 'Punishing Disadvantage', focused on 'Who are the children who end up in custody?', and 'What crimes have they committed that necessitate being detained?' Around 39 per cent of those children had been on the child protection register (Jacobson et al., 2010). Around 70 per cent were already known to social services. High numbers had truanted and experienced parental neglect or untimely bereavement. Many had early onset mental health problems or a learning disability or difficulty, and so on and so forth. Their stories are all too familiar. Their offending profile would be familiar – a gradual spiral of getting into more trouble and difficulty, not getting the interventions, the support and backup, needed at a time when it could have helped to divert them from their path.

Colin Moses gave his views as he stepped down as longstanding Chairman of the Prison Officers' Association:

> What we are doing in this country currently is sending people to prison, many of whom are victims themselves, many of whom have been bullied, and will continue to be bullied in prisons. When it comes to lights out time and you then could stand outside those prison wings and hear the chatter that goes on from the windows and those who've been bullied at school, those who've been bullied in their homes, many of whom have been sexually abused before they've come to prison and you hear them themselves being bullied again or taunting and that is the 24 hour cycle in a prison. The cries for help, those young men who go to bed at night and become bedwetters. Those young men who go to the library and pick up the book with the biggest pictures in, because they don't want people to know that they can't read and write. They may have the muscles of an adult, but what they really are are young men crying out for help. Yes there are some bad offenders in there, there are people who've done some horrendous things, but what we have is a system that is totally overburdened and under resourced that will not work in those circumstances (Prison Reform Trust, 2011a).

A lasting mark

Many people involved in reform want to help people in need. There is a real risk that they will use the justice system, or the resources available within it, in order to help those people in need – thus condemning them to a long period of time in some form of custody. To some form of existence within the justice system that will mark them indelibly.

The Offender Rehabilitation Bill currently before Parliament will, if passed, consign everyone serving a prison sentence of two days or more to an additional one year of mandatory supervision in the community to enable them, during this period of unjust and disproportionate punishment, to become rehabilitated. On government's own assessment of impact this is likely, mostly through breach and recall, to add an extra 13,000 people to the prison population.

If one views both community sentences and prison sentences in parallel, the outcomes are quite poor for both. Around half the people sentenced reoffend within one year of release – and for young offenders the figure is much higher than that. A case could be made for avoiding short prison sentences simply in order to avoid that indelible marking.

If you've served a prison sentence, then you are a former prisoner. I work with colleagues at the Prison Reform Trust who have, themselves, spent time in prison. They point out that custody throws a long shadow – at what point are they no longer a former prisoner? At what point do they lose that identity?

On a practical level, amendments have been made to the Rehabilitation of Offenders Act which, when implemented, will slightly reduce disproportionate disclosure periods. But banking, credit rating and insurance continue to prove difficult to access and many former prisoners and their families find themselves financially excluded (Bath and Edgar, 2010).

The punishment of imprisonment is the loss of liberty. It is not meant to be loss of identity, or the loss of a future. Yet only a quarter of people leave prison with a job or any kind of training course to go to. Far too many are released homeless, jobless, isolated and in debt.

Talk of punishment

It shouldn't surprise us that reconviction rates are so high. Criminologists have written about this time and again.

Brodeur commented:

Punishment is the one policy that is never discredited by
its failure to achieve its stated objectives. If it fails to meet
its goals, the only reason is that there is not enough of it
(2007).

In the last few years a justice reform programme has been introduced in which the language has begun to change. New words
are being introduced. The last Ministry of Justice consultation on
community sentencing and the probation service was peppered
with the word 'punitive'. Some politicians or civil servants will say
that we must put this 'gloss' on it – which I would describe alter-
natively as an 'acid wrap'. They say we have to wrap prison reform
in these words, because then it will be more palatable to the public.

The fundamental principle that governs a healthy prison system
that you are sent to prison as a punishment not for punishment is
being undermined by a steady stream of headline-grabbing justice
announcements. These range from toughening up the incentives
and earned privilege programme to introducing more indeterminate sentences.

The question arises, does the language of punishment matter?
I would say that yes it does. The way we describe imprisonment is
important to how we see ourselves as a society. It is important for
the people within the justice system, both on the receiving end of
those punishments, and the people who are employed on our behalf to try and manage that environment. The growing emphasis
on punitive language is damaging. It can lead to harsh, inhumane
treatment. And it can fuel scaremongering by politicians and the
press. So as crime continues to fall, we see an increase in the damaging and erosive fear of crime.

Another language that has been developing, parallel to punitive, is the language of the market. This, I would argue, is similarly
devaluing and demoralising. Terms like the 'stock-and-flow' of
prisoners – which refers to the movement of people in an overcrowded system, and 'creaming and parking' of people which has
cropped up in various commissioned pieces of work. You would

'park' someone who does not meet their targets, and you would 'cream off' those who would, because payment is measured by results. Voluntary organisations must put themselves forward in the hope of being chosen as 'sub-primes' by the 'primes' to be part of the rehabilitation 'supply chain'. The Prime Minister recently referred in Parliament to the success of 'contractorisation'.

Regulation and oversight

In tough economic times, government ministers have hard choices to make. Under financial pressure, efforts to ensure that the criminal justice system is fair and reasonable may be put at risk by spending cuts. However, there are a number of safeguards in place to promote the fair treatment of vulnerable and minority groups. Any re-imagining of imprisonment must pay due regard to the importance of the regulation and oversight of prisons, often the least visible and most neglected of any public service.

The Universal Declaration of Human Rights prohibits torture and any other cruel, inhumane, or degrading treatment or punishment. Many states have signed up to the Optional Protocol to the Convention, under which each state is obliged to provide a National Preventative Mechanism. NPM's are required to be functionally independent with independent personnel. Some countries, like France, have created a post to inspect places of custody. Other countries like Spain, Georgia and Denmark have assigned the NPM role to their Ombudsman. In the UK the prisons inspectorate coordinates a large network of NPM bodies.

The Prisons Inspectorate (in addition to its obligations under OPCAT) has created – drawing on the work of the World Health Organisation on 'healthy' prisons – the four tests of a healthy prison. This asks, where prison must exist, what would a healthy prison look like? The four tests outlined by the inspectorate are safety – that prisoners, particularly the most vulnerable, are held safely; respect – that prisoners are treated with respect for their human dignity; purposeful activity – that prisoners are able and expected to engage in activity that is likely to benefit them; and lastly, resettlement – prisoners are prepared for release into the community, and the likelihood of reoffending is reduced.

There is scope to amend and improve the terms of the UN standard minimum rules for the treatment of prisoners. The Bangkok rules, which focus entirely on women, have recently been ratified by the UN. This has plugged a gap in the Standard Minimum Rules where women were scarcely mentioned at all. Women now have their own set of rules which cover not only imprisonment, but also community penalties. The Bangkok rules refer to violence against women, and the specific implications for women's contact with the justice system in terms of physical and psychological safety. The Standard Minimum Rules, which were agreed in 1955, has no such reference to safety. This creates an opportunity now – one arguably in a generation – to revisit these rules in order to establish protection from harm, rules that enable prison authorities to ensure the safety of prisoners, staff and visitors.

If one looks at local boards – like the Independent Monitoring Boards, for example, the role of inspectorates, the role of the Ombudsman, and the role now of the UN rules and OPCAT, one can see how a set of concentric circles around imprisonment can be established that ensures that prison can be the humane and decent place we expect it to be.

Barred citizens

At the heart of prison reform lies the recognition that people behind bars are still people. If we focus for a minute on improving treatment and conditions, bearing in mind the warnings mentioned earlier, there are certain practical things that can be done. One such example took years to achieve, but has now had an impact across the UK. Our advice and information service that responds to over 5,000 prisoners a year informed us that prisoners and their families were very concerned about high phone charges – six times higher than they would be for someone using a phone outside. It is well known that good family contact reduces the risk of further offending by a factor of about times six. It made sense to try and reduce this cost, both for the prisoners who were trying to survive a sentence and still have contact with their family, and for the authorities in order to reduce reoffending.

After trying negotiations with BT, the monopoly provider, and with the Prison Service, the commissioner and after securing press exposure, the route that actually got a result is interesting, and has some bearing on re-imagining imprisonment – the consumer route. It was to reaffirm that people who are in prison are people. They may have lost their liberty, but they have not lost their humanity, nor their rights as consumers of services. Within prison, consumers have no choice about their telephone services. Therefore, we took a case under the Enterprise Act (2002) with the then Consumer Council in each of the different countries within the UK, and won each one. This resulted in a reduction of around half for the cost of calls to mobile phones, and some reduction for landlines.

Can people in prison represent themselves, and if not, who represents them, is an important question. The development of prisoner councils and peer mentoring schemes opens up scope for personal responsibility and people helping one another (Edgar et al., 2011). Interviewed for our report on active citizenship, one man said:

> It helps you for the outside world, if you are given responsibility. They give you responsibility in here. No one is giving up on you. Some of us, no one has given them responsibility.

And a prison governor in charge of resettlement confirmed:

> Prisons should not be about turning offenders into good prisoners, but about turning prisoners into good citizens (Edgar et al., 2011).

One can look through the same lens for prisoner voting. Voting is a right and arguably a responsibility not a privilege. Yet there has been absolute resistance within the Westminster Parliament to enact the European Court of Human Rights judgment from the John Hirst case in 2004 which declared that the blanket ban on prisoners voting was unlawful. The Parliamentary debate flushed out some very grim, unacceptable views about people in prison. The reason for this resistance is, in part, the same reason we have such high numbers in prison. It is this toxic mix of politicians who have found that talking 'tough on crime' is a way to win votes, and the press who have found that profiling the worst crimes is a way to sell media space.

In South Africa when under universal suffrage everyone in prison was granted the vote; it was described as a 'badge of dignity and personhood' which shows that 'everybody counts' (Prison Reform Trust, 2010). The Catholic Bishops of England and Wales support the view that prisoners should have the right to vote. In their report, *A Place of Redemption*, they stated:

> Prison regimes should treat prisoners less as objects, done to by others, and more as subjects who can become authors of their own reform and redemption. In that spirit, the right to vote should be restored to sentenced prisoners (Catholic Bishops' Conference of England and Wales, 2004).

No place for children

One of the most hopeful footholds for reform is the marked reduction in child custody in England and Wales – with similar drops in Scotland and Northern Ireland. The number of under-eighteen year olds held in the prison system over the last seven years has dropped by more than half. This has been achieved through a range of methods. The Prison Reform Trust has been privileged to have the support of the Diana, Princess of Wales Memorial Fund, which allowed us to run a five-year programme that focused entirely on reducing child imprisonment. We have been able to map out what is driving up use of imprisonment for the high custody local authorities – not to publish, but to hand it back to these authorities as a catalyst for change. Some of the drivers are so ordinary. Things like communication between people who work in youth offending teams and magistrates; returning timely reports to the courts; knowing what other options are available.

Within the local authorities with which we've worked most closely the drop in child imprisonment has been even more marked than the average. Another significant reform is the Home Office changes to the police target policy which are no longer incentivised to 'meet targets'. The Youth Justice Board is reducing its ambit and consistently working to support the reduction of the number of children entering the youth justice system for the first time, rather than using the justice system as a preventative mechanism or a means of rehabilitating children at risk. Rightly that task belongs to families, children's services, youth work and children themselves.

Care not custody

There are some particularly vulnerable people who have ended up in the justice system.

The first group are prisoners who have a learning disability or a learning difficulty. A Prison Reform Trust report, *Prisoners' Voices*, gave harrowing accounts of what it was like for offenders with learning disabilities to go from police stations to courts to prison in a fog of anxiety and well-founded fear of bullying, not understanding, or half-understanding, what was happening to them (Talbot, 2008).

In court, their lives were taken over by opaque court procedures and legal terminology. *No One Knows* (Prison Reform Trust, 2007) found that in court over a fifth of the defendants who had learning disabilities did not understand what was going on. Some did not know why they were in court or what they had done wrong, which raises questions about fitness to plead and the risk of miscarriage of justice. Most said the use of simpler language in court would have helped them. One young offender talking about his experience at court said:

> I couldn't really hear. I couldn't understand, but I said 'Yes, whatever' to anything because if I say, 'I don't know' they look at me as if I'm thick. Sometimes they tell you two things at once.

In prison, many were left to fend for themselves in a shadowy, threatening world of not knowing what was going on around them or what was expected of them.

These prisoners were five times as likely as others to have been subjected to control and restraint techniques and three times more likely to have spent time in segregation. They were generally uncertain about where they would go for help as they prepared to leave prison. One prisoner told of the difficulties he had keeping in touch with his family:

> Nobody told my mum I was going to jail, she thought I was dead. I asked how they were going to tell my mum, but it took three months for anyone to contact her. I finally found someone to help me write a letter.

A second group of people who have particular needs are those who have mental health problems. In a 2005 report, *Troubled Inside*, the Prison Reform Trust showed how inappropriate the prison setting is to help people recover from mental illness. More recently, the Prison Reform Trust surveyed the independent monitoring boards to gather evidence about the problems prisons have in meeting the needs of mentally ill prisoners.

Dr Peter Selby, then president of the National Council for Independent Monitoring Boards, and former bishop to prisons, wrote in his foreword to the report:

> There is no more distressing a mismatch in our criminal justice system than mental illness and prison. Would anybody prescribe for a mentally ill person the kind of envi-

ronment that a prison needs to be, let alone the kind of environment that actually exists in our oldest and most unsuitable prisons? Yet this mismatch is what tens of thousands of prisoners experience (Edgar and Rickford, 2009).

As a group, the boards described a system under pressure struggling to respond to the complex needs of people, many of whom, they felt, should not have been sent to prison. Earlier intervention, well resourced mental health and social care in the community, residential care, including for those suffering from dementia, and, in some cases, in-patient or secure psychiatric provision could have saved many vulnerable people from the damaging rigours of imprisonment.

There are footholds for hope and for change. In response to the Bradley review of Mental Health and Learning Disability, and the Women's Institute's powerful campaign 'Care, not custody', there has been an agreement between the Departments of Health and Justice to set aside an initial £50 million for diversion schemes in every police station and court across England by 2014. That would mean that people, on arrival, could have an assessment if such was thought to be needed, and could then be diverted into necessary treatment. If the offending is such that they must stay within criminal justice, then the treatment will follow them through the system.

Complex problems require complex solutions. The needs of vulnerable people should be the concern of every department of government, not monopolised by justice. Prisons cannot and should not continue to pick up the tab for a range of social and health needs A more effective and far-sighted use of public monies would see people with addiction receiving treatment in the community or in residential centres and people who are mentally ill, or those with learning disabilities, getting the health and social care they need to lead healthy responsible lives in their communities.

Reparation not retribution

Four weeks after the riots in summer of 2011, the Prison Reform Trust commissioned ICM to conduct a poll of 1,000 people across the UK to see how they felt about crime and punishment (Prison Reform Trust, 2011b). We expected a hardline approach given the level of public disorder in some towns and cities. It was remarkable how many people were interested in restorative justice, and reparative solutions to crime. The vast majority (80-90 per cent) said that they wanted people to account to victims for what they had done. Almost all could see that measures like treatment for addictions, mental health care, and better supervision by parents of young people would prevent crime and disorder in the future. There is a much greater public appetite for a change of direction than politicians or press acknowledge.

There will be the few people who feel that more punishment is all we need. But there are others who see that route as a *cul de sac*. The people we punish know what punishment is. Long before they get into trouble and caught up in the justice system, very many offenders are used to punishment, not as a measured, proportionate response to wrongdoing but as random acts of cruelty often born of frustration and ignorance. What has not been part of their lives is restoration, reparation, and gaining that empathic insight that can help you see how somebody else feels. Strands of that can be found within prison, in restorative justice conferences in custody and in the work of Samaritan listeners in prison – they do exist there. But where they flourish is outside of prison in the community.

You can see the success of restorative justice if you look to Northern Ireland, and the work that is done with under-eighteen year-olds (Jacobson and Gibbs, 2009). This has reduced child prison numbers markedly. Victim satisfaction is running at around 90 per cent, and there is high attendance at restorative conferences. That is the integrated and best way of dealing with most children and young people in trouble with the law. We need to look to those examples of reparation, of restoration. If we only look at punish-

ment, it darkens our lives as well as the lives of the people subjected to it.

And it is futile to pretend that punishment is what good people
do to bad people. Solzhenitsyn, in his Nobel address 'One word of
truth', wrote:

> If only there were evil people somewhere insidiously com-
> mitting evil deeds, and it were necessary only to separate
> them from the rest of us and destroy them. But the line
> dividing good and evil cuts through the heart of every hu-
> man being. And who is willing to destroy a piece of his own
> heart? (Newell, 2000).

Re-imagining imprisonment

We will not solve the problems of imprisonment by looking within
prison. Solutions do not lie behind prison walls, instead they lie
largely within communities, within housing, within education,
within work, within families. If we are to re-imagine imprisonment, we must reintegrate prison back into communities. We
must make prison smaller – smaller in our minds, and smaller in
number and capacity.

The reduction in child imprisonment in the UK has also happened in other countries, sometimes coupled with a reduction in
imprisonment as a whole. Denmark, for example, now imprisons
63 people in 100,000 and in Germany it's 83 in 100,000. In England
and Wales we imprison 155 people in 100,000. Other European
countries can tell us much more about a sparing use of imprisonment. Current and former prisoners, prisoners' families and prison staff, past and present, have informed views on what needs to
change. Yet their voices are rarely heard.

The growing level of competition and privatisation within the
system diminishes the incentive to share good practice. In order
to have a competitive edge, you cannot share what you do best.
A public service becomes demoralised when you not only cut its
budget to the bone, but also ask it to compete within the market.

Competition rarely feels like it is on a level playing field. With competition you also create a language of marketisation that mystifies what should be a common sense debate about crime and punishment and the use of imprisonment.

The decisive factor here is the cost of an individual going to prison. We cannot afford to have this huge prison population any longer, because of the economic situation in Europe and beyond. I think most of us would prefer a humanitarian argument – hearts and minds instead of wallets – but looking to the United States we can find, along with the opportunity to learn from their mistakes, some positive ways to reduce an unacceptably expensive prison population. Many penal reformers in the US are pragmatists, and they have accepted the idea that prison reform can be achieved through economic imperatives, legal challenge and justice re-investment. Of course it would be right to win the argument on hearts and minds, but it is better to win. It is more important to reduce the number to an 'unavoidable minimum', it is better to prevent that indelible mark being placed on so many people. We may say that the prison system is unsustainable emotionally, but many would say it is unsustainable economically.

I promised that I would return to Winston Churchill's seminal speech in Parliament. He said:

> ... when the doctors, chaplains and prison visitors have come and gone, the convict stands deprived of everything that a free man calls life. We must not forget that all these improvements, which are sometimes salves to our consciences, do not change that position.

The only way to re-imagine imprisonment is to put it where it belongs – at the far end of any justice system as a punishment of absolute last resort.

Bibliography

Bath, C. and Edgar, K. (2010) *Time is Money: Financial responsibility after prison.* London: Prison Reform Trust.

Brodeur, J.P. (2007) 'Comparative Penology in Perspective'. In: Tonry, M. ed. *Crime, Punishment and Politics in a Comparative Perspective.* Chicago: University of Chicago Press.

Catholic Bishops' Conference of England and Wales (2004) *A Place of Redemption.* London: Burns and Oates.

Edgar, K., Jacobson, J. and Biggar, K. (2011) *Time Well Spent: A practical guide to active citizenship and volunteering in prison.* London: Prison Reform Trust.

Edgar, K. and Rickford, D. (2009) *Too Little Too Late: An independent review of unmet mental health need in prison.* London: Prison Reform Trust.

Hough, M. and Jacobson, J. (2010) *Unjust Deserts: Imprisonment for Public Protection.* London: Prison Reform Trust.

Jacobson, J. and Gibbs, P. (2009) *Making Amends: Restorative youth justice in Northern Ireland.* London: Prison Reform Trust.

Jacobson, J., Bhardwa, B., Gyateng, T., Hunter, G. and Hough, M. (2010) *Punishing disadvantage: A profile of children in custody.* London: Prison Reform Trust.

Newell, T. (2000) *Forgiving Justice - A Quaker vision for criminal justice.* London: Quaker Home Service.

Prison Reform Trust (2013) *Bromley Briefings, Prison Factfile.* Available at: http://www.prisonreformtrust.org.uk/Publications/Factfile (Accessed 23 January 2014).

Prison Reform Trust (2011a) *Talking Justice: Talking Sense.* Available at: www.prisonreformtrust.org.uk/TalkingJusticeTalkingSense/talking justicebestoffilm (Accessed 23 January 2014).

Prison Reform Trust (2011b) *Public want offenders to make amends briefing paper.* London: Prison Reform Trust.

Prison Reform Trust (2010) *Barred from voting: The right to vote for sentenced prisoners.* London: Prison Reform Trust.

Prison Reform Trust (2007) *No One Knows.* London: Prison Reform Trust.

Talbot J. (2008) *Prisoners' Voices: Experiences of the criminal justice system by prisoners with learning disabilities and difficulties.* London: Prison Reform Trust.

3

Why Do We Send People to Prison? A View from Ireland

Peter McVerry

Introduction

Why do we send people to prison? While books have been written about the objectives of imprisonment, most people have, understandably, a more limited understanding of imprisonment. There is a belief that the more offenders that are locked up, for the longest possible length of time, the safer the rest of us will be. This appears to be self-evident. Most of us have been a victim of crime at some point in our lives, so we may have little appetite for a rational discussion on the causes of crime or the objectives of imprisonment – we just want the perpetrator punished. So, many people may have little time for do-gooders or the usual left-wing brigade who might point out the limitations or contradictions of such an understanding.

Here I wish to reflect on and question some of the conventional thinking around imprisonment from my own experience. I cannot claim that my reflections are in any way original. I have no doubt that you will have heard them before, perhaps often before, but I raise them again in the context of my experience.

I started working with young people who were homeless, many of whom have an addiction problem, when I was a young, handsome man with black hair – and time has taken its toll on two of those characteristics! Most of these young people have spent some time in prison, some have been there many times. I maintain contact with them by regularly visiting the prisons, a contact which is much appreciated. They have challenged me in so many ways; indeed, I would say that they have totally and radically changed me. They have challenged my attitudes, my values and my understanding of society. So these are my own personal reflections on those challenges.

Crime and fear and the 'offender'

While the detection rates for some categories of crime, such as murder, are high, most of us are not going around worried about being murdered. Our worries are having our houses burgled, or being assaulted and robbed while walking home some evening. And the conviction rate for burglaries can be less than 10 per cent; for other street crime perhaps 35-40 per cent. Of those who have been detected, most are on bail; many have served their sentence and have been released. This of course suggests that most offenders are, in reality, walking around amongst us. We pass them every day on our streets, but they are mostly unknown to us. Unless we want to spend vast amounts of money on our prison system, which would necessitate reductions in the amount we spend on education, health and social services – as the US seems to be happy to do – we can ever only lock up a small minority of offenders.

Indeed, even as more and more people end up behind bars, our fear of crime may still continue to increase, often fuelled by some media who make profits from the fear of crime; and some politicians who see votes in their promises to make the streets safer. Despite dramatic increases in the number of people being incarcerated in the past decade or so, selling burglar alarms is a growing industry, gated communities continue to increase and many people fear leaving their homes at night. Our sense of security has little or nothing to do with the number of people behind bars. Indeed, research suggests that a large increase in the numbers being sent to prison produces only a small decrease in the actual level of crime (Tarling, 1993).

Again, the consequences of the crimes committed by burglars and robbers – while they can often distress and even traumatise the victim – pale into insignificance when placed alongside the consequences for the whole of society of crimes such as tax evasion, flouting of environmental laws, corruption in the planning process, breaching company legislation and other white collar crime. We are all victims of such crimes through increased taxes, reduced services, increased unemployment, a lower quality of life and restricted life opportunities. But these crimes do not generate the same anger or fear amongst the public or media as those crimes where the victim is more clearly identifiable.

We often draw a sharp distinction between the offender – 'them' – and the victim – 'us'. However, this tends to ignore the fact that we are actually all both victims and offenders. Speeding, which is a crime most of us have committed, (myself, of course, excluded, in case anything I say may be written down and used as evidence against me) is a major cause of death and injury on our roads. Yet our attitude to such crimes, which 'we' are more likely to commit, is very different to our attitude to crimes, which 'they' are more likely to commit, such as joyriding which causes far less deaths and injury on our roads.

So why do we send people to prison? The stated objectives of imprisonment are also just as confused and confusing as our attitudes to prison and offenders.

Prison as punishment

The first and most obvious aim of imprisonment is to punish the offender. However, while the law states that offenders go to prison *as* punishment not *for* punishment, the distinction is generally lost on most people who believe and hope that the experience in prison is one of great hardship. Media reports of flat-screen televisions and PlayStations to pass away the hours fuel a belief that prison has lost its way and just isn't working. A very high recidivist rate confirms this belief and further fuels their demand for harsher conditions.

I have always held the theory – without any evidence, I have to say, but which suits my ideological bias – that the humane prison conditions in Scandanavian countries may be partially related to the fact that they have a mandatory 30-day imprisonment for drink driving, which means that many middle class people end up in jail and experience the intolerable conditions which they may have previously supported.

While imprisonment is certainly a punishment for some of those who go there, the punishment is proportional to the loss which they experience. Those who had a job, or status, or place in society may lose that on going into prison and the greater the loss, the greater the punishment. But the reality is that the majority of people who go to prison in Ireland have little or nothing to lose. Punishment is not an appropriate response: they have already been punished all their lives. The profile of most people going to prison is clear: early school leaver, few skills or qualification, no history of employment, poor literacy levels, often with an addiction to drink or drugs; a significant number also have a history of homelessness or insecure housing, and some have a history of mental health issues. Many will also have experienced abuse in childhood or violence at home.

On a visit to Ireland's most well known prison, Mountjoy Prison, some years ago, I reflected afterwards on the nine prisoners I had met that day. Six of them were known to me to have been sexually abused as children, and the other three I just did not know well enough to be able to say. And I said to myself, if this runs through the whole prison system, what on earth are we doing to these people? They developed an addiction because they could not cope with their experience of abuse and committed crimes as a result of their addiction. They were victims then, and we victimise them again by sending them to prison instead of trying to help them deal with the effects of that abuse. Many have been failed by all the structures in society, the educational system, the housing system, the health system, the labour market. Some will also have been failed by the child care system. When I was working in a poor inner-city parish, we priests used to say that we could predict, with 90 per cent accuracy, which children would end up in prison when we were baptising them. The prison system is the only publicly-funded service available to the poor for which there is no waiting list!

One young man I know, who has been in and out of prison all his life rarely attended school. Instead, from the age of six his parents took him into town, where his job was to distract the security guards while his parents shoplifted. By his early teens, robbing was as much a part of his life as eating or sleeping. It was the only thing he was good at, the only skill he had acquired.

Another young man I know who had been homeless most of his life finally got a very modest apartment of his own. His child, who had been in care returned to live with him. A few weeks later, he received a three month prison sentence for some offence he had committed many months earlier when he was homeless. He lost his accommodation and his child was taken back into care. Imprisonment affects more than the person who has committed the offence. The family of the person imprisoned is also punished. Spouses will find themselves in difficult financial circumstances, having to bring up their children without support, and suffer the same prejudice and discrimination from society as if they had committed the offence themselves. Relationships with their children may become strained as a result of the stresses they are now experiencing and their relationship with their partner may end up being irreparably damaged or destroyed.

So for a large majority of those we send to prison, punishment as an objective or purpose of imprisonment does not seem to me to be an appropriate response to their offending.

Prison as deterrence

One of the objectives of imprisonment is to act as a deterrent to criminal behaviour, both for the offender in committing further crime and for the wider society. There is no doubt that those who will be most deterred by the prospect of going to jail are those who have most to lose by going to jail. And they include the very people who make the laws and determine the sentences of those who break the laws. But prison is not much of a deterrent to many of those who end up there, as is evident by the recidivist rate. In Ireland, 50 per cent of those released from prison return there within four years (O'Donnell et al., 2008). One of the saddest experiences I have is to see someone at the end of their sentence looking forward to getting out in the next day or so, and then to meet them, 24 hours after release, depressed and asking: 'Why did I bother coming out?'

Many of those who go in and out of prison tell me that life outside prison is pretty much the same as life inside prison, except you don't have the bars. They feel trapped within the structures of society, unable to influence them or find a way out of them.

I went to a boarding school when I was 12. I didn't particularly want to go, I wasn't asked if I wanted to go, but it was just my destiny or something over which I, at 12 years of age, had no say and no control. Most of the people I know who go to prison feel much the same. Their friends have been to jail, members of their family may have been to jail. For them, going to jail is just destiny, a part of their life, not chosen, but unavoidable. For a small few, it may even be a badge of honour.

Going to prison may sometimes not be a deterrent, but may make it more likely that a person will return there. Despite the best efforts of the Irish Prison Service to keep drugs out of prison, drugs continue to be readily available within most of our prisons and a drug culture exists, into which newly sentenced prisoners are inserted. Despite the often excellent education and training services available within some of our prisons, and an innovative and successful Community Return Programme, all of which have an inadequate number of places for the number of prisoners. The reality is that most prisoners have little constructive activity during most of their days in prison, so the boredom, even meaninglessness, of prison life becomes a primary driver of drug misuse. Furthermore, the now official, but unstated, policy in Ireland of doubling up cells (in contravention of the European and UN best practice) makes it impossible for someone to remain drug free if they are sharing a cell with an active drug user.

I personally know about 40 young people who never touched a drug prior to going to jail and came out addicted to heroin. They will almost certainly return to jail, as a direct result of their prison experience.

There is also a lot of violence within prison. Assaults on prisoners by other prisoners have become a regular feature of prison life. The Irish Prison Service *Annual Report 2010* recorded that there were '1014 incidents of violence among prisoners during the year' – but added that this included 'very minor incidents' (2011). Interestingly, no information about the incidence of inter-prisoner violence is provided in the Annual Report for 2011 (Irish Prison Service, 2012). No figure is given for assaults on prison officers – but these do, of course, occur, and anecdotal evidence suggests they are increasing. One prison officer to whom I was talking casually when visiting one of our prisons recently remarked that he had been working now for 20 years, but for the first time in his career, he no longer felt safe coming in to work.

Many of the serious assaults on prisoners by other prisoners involve 'striping' a prisoner's face with a blade, leaving a permanent scar which may run down the whole side of the face.

Apart from the actual recorded incidents of violence, there is considerable bullying and intimidation of prisoners within our prisons. This was a very prevalent and very worrying feature of life within St. Patrick's Institution for young offenders. Huge pressure is placed on vulnerable prisoners to bring back drugs when attending court or hospital. Gang feuds outside prison continue within prison. Scores are settled within prison. Some people going into prison align themselves with one or other of the criminal gangs within prison for their own protection – but on release, they cannot then dissociate themselves from the gang.

The fear of assault has resulted in a significant number of prisoners requesting to be placed in isolation from others. For example, in November 2011, there were 364 prisoners (that is about 8 per cent of the prison population) on extended lock-up, most of them on 23-hour lock up, and, most worryingly, 44 of them were young people, under 21 years of age, in St. Patrick's Institution (Deputy Lynch asks Minister Shatter, 2011). One prisoner, well known to me, completed four years on 23-hour lock up and is now seriously damaged, emotionally and psychologically.

In order to deal with high levels of violence and gang culture one particular prison introduced a complex colour coded system for prison groups. The red prisoners were not allowed out of cell at the same time as yellow prisoners, but they could mix with blue prisoners; blue prisoners were not allowed to mix with green prisoners but could mix with yellow prisoners. Increasingly prison development in Ireland is attempting to 'maximise capacity' into 'economies of scale', however, the lived reality is that the larger the prison, the more difficult it is to manage potential violence.

Going to prison is, for many people, not a deterrent to further criminal activity on release but may make their future involvement in crime more likely.

Prison as rehabilitation

One of the objectives of imprisonment is rehabilitation. Rehabilitation ought to be a central objective of the prison system but for the most part, rehabilitation of prisoners is often little more than an add-on to the system, in so far as limited resources allow. While the education and training services within Irish prisons is often of a very high standard, with very committed teachers and staff, they can only cater for a small minority of prisoners at any one time. Most people in prison spend the majority of their time just walking around a yard, or playing snooker or just lying on their cell beds. Given the profile of the majority of prisoners, a prison sentence is an ideal opportunity to increase the training and educational achievements of people who have, in many cases, achieved or received very little in life.

However, even if rehabilitation were to be the central priority of the Irish Prison Service, rehabilitation in prison doesn't work. Most people, even those few who have the slightest interest in what happens to prisoners, judge the success of rehabilitation in prison by the reduction in the recidivist rate. By this criterion, rehabilitation doesn't and cannot work. It is likely that a substantial investment in education and training opportunities within prison will lead to a very small reduction in recidivism, as some individuals will use the skills learnt to find employment and change their life around. But the recidivist rate is primarily determined by what happens outside prison, not what happens inside prison. No matter how much education and skills training we give to people, if we send them out of prison into the same chaotic conditions from which they came, to the same deprived communities with limited opportunities, to communities where drugs are readily available, out to homelessness or insecure housing, then we cannot realistically expect people to turn their lives around.

This is not to say that rehabilitation should not be the central priority of the prison service. To judge the value of our investment in rehabilitation by the reduction in the recidivist rate is to value that investment by its effect on *us,* the extent to which *we* become safer. But the value of rehabilitation is in its effect on the *offender.* It is to seek to expand the skills and knowledge and personal development of people who have often had very little opportunity to acquire them during their childhood and adolescent years. Rehabilitation is a matter of justice for them, not about making society safer for the rest of us. It is about acknowledging that many of those in prison have been failed by society and we now take the opportunity to try to restore the balance a little bit.

One of the most important outcomes of a focus on rehabilitation is an increase in the self-esteem of people who may have little self-esteem.

Recently, when I was in one of our prisons, a guy came up to me and told me with great pride that he had passed his Leaving Certificate, our final State exam. I asked him what subjects had he done, and he said 'English – I got a grade C'. Passing that one subject gave him the same sense of achievement and pride as someone else might get from passing their degree exam in college. And he got a certificate to prove it. He gave me his certificate to keep safe for him until his sentence was over. He had never received a certificate for anything in his life before. To him, the certificate was society's acknowledgement of his achievement. That is the value of rehabilitation. The value of this increase in self-esteem is unquantifiable and we tend not to value what is unquantifiable. But it is evident to all who know the person and it is of huge value to the person themselves and to the rest of society.

Prison as prevention

So punishment is inappropriate for most of those going into prison, imprisonment has little deterrent value for most, rehabilitation doesn't work by our criterion, and that just leaves prevention. Most people would say that people in prison cannot commit crime. But again, our centre of concern is ourselves. It is true that those in prison are prevented from committing crimes against us outside of prison, except perhaps by proxy, but people in prison can still commit crime. Assaults, drug dealing, drug misuse, thefts all occur on a daily basis within prison. But as long as these crimes are committed against other prisoners, we can dismiss them as of no relevance to us.

So the primary objective of our prison service is to contain people, in reasonably humane conditions, at enormous expense.

The average cost of keeping a person in prison in Ireland in 2011 was €65,359 (Irish Prison Service, 2012), a substantial decrease on the cost of almost €100,000 some years ago (Irish Prison Service, 2008). This decrease in average cost results from 'reduced expenditure and an increase in the provision of bed capacity', which is prison-speak for cuts in services and overcrowding.

Of 12,990 persons sentenced to imprisonment in 2011, 8,070 were sentenced to less than three months (Irish Prison Service, 2012). While those serving less than 3 months represent only 1.2 per cent of the prison population on any one day, nevertheless it imposes a huge administrative and financial burden on an already overburdened and underfunded system.

A vital key to reducing the numbers going to prison and particularly those going for shorter sentences is the judiciary. Most of the judiciary have seldom or never been in prison, have no idea of the reality of the conditions in prison and yet are the gateway into prison. Imprisonment is meant to be the penalty of last resort, yet a few judges use it to teach someone a lesson, or to give someone a taste of prison or to send a message to the wider community, which is a totally inappropriate use of a very expensive resource. The judiciary rightly defend their independence but this sense of independence can also make it very difficult to challenge or change attitudes. We could legislate that all sentences less than six months be substituted by an alternative to imprisonment, but these same few judges will then start giving sentences of seven months! However, in fairness to the judiciary, sometimes the reason why they do not use alternatives to prison more often is that they may have no confidence in them, often because they are under resourced and therefore less effective.

Need to restore relationships

In my view, at the centre of any reform of the penal system must be restorative justice. Restorative justice has the potential to change attitudes of both victims and offenders. Often offenders have little appreciation of the effect of their crime on the victim.

A young lad, on a night out with his mates, decided to rob a car and drive around town for a while. The car crashed and was a total write off. The young lad was asked, 'Did he not think of the person who owned the car, and how they would be affected by its loss, when he was robbing it.' 'Ah, sure,' he replied, 'the insurance will buy them another car, so there's no big deal.'

The young lad was brought to court, and both the victim and the car thief agreed to meet face to face. The car owner explained that she was not covered by insurance for theft, so she couldn't replace the car. She needed the car to go to work. As the nearest bus stop was 30 minutes walk away and she had a physical disability and couldn't walk that far, she had to give up her job. She now lives on Disability Allowance, is confined to her home, and is very depressed and lonely. The young lad was lost for words. He had never thought of the consequences for her. It was a real eye-opener for him.

A person who commits a crime does so not out of freedom but out of a lack of freedom. If I rob or assault you, I reveal in myself a lack of awareness and sensitivity to the impact of my crime on you. This lack or defect limits my freedom to act differently towards you. Restorative justice can help to expand the freedom of the offender by increasing their awareness and sensitivity.

Restorative justice can also sometimes challenge the victim. One businessman, whose offices had been burgled, agreed to meet the offender. The offender had the opportunity to explain what had led him to commit this crime, along with many others that he had previously committed. At the end of the session, the businessman offered the offender a job.

Restorative justice gives the victim a sense of being involved in the justice process. It is also, and most importantly for our politicians, much cheaper. Every institution, every project, is being analysed in depth to ensure that society is getting value for its money.

The Peter McVerry Trust have a project that receives €70,000 – equivalent to imprisoning one person for a year – annually from the State to provide accommodation for up to 30 people a year who are leaving prison. This requires form-filling and financial returns on a monthly basis to ensure that the funding is being wisely and appropriately used.

But the prison system as we have it today is, by any rational criterion, an enormous waste of money. For the majority of prisoners, it achieves none of its objectives and, for society, who sees imprisonment as indispensible for making society safer, it is often counter-productive.

And so we are back to where I began: we lock people up just to get rid of them. What happens to them when they are behind walls we simply don't care, even though we know, regretfully, that they will have to return to the community one day. It is in society's own interest to ensure that they return to the community less alienated and better skilled and educated.

It is patently obvious that what we are doing with our prisons just isn't working. But we don't seem to have much interest in changing it.

Bibliography

Deputy Lynch asks Minister Shatter. (2011) 24 November, 747(5): q. 165, PQ 36794/11.

Irish Prison Service. (2012) *Annual Report 2011.* Longford: Irish Prison Service Print Unit.

Irish Prison Service. (2011) *Annual Report 2010.* Longford: Irish Prison Service Print Unit.

Irish Prison Service. (2008) *Annual Report 2007.* Longford: Irish Prison Service Print Unit.

O'Donnell, I., Baumer, E. P. and Hughes, N. (2008) 'Recidivism in the Republic of Ireland'. *Criminology and Criminal justice*, 8(2):123-146.

Tarling, R. (1993) Analysing *Offending: Data, Models and Interpretations.* Home Office Research and Planning Unit, London.

4

How to Reduce Prison Numbers: The Experience of Finnish Penal Policy

Tapio Lappi-Seppälä

Introduction

The Nordic family

Finland is a small Nordic country with a population of 5.4 million. The Finnish juridical system is manifestly rooted in western, continental legal culture with strong influence from neighbouring Nordic countries. Today, Finland profiles itself – together with the other Nordic countries Denmark, Iceland, Norway and Sweden – as a county with internationally high levels of social security and equality, high social trust and political legitimacy, and a low level of penal repression.

Criminal justice systems do not exist outside of historical, cultural, social and political contexts. In particular, the Nordic political systems and welfare states are crucial to understanding Nordic crime patterns and criminal justice system policies and operations today.[1] Consensus political systems and career judges and prosecutors are associated with moderate penal policies and

---

[1] The central social and political characteristics of the Nordic countries and their relevance on national penal policies are discussed in more detail in Lappi-Seppälä and Tonry (2011) and Lappi-Seppälä (2007; 2008).

low imprisonment rates. So are low levels of income inequality and high levels of welfare expenditure, trust and legitimacy (Lappi-Seppälä, 2008). Perhaps not surprisingly, the most recent International Crime Victimization Survey and European Crime Survey showed that, compared with other developed countries, residents of the Nordic countries were among the least punitive, and the least fearful about crime (van Dijk et al., 2007).

Moreover, these social and political features are crucial to the understanding of the major changes in Finnish criminal justice policies that took place in the last century. Finland has not always been a member of the 'Happy Nordic Welfare Family'. Not too long ago, Finland was a poor agricultural country, struggling in the midst of social, economic and political crises. During the last century, Finland experienced three wars (the 1918 Civil War and the two wars against the Soviet Union between 1939 and 1944). These crises have left their marks on Finnish society and its criminal justice policy. The trends in prison rates – a commonly used basic indicator for changes in penal policy – have been more turbulent than in almost any other Western European country.

Major phases in the use of imprisonment

The harsh history of Finland can be read from her prison statistics. Figure 1 displays the trends in prison rates (relative to 100,000 of the population) throughout the last century. The role of political, social and economic crises is highlighted by dividing prisoners into three categories: (1) prisoners serving their sentences for ordinary crimes, (2) prisoners placed in prisons for political crimes (treason-like activities) or those sentenced by the martial courts during war-times, and (3) prisoners placed in prisons for unpaid fines (fine defaulters).

Three main phases are identified. The period from the civil war of 1918 until the end of war with the Soviet Union (1945) is characterised by recurring political, social and economic crises –and hugely varying incarceration rates. From the early 1950s, there

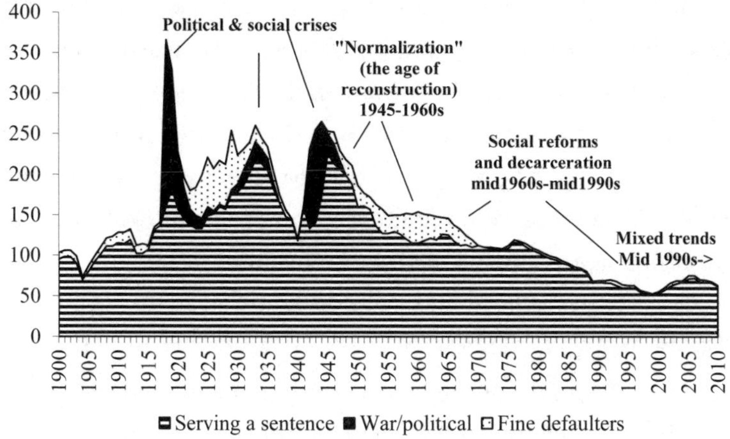

Figure 1: Prisoner rates in Finland, 1900–2010 (annual averages) (Source: National Statistics).

started a period of normalisation (known as the 'age of reconstruction'). Finland was recovering from the damages of war and paying war compensations; this led to the development of industrial infrastructures which formed the foundations of the welfare state.

The dire economic circumstances were reflected also in the prison administration. In general terms, the criminal justice system of Finland in the 1950s and into the 1960s was less resourceful, less flexible and more repressive than that of its Nordic neighbours. This was all about to change during the third phase, the period of social reform from the 1960s onwards, which will be discussed below.

The reform ideology of the 1960s and the 1970s

Against coercive care

In the 1960s, the Nordic countries experienced heated social debate around the effects of, and justifications for, involuntary treatment in institutions, both penal and otherwise (such as in health care and in the treatment of alcoholics). In Finland, the criticism of the treatment ideology was merged with another reform ideology that was directed against the overly severe Criminal Code and the excessive use of custodial sentences. The resulting criminal political ideology, 'humane neo-classicism', stressed both legal safe-guards against coercive care and the goal of less repressive measures in general. In sentencing, the principles of proportionality and pre-dictability became the central values. Individualised sentencing, as well as sentencing for general preventive reasons or perceived dan-gerousness, was severely limited (see in more detail Anttila, 1971; Lahti, 2000; Lappi-Seppälä, 2007 and Törnudd, 1996).

Broadening the aims and means of criminal policy

Behind the shift in the strategies in criminal policy were more pro-found changes in the way the entire problem of crime was con-ceived. The theoretical criminal political framework and the con-ceptualisation of the aims and means of criminal policy underwent a change, as the social sciences and planning strategies merged with the criminal political analysis. The aims of criminal policy were defined as part of the overall aims of general social policy. Cost-benefit analysis was introduced into criminal political think-ing. The result of all this was that the arsenal of criminal policy re-sponses expanded to include general social welfare interventions, environmental planning and situational crime prevention. This new ideology was crystallised in slogans such as 'criminal policy is an inseparable part of general social development policy' and 'good social development policy is the best criminal policy'. The role of punishment came to be seen as relative. Once regarded as the primary means of criminal policy, punishment came to be re-garded as only one option among many.

The function of criminal justice: Indirect general prevention

After the fall of the rehabilitative ideal and a re-evaluation of the justification of punishment, there was a shift, once again, towards general prevention. However, this concept was now understood differently. It was assumed that general prevention could be reached not through fear (deterrence), but through the moral-creating and value-shaping effect of punishment. According to this idea, the disapproval expressed in punishment is assumed to influence the values and moral views of individuals. As a result of this process, the norms of criminal law and the values they reflect are internalised; people refrain from illegal behaviour not because such behaviour would be followed by unpleasant punishment, but because the behaviour itself is regarded as morally blameworthy (Törnudd, 1996). This, too, had a number of policy implications. Indirect prevention is best served by a system of sanctions which maintains a moral character, demonstrates the blameworthiness of the act and follows procedures perceived as fair and just by all parties. Instrumental compliance based on fear and sentence severity was given but a marginal role.

Sentencing: Humane neo-classicism

The classical element in humane neo-classicism was the revival of the old principle of proportionality in a new sentencing ideology. The humane elements were to be found in systematic efforts towards leniency. Minimisation of the suffering caused by the crime control system was one of the generally accepted crime policy goals. The role and functions of the principle of proportionality were also seen in this spirit: it had its roots in the rule of law and the guarantees against the excessive use of force. The main function of the proportionality principle in Finland was to introduce an upper limit which the punishment may not exceed. (Lappi-Seppälä, 2001).

This theoretical framework provided a starting point for a broad legislative reform program that took off in the 1970s and 1980s.

Legislative reforms and sentencing practices

Systematic legislative reforms started during the mid-1960s, and continued until the mid-1990s. They dealt with the general sanction system as well as specific offences. The major law reforms affecting the number of prisoners are summarised below (and in Figure 2, where DWI refers to drunk driving and CSO refers to Community Service Orders).

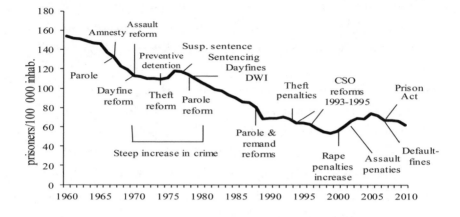

Figure 2: Prison rates and policy reforms in Finland, 1960–2010.

General structure of sanctions, 1950-1990

The general structure of the sanctions system remained untouched between 1950 and the 1990s. This consisted of fines, conditional sentence and imprisonment. The decrease of prisoner rates between 1950 and the 1980s was technically a result of the general decline in the length of prison sentences and the expansion in the use of fines and conditional sentences. In 1950, the average length of all sentences of imprisonment imposed for theft was 12 months; in 1971, it was seven months; and in 1991, three months. Similar changes occurred in other major crimes, such as robbery, assaults and drunken driving (Figure 3). Up to about 1970, these reductions were court-initiated; from the 1970s onwards the trend was supported also by legislative reforms.

From the late 1960s onwards, all major offences tended to increase. The increased number of property and violent offences were punished either by conditional prison sentences or fines. In 1977, the use of fines was expanded as a substitute for short-term imprisonment; this was done by raising the monetary value of fines. The scope of *conditional imprisonment* (suspended sentence) was extended by relaxing the prerequisites for the use of this sanction. The number of annually imposed conditional sentences rose from 4,000

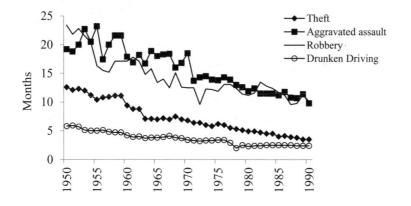

Figure 3: The average length of sentences of imprisonment for four differ-ent offences 1950 to 1990 (Source: Statistics Finland).

(1960) to 18,000 (in 1990, Table 1, section B). *Sentencing reform* in 1976 restricted the relevance of a prior record in sentencing. This reduced the length of prison sentences especially among chronic property offenders.

The expansion of petty traffic and property offences increased the use of fines. This expansion also forced the legislator to adopt different forms of summary proceedings (see Table 1, section A). The number of prosecutor fines expanded from 80,000 in 1950 to over 300,000 in the 1990. To ease administrative pressures, an even more simplified fixed police fine was introduced in the late 1980s. Today, both the police and the prosecutor impose about half a million small fines, mainly for traffic and small property offences.

The adoption of summary proceedings has kept the annual number of court-imposed penalties on a fairly stable level (50,000–80,000). The absolute number of prison sentences imposed is to-day at the same level as over 50 years ago, and at a much lower level than some 30 years ago (see section B). An increased number of people guilty of medium rank offences have received a fine or been given a community sanctions. Comparison between other court-ordered sanctions (excluding fines), shows how the relative share of prison has reduced from 70 per cent in 1950 to 25 per cent in 2008 (see Table 1, section C).

Reducing the penalty-scales for specific offences

In 1977, the law on drunken driving was changed whereby unconditional prison sentences were replaced by conditional sentences and fines. In a short period of time, the proportion of prison sentences dropped from 90 per cent to 20 per cent. The introduction of community service in the mid-1990s brought another drop in the use of imprisonment to around 10 per cent (Figure 4).

Aside from the impact of drunk drivers, Finnish prisons in the 1950s to the 1970s were crowded due to property offenders, especially those committed for theft. Penalties for theft were reduced both in 1972 and 1991. These reforms decreased the share of unconditional imprisonment from 50 per cent to 25 per cent, while the share of fines increased from 20 per cent to 50 per cent.

This de-penalisation had a dramatic effect on prison numbers. While, in the mid-1970s, two out three prisoners were sentenced either for drunk-driving or theft, today the relative share of these offences is about one-third. In 1975, there were 1,800 prisoners serving a sentence for theft; today their number is around 450. For drunk driving the corresponding figures are 1,000 and 300.

Specific offender-groups

Targeted actions were taken to reduce the size of prison populations in three groups of inmates: fine defaulters, people who repeatedly offend and young people. The use of *default imprisonment for unpaid fines* approached record levels in the 1960s, with almost 1,800 fine-defaulters on any given day. In 1969, the use of default imprisonment was restricted and the major offence for which fines were issued was removed when public drunkenness was decriminalised. The daily number of fine-defaulters fell from over 1,000 to less than 50 (Figure 5).

	A. Summary fines N		B. Courts: all sanctions N					C. Courts: other than fines %			
	Prosecutor	Police	Prison	CSO	Conditional	Fines	All	Prison %	Condit. %	CSO %	All N
1950	80,000		6,741		2,812	39,027	48,580	70.6	29.4		9,553
1960	148,000		6,900		3,686	40,812	51,398	65.2	34.8		10,586
1970	150,000		10,212		5,215	42,248	57,675	66.2	33.8		15,427
1980	250,000		10,326		14,556	47,401	72,283	41.5	58.5		24,882
1990	312,000	70,000	11,657		17,428	52,542	81,627	40.1	59.9		29,085
2000	196,000	104,000	8,147	3,413	13,974	37,504	63,038	31.9	54.7	13.4	25,534
2008	255,000	202,000	6,872	3,222	15,998	37,615	63,707	26.3	61.3	12.3	26,092

Table I: The use of different sentencing alternatives and processes, 1950 to 2008

55

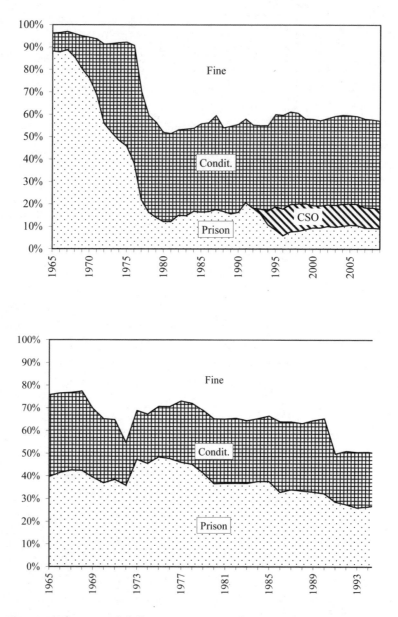

Figure 4: The use of different sentencing alternatives for drunk driving (top) and theft (bottom) (Source: Statistics Finland).

In the course of the 1960s, the use of *preventive (secure) detention* for repeat offenders had expanded to include large numbers of property offenders, with a prison daily rate of 400 persons (5

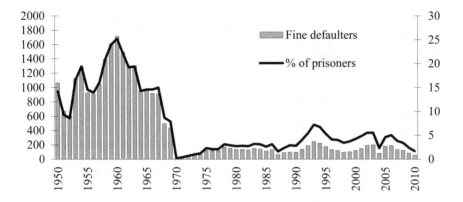

Figure 5: The number of fine defaulters, 1950–2010 (absolute figures and as percentages of all prisoners) (Source: Criminal Sanctions Agency).

per cent of the prison population). In 1971, the use of preventive detention was restricted only to serious violent recidivists, and the number of people held in preventive detention fell overnight from 250 to less than 10 (see trend in Figure 6).

By the late 1970s, the use of imprisonment for *young offenders* started to fall, reflecting court sentencing practices, as the number of prison sentences imposed for juveniles started to decrease – only to rise again during the 1980s. Two law reforms during the 1990s contributed to a renewed reduction in the number of young people in prison. The Conditional Sentence Act was amended in 1989 by including a provision which allows the use of unconditional sentence for young offenders only if there are exceptional reasons for this. Also, the reduction of minimum penalties for car-thefts (joy-riding) in 1991 had an impact on younger age groups, as this offence is typically committed by youths (one-third of prison sentences in the age group of 15-17 were imposed for this offence – see Figure 7).

In 1975, the courts imposed over 2,000 prison sentences for young adults (18-20 years) and more than 700 sentences for juveniles aged 15-17 years). In 2010, the corresponding figures were

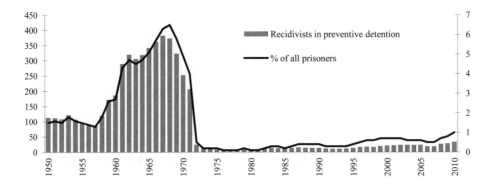

Figure 6: The number of recidivist in preventive detention, 1950–2005 (absolute figures and as percentages of all prisoners) (Source: Criminal Sanctions Agency).

500 and 50. In 2010 also, there were about 70 prisoners between the ages of 18 and 20, and 5 in the 15 to 17 age group. In the mid-1970s, the numbers were five to ten times higher.[2]

Community service

The next major sanction reform was the introduction of community service in the mid-1990s. In order to ensure that community service would really be used in lieu of an unconditional sentence of imprisonment (and not instead of other more lenient penalties), a specific two-step procedure was adopted. First, the court is supposed to make its sentencing decision without considering the possibility of community service. If the result is unconditional imprisonment, then the court may commute the sentence into community service under certain conditions prescribed in the law. The duration of community service varies between 20 and 200 hours. In commuting imprisonment into community service, one day in prison equals one hour of community service.

---

[2] One needs to remember that in the age-group 15-17 child welfare bears the basic responsibility for rehabilitative actions including institutional care when necessary. Finnish juvenile justice system is discussed in more detail in Lappi-Seppälä, 2011a.

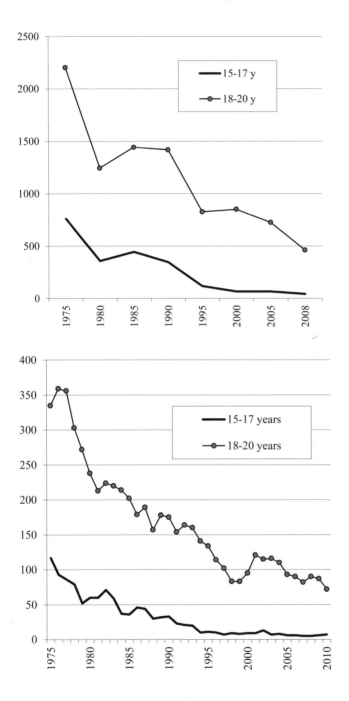

Figure 7: Imposed prison sentences (top) and the number of juvenile prisoners (bottom), 1975–2010 (annual averages, absolute figures, remand included) (Sources: Statistics Finland, Criminal Sanctions Agency).

Within a short period of time, community service proved to be an important alternative to imprisonment. Today community service replaces around 35 per cent of short term (maximum 8 months) prison sentences.

Parole

The system of parole and early release has also proven to be a very powerful tool in controlling prisoner rates. In Finland, practically all prisoners are released on parole on a routine basis. The minimum time to be served before the prisoner is eligible for parole is 14 days. A series of reforms have brought it down to this. In the mid-1960s, this period was shortened from six to four months; in the mid-1970s, from four to three months; and finally in the late 1980s from three months to 14 days. Also, the criteria for early release were relaxed and the conditions for the revocations of parole were made more strict. All this had a substantial effect on the overall scope of parole and early release. In the early 1960s, less than 40 per cent of annually released prisoners were released on parole. By the late 1960s, their share increased to 50 per cent, and during the 1970s to 75 per cent. After parole reform in 1989 practically all prisoners are released on parole before their sentence is complete (see in more detail Lappi-Seppälä, 2011b).

Explaining penal liberalisation

The decrease in the Finnish prison population was a result of a conscious, long term and systematic criminal policy. This policy was backed up by criminal political ideology that combined the pragmatic aims of criminal justice with the ideas of fairness and respect for legal safeguards. What resulted was a broader view than previously of the general aims of criminal policy which emphasised the role of both social and situational strategies in crime control. But this still raises the question as to what were the driving forces behind this ideological change, and what made it possible to realise this policy in political practice.

Historically, the period of penal liberalisation coincides with the growth of the welfare state in Finland. From 1950, there was a period of radical social, economic and structural change. From 1950 to 1970, the gross domestic product of Finland increased by 125 per cent compared to the OECD average growth of 75 per cent, and considerably less growth in the UK and the USA. Between 1960 and 1998, the total public social expenditure as a percentage of GDP increased in Finland by 18 percentage points, in OECD countries by 13, in the UK by 11 and in the US by 7. Between 1966 and 1990 the income differences – measured by GINI-index where the lower the figure the less income inequality in a nation – reduced in Finland by 8.3 points (from 33.4 to 25.1). In short, Finland was joining the Scandinavian welfare family in terms of the level of economic prosperity, welfare provision and income equality. This change was reflected also in our penal policies. In contrast, imprisonment expansion in the Anglo-Saxon world coincides with the concomitant general scaling down of the welfare states (Garland, 2001).

Part of the answer can also be found in the structure of our political culture. There was clear political will and consensus to bring down the prisoner rate (Törnudd, 1993: 12). Another closely related way of characterising the Finnish criminal policy would be to describe it as exceptionally expert-oriented: reforms have been prepared and implemented by a relatively small group of experts whose thinking on criminal policy, at least on basic points, has followed similar lines. The impact of these professionals was, furthermore, reinforced by close personal and professional contacts between some politicians, state officials and academic research. Consequently, and unlike the situation in many other countries, crime control has never been a central political issue in election campaigns in Finland. At least the 'heavyweight' politicians have not relied on populist policies, such as 'three strikes' and 'truth in sentencing'.

Nordic co-operation also matters. The early 1960s was a period of intensifying Nordic co-operation in legal matters, including criminal justice. The reform work of the 1960s and 1970s in Finland was heavily influenced by this exchange of ideas and legislative models. In many instances liberal reforms could be defended by reference to positive experiences gained in other Nordic countries and the need for Inter-Nordic harmonisation. The results of this co-operation were manifested in legislative acts that have been adopted separately in each Nordic country, but with identical contents.

In this setting, the *role of the media* is also of crucial importance. In Finland, the media have retained quite a sober and reasonable attitude towards issues of criminal policy. The Finns have largely been saved from low-level populism. There is a striking difference between the British and Finnish crime reports in the media. The tone in the Finnish reports is less emotional, and even reports of singular criminal events are often accompanied by analysis based on research.

Further, collaboration with and assistance from the judiciary was one of the key factors in explaining penal liberalisation. In many cases the legislature was strongly supported by the courts. Different training courses and seminars arranged for judges (and prosecutors) in co-operation with the universities have also had an impact on sentencing and prosecutorial practices. The Finnish *sentencing structure*, which treats sentencing as an area of normal judicial decision making, guided by valid sources of sentencing law, may also function as a shield against political pressures (for discussion, see Lappi-Seppälä, 2001).

Imprisonment rates and crime rates in Nordic countries

A profound change in the use of imprisonment naturally raises questions about its effects on crime rates. There are several well known methodological difficulties in measuring causal relations between crime rates and prison rates. However, the possibility of comparing the Nordic countries, with strong social and structural similarities but with very different penal histories, provides an unusual opportunity to see how drastic changes in penal practices in one country have been reflected in crime rates, compared with countries which have kept their penal systems more or less stable. Figure 8 shows incarceration and reported crime rates in Finland, Sweden, Denmark and Norway, from 1950 to 2010.

Except in Finland, imprisonment rates were remarkably stable during the entire period, ranging between 40 and 80 per 100,000. By the late 1980s, Finnish rates had fallen to the Scandinavian level, where they have since remained.

All in all, there is a striking *difference* in the use of imprisonment (top), and a striking *similarity* in the trends in recorded crime (bottom). That Finland has substantially reduced its incarceration rate has not disturbed the symmetry of Nordic crime rates. These figures, once again, support the general criminological conclusion that crime and incarceration rates are fairly independent of one another; each rises and falls according to its own laws and dynamics.

Nordic Prison Policies in International Comparisons in 2010

How does all this appear in a wider comparative perspective? Figures 9a nd 9b present data on imprisonment rates in 2006/07 and 2012/13 for 25 European countries, Russia and the United States.

Both individually and collectively, Scandinavian rates are amongst the lowest. Individually, the Scandinavian countries occupy five of the six bottom spots. In recent years Scandinavian rates have varied between 60 (45 in Iceland) and 75, with an average in 2013 of 63. For other Western European countries in 2010 the average rate was 107 per 100,000, in Eastern Europe 185, in the Baltic countries 288, in Russia 470, and in the United States 707. Over the last five to six years the imprisonment rate in most countries has increased with the exception of Finland, Sweden,

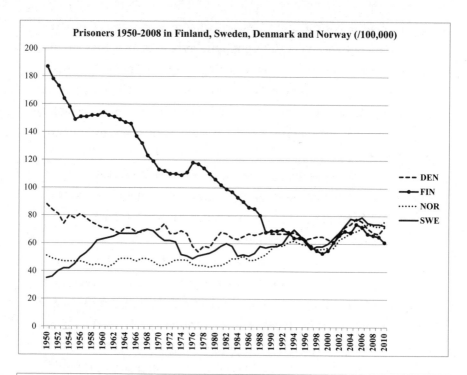

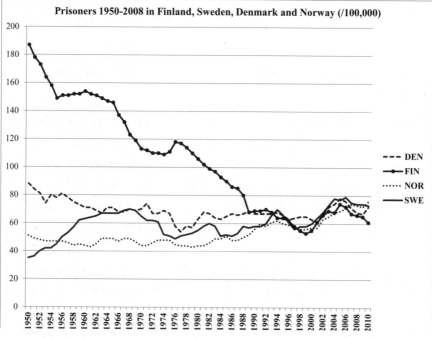

Figure 8: Prison rates (top) and crime rates (bottom), 1950–2010 (compiled from von Hofer et al., 2012).

Germany, the Netherlands, Spain, Czech Republic, Poland, Estonia, Russia and the US. The most substantial annual decreases have taken place in Russia and while prison numbers are declining in the US does not risk US's leading position. Sharp increases have taken place in Slovakia, Hungary and Lithuania.

These differences in imprisonment rates cannot be explained by differences in crime. Nordic homicide rates are low (except in Finland), but not remarkably so compared with those in other western European countries. Rates for other crimes are comparable to those in other developed countries. Wider cross-national and comparative evidence suggests, instead, that penal severity is closely associated with the extent of welfare provision, differences in income equality, trust (and other social sentiments), and political cultures (Lappi-Seppälä, 2008). The Nordic Penal Model has its roots in a consensual and corporatist political culture, in high levels of social trust and political legitimacy, and in a strong welfare state.

Strong welfare states sustain less repressive policies by providing workable alternatives to imprisonment. Extensive and generous social service networks often function as effective crime prevention measures, even if that is not a direct motivation for them. Consensual politics also lessen controversies, produce less crisis talk (moral panic), and sustain long-term policies. They are less vulnerable to 'penal populism' compared with more polarised conflictual (majoritarian) political cultures in which differences are exaggerated and controversies are sharpened, and in which more polarised political systems tend to give rise to complete turnovers of governmental power, short-term solutions, and more direct appeals to public emotion and demands.

The future: Will the Nordic model survive?

Nordic penal policy has a pragmatic and non-moralistic approach, with a clear social policy orientation. It reflects the values of the Nordic welfare state ideal. Measures aimed at reducing social

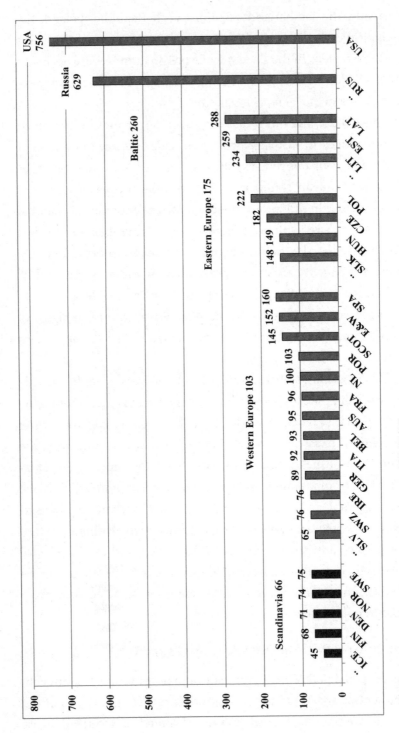

Figure 9a: Imprisonment rates by regions 20007/07.

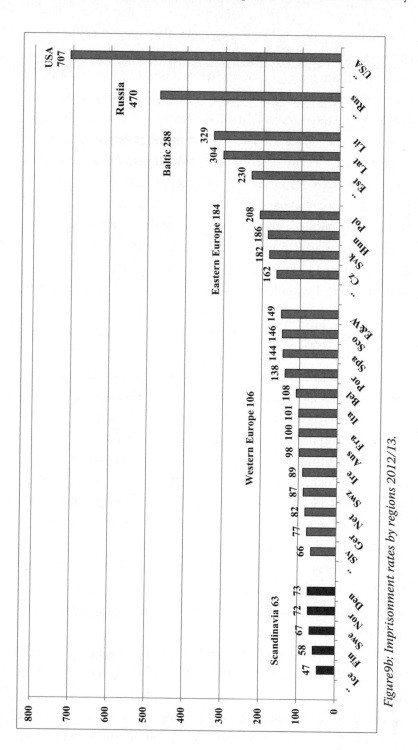

Figure9b: Imprisonment rates by regions 2012/13.

marginalisation and achieving equality also operate as measures against crime. These policies are to a large extent a byproduct of an affluent welfare state and of consensual and corporatist political cultures. However, we are ultimately faced with the question, will the 'Nordic Model' survive the future, and will the Nordic countries retain their 'exceptional' position in the global penal chart?

The Nordic welfare states – and Finland perhaps more so than the others – have also suffered from economic crises. Nordic welfare States were not spared from general global trends such as cutbacks in the public sector, general scaling down of welfare provisions and increases in income differences. Furthermore, the Nordic criminal justice systems have received their share of the global 'punitive turn'. These changes may not be comparable in type and magnitude to those that have taken place elsewhere in Europe and beyond, but they are still real for the Nordics (Tham, 2001; Balvig, 2004).

The question as to whether Finland will face similar growth in the prison population as is found in so many other countries would probably receive different answers from different observers. An optimist would point out that very few of the social, political, economic and cultural background conditions which explain the rise of mass imprisonment in the United States and United Kingdom apply to Finland. The social and economic security granted by the Nordic welfare state model may still function as a social backup system for tolerant criminal policy. Political culture still encourages negotiations and appreciates expert opinion. Social security, equality, trust and legitimacy granted by an affluent, universalistic welfare state will dampen public fears, punitive projections and reactive populist posturing.

For a pessimist, neoliberalism has already gained a firm foothold in Finland since the early 1990s and will tighten its grip in the coming years. Punitive and populist trends – more visible in Sweden and Denmark – will also invade Finland. Right-wing protest parties are increasingly popular in all Nordic countries (most recently in the 2011 national elections in Finland). An optimist might argue that the tone is still different compared to similar changes in many other countries (and that the Finnish right wing party has not so far shown any major interest in criminal justice policy). The Nordic welfare model may be under threat, but it certainly has not been abnegated or rejected. On the contrary, it has become a part of the 'Common Nordic Identity' and is widely supported across the whole political field, at least on the level of political rhetoric. Uncontested as this model is, it may well prove to be one of the cornerstones for the argument in maintaining a more social and human penal policy. However, making predictions on penal policy is a risky business. And the same applies to predictions about the survival of the Nordic welfare model, particularly in the light of the recent European and global economic crisis.

Bibliography

Anttila, I. (1971) 'Conservative and Radical Criminal Policy in the Nordic Countries'. *Scandinavian Studies in Criminology*, 3: 9-21.

Balvig, F. (2004) 'When Law and Order returned to Denmark'. *Journal of Scandinavian Studies in Criminology*, 5(2): 167-187.

Garland, D. (2001) *The Culture of Control: Crime and Social Order in Contemporary Society.* Chicago: University of Chicago Press.

Lahti, R. (2000) 'Towards a Rational and Humane Criminal Policy – Trends in Scandinavian Penal Thinking'. *Journal of Scandinavian Studies and Crime Prevention.* 1(2): 141–155.

Lappi-Seppälä, T. (2011a) 'Nordic Youth Justice: Juvenile Sanctions in Four Nordic Countries'. In: Tonry, M. and Lappi-Seppälä, T. eds. *Crime and Justice: A Review of Research, Volume 40.* Chicago: University of Chicago Press.

Lappi-Seppälä, T. (2011b) 'Changes in Penal Policy in Finland'. In: Kury, H. and Shea, E. eds. *Punitivity. International developments. Vol. 1: Punitiveness – global Phenomenon?* Bochum: Universitätäverlag Dr. N. Brockmeyer.

Lappi-Seppälä, T. (2008) 'Trust, Welfare, and Political Culture: Explaining Differences in National Penal Policies'. In: Tonry, M. ed. *Crime and Justice: A Review of Research, Volume 37.* Chicago: University of Chicago Press.

Lappi-Seppälä, T. (2007) 'Penal Policy in Scandinavia.' In: Tonry, M. ed. *Crime, Punishment, and Politics in Comparative Perspective: Crime and Justice, Volume 36.* Chicago: University of Chicago Press.

Lappi-Seppälä, T. (2001) 'Sentencing and Punishment in Finland: The Decline of the Repressive Ideal.' In: Tonry, M. and Frase, R. eds. *Punishment and Penal Systems in Western Countries.* New York: Oxford University Press: 92-150.

Lappi-Seppälä, T. and Tonry, M. (2011) 'Crime, Criminal Justice, and Criminology in the Nordic Countries.' In: Tonry, M. ed. *Crime and Justice: A Review of Research, Volume 40.* Chicago: University of Chicago Press.

Tham, H. (2001) 'Law and order as a leftist project?' *Punishment & Society: The International Journal of Penology*, 3(3): 409-426.

Törnudd, P. (1996). 'Facts, Values and Visions'. In: Anttila, I., Aromaa, K., Jaakkola, R., Lappi-Seppälä, T. And Takala, H. eds. *Essays in Criminology and Crime Policy.* Helsinki: National Research Institute of Legal Policy.

Törnudd, P. (1993) 'Fifteen Years of Decreasing Prison Rates in Finland.' In: National Research Institute of Legal Policy. ed. *Research Communication 8.* Helsinki: The National Research Institute of Legal Policy.

Van Dijk, J., van Kesteren, J. and Smit, P. (2007) *Criminal Victimisation in International Perspective. Key Findings from the 2004-2005 ICVS and EU ICS.* Meppel: Boom Legal Publishers.

Von Hofer, H., Lappi-Seppälä, T. and Westfelt, L. (2012) *Nordic Criminal Statistics 1950–2010.* Stockholm: Stockholm University.

5

The Societal Impact
and Role of Imprisonment:
An Example from Slovenia

Dragan Petrovec and Mojca M. Plesničar

Introduction

Different societies establish different hierarchies of values. Their attitudes towards specific pertinent issues vary tremendously: questions on the role of the welfare state, or the legitimacy of capital punishment, receive very different answers across different societies and even within them. Within our topic of discussion, attitudes to imprisonment and the treatment of offenders are equally divisive. By presenting the experience of our country, we attempt to illustrate how ideology can make all the difference in any given system and how rapidly and dramatically things can change, unfortunately not always for the better.

The setting

Slovenia is a country that has long been part of the central European legal reality, retaining much of its Austro-Hungarian juridical legacy even through its half century long socialist experience. A fact that might surprise people about this small jurisdiction in the middle of Europe is its remarkably low imprisonment rate, comparable to Scandinavian countries. What is even more surprising is the fact that the current imprisonment rate of 63 per 100,000 of the population (Walmsley, 2011) is on the back of a rapidly increasing prison population trend in the past two decades. The imprisonment rate used to be much lower in the early days after the country gained independence in 1991.[1]

The Slovenian penological experience, which will be discussed below, is based on values established prior to the country's independence, under the communist regime. The shape of criminal justice has changed dramatically over the 20 years since independence. Even prior to independence, Slovenia was very different from other Yugoslav states with respect to punishment. For example, while federal legislation provided general rules (and settled specific politically important issues), states were left to develop their own criminal justice and penal sanctions. In this context Slovenia opted for a rather lenient system of punishment; first becoming a de-facto abolitionist country after its last execution in 1959, followed by the definitive abolitionist move in 1989. The maximum penalty provided by the Penal Code prior to independence was 20 years of imprisonment; the sentence length was rarely questioned. From the 1970s onwards, the penal system functioned much in line with a humanistic ideology, sponsoring humanising social experiments and socio-therapeutic treatment (Petrovec and Meško, 2007; Meško et al., 2011).

The general leniency and humanity of the criminal justice system may seem rather misplaced in a setting of a totalitarian regime, but two remarks might make it less so. Firstly, when discussing leniency and humanity what is meant is the *general* outlook on criminal justice and penal institutions specifically. In spite of great differences in the types of communism that existed in our European surrounding, any totalitarian regime must necessarily deal with its opposition in order to survive and the social repercussions

---

[1]The rapid increase is due to multiple factors, beginning with a very low starting point after a system 'reboot', and continuing with changes in sentencing, the introduction of fine enforcement by imprisonment, the increase in pre-trial detention, a decline in the use of conditional release, etc., but explaining the complex issue of this sadly common occurrence in the Slovenian setting is outside the remit of this chapter.

(not necessarily of a legal nature) of opposing mainstream ideas were important and very much present. The Slovenian Penal Code thus acknowledged political crimes, there were political prisoners and the ideology was also safeguarded through legal instruments. However, criminal justice generally managed to position itself away from political issues, thus constructing a rather modern system with a multitude of safeguards and checks preventing extreme abuses. The system was dominated by professionals, with officials generally leaving (the non-politically) criminal justice issues to be resolved by professors and researchers, who functioned much like Loader's 'platonic guardians' (Loader, 2006).

Secondly and perhaps even more surprisingly, the very authoritarian nature of the totalitarian regime worked as a deterrent to those coveting a harsher system. The paradox, one could only expect in a (probably comical) fictional setting, was however very real: because the official stance was that of humanism and tolerance, opposing it would have been rather inappropriate if not outright dangerous (Petrovec and Muršič, 2011).

Within this context open prisons were established allowing for inventive approaches to be developed: a humane regime was advanced in prison institutions, including a specific treatment of prisoners which led to a slow but steady opening of at least some of the twelve prison institutions.

While severe sentencing, inhumane prison conditions, and prison overcrowding are regularly criticised by a large body of academic literature (Tonry, 2004), there is little support for the view that prison institutions can be humanised and 'opened up' (Petrovec and Muršič, 2011). We would like not only to propose, but also show that they can. The following account is thus not merely wishful thinking, but empirically founded knowledge, based on the experience of our own penological past. In the seventies and eighties Slovenia succeeded in doing just what today seems utterly impossible: changing a formerly closed prison to an open prison. There was no pre-selection of inmates; the only pre-selection was that of the team put in charge of running the institution. The experiment proved, at least in the Slovenian context of that period, that the fear of prisoners is much exaggerated and strongly suggested that this example could and should be followed in other prison institutions (Petrovec and Muršič, 2011).

An initial experiment

The developments in Ig prison will be the main focus of this chapter. However, it is important to first make reference to an experiment conducted by the Institute of Criminology at the Faculty of Law in Ljubljana and led by a prominent Slovenian criminologist, Professor Katja Vodopivec from 1967 to 1971. Vodopivec's study was a catalyst for the subsequent developments in Ig.

The tenet of Vodopivec's experiment was a strong belief in the option of loosening the authoritarian grip of the institution, while still providing a safe and stimulating environment for those detained and for prison staff. The experiment confirmed the hypothesis that permissiveness in the treatment of juveniles did not in any way have a negative impact on their rehabilitation, quite the contrary. Group counselling proved an efficient method of working in the institution.

The social climate in the institution showed a marked improvement: through a decrease in tensions between inmates, in antisocial behaviour, and, accordingly, in the need for punitive or correctional measures. Furthermore, the impact of the changed attitude proved to be welcomed by the staff as well as those detained.

Among the core features of the experimental approach were group counselling, designed in a way to give the youth in the correctional home more room for independent decision-making, as well as the personal attitude and characteristics of the staff (Vodopivec et al,. 1973; Vodopivec et al., 1974; Petrovec and Muršič, 2011).

Opening up the prison of Ig[2]

Stemming from the encouraging findings of that experiment, a group of Slovene penologists in the Ministry of Justice began another experiment in the mid seventies attempting to improve the social climate in a closed prison institution.

Theoretic framework

The experiment was based on rehabilitative concepts of treatment, and humanistic psychology and penology, fostered at the time by groundwork done by Maslow (1954), Rogers (1961) and Fenton (1965). It involved above all a shift in attitude towards inmates, resulting in the democratization of the institution, but its goals were broadly defined. No one did or could have predicted exactly what changes the program might bring about in the long-term; the desired outcomes were set rather reservedly to merely improving the existent social and emotional climate in the institution.

In fact, contrary to the Vodopivec's experiment, this was not an experiment conforming to academic standards, but rather a radical change of practice fuelled by the curiosity and optimism of the leading officials in the prison administration (Petrovec and Muršič, 2011).

Practical requirements

In order to implement the new practice it was necessary to find an institution that would fulfil several conditions (Petrovec and Muršič, 2011):

• The number of inmates should not exceed 100.

• There should be no pre-selection of prisoners with regard to their prison status, length of sentence, or criminal offence (including no distinction between people who were in prison for the first or multiple times).

---

[2] Parts of this section of the chapter are based on Petrovec and Muršič, 2011, pp. 429-438.

- The personnel, especially the warden, should favour the idea of the re-integration of prisoners into society by opening up a formerly closed institution, as well as liberalizing its regime. Leading personnel should advocate a non-authoritarian attitude while being brave and firm in deciding on problematic issues.

In order to meet these requirements a female prison was selected as the first institution to run the new programme, named Ig prison because of the town nearby. The institution was (and still is) the only Slovenian women's prison, housing at the time slightly less than 100 prisoners, and about 40 at present (Plesničar, 2012).

Group work

Starting with group work, as Fenton (1965) suggested, the team divided the inmates into four groups, each of these being led by a therapist (defined as someone capable of leading a group where dynamic psychological processes occur). The groups were heterogeneous with regard to criminal categories and the only requirement imposed was a regularity of meetings: they were held once a week at the same time and place.

The inmates initially rejected the idea of solving problems within a group. Most of the discussions were about house order, discipline, and cleaning. Later on, conflict situations emerged causing major problems for the therapists, at whom much criticism was then directed. Each therapist had to adapt their own behaviour as well as expecting the inmates to moderate their hostility. What is important to emphasize is that there was no consequence whatsoever for the inmates when presenting their criticism, regardless of any improper behaviour in group meetings. This was a precondition of creating mutual trust and confidence.

The therapists themselves faced significant stress. They were required to loosen the authoritarian grip that had so far offered them a sense of security and approach normal as well as conflict situations in a therapeutic, problem-solving way. In doing that they felt somewhat vulnerable, more so due to the lack of clarity in the set goals and the high expectations of their supervisors. Some team members could not cope with the changed circumstances and left the institution. However, the vast majority were able to adapt.

After a period time and continued group work things began to change. The topics discussed at group meetings slowly transitioned to more substantial ones. Problems of house order were replaced by discussions about benefits, mostly day release from the prison. Groups were not in a position to decide on this, but could suggest it to the expert team. The more their suggestions were accepted, the more inmates felt that they could decide on significant parts of their lives, which slowly undercut their traditional distrust of prison personnel and their reluctance to rationally discuss issues and propose realistic measures.

Group meetings were followed by weekly community meetings, involving all inmates and all prison personnel. Those meetings offered a setting where problems pertinent to the larger community were settled after a broad discussion. In the course of time, a shared decision-making process was established, where inmates felt that they had power – albeit 'de facto' only and not 'de jure' (Petrovec and Muršič, 2011) – to decide on important issues regarding their life in prison and outside as well. Later on, when mutual trust increased, even conditional release was subject to an open discussion.

Each community meeting was followed by an exhaustive discussion by the institution's expert team (the warden, the institution psychologist, educators, social workers, the nurse, a representative of the guards, along with official instructors), where significant events and matters of importance that arose during the meeting were re-examined. However, decisions that were adopted at community meetings were always allowed to stand and were never altered or revoked at the experts' meetings.

Effects

Slowly, a traditional closed institution turned into an open one, which had a number of significant effects. Firstly, a hierarchic model of communication was substituted by a horizontal one. This occurred at two levels – among the different services within the prison institution, as well as in communication with prisoners. The prison personnel (psychologists, educators, doctors, guards, etc.) were expected to share all information that had an impact on decisions brought about or concerning inmates. Moreover the communication with prisoners was much improved by the changed stance of the personnel, which removed the typical authoritative tone.

Furthermore and more importantly, within two years from the beginning of the experiment, 90 per cent of the inmates enjoyed the privilege of an open regime, which among other things means that they would normally leave the institution on Friday afternoon and come back on Sunday evening. There were very few inmates who abused this privilege by returning late or not at all or by committing further offences. As a consequence traditional disciplinary sanctions fell out of use for the next fifteen years, until the early 1990s.

Moreover, largely as a result of the new practice, the recidivism rate in the prison decreased to 20 per cent, whereas the average number in other Slovenian prison institutions was 60 per cent. While recidivism is too complex an issue to be discussed here (Farabee, 2005; Ward and Maruna, 2007; Filipčič and Prelič, 2011; Ramdhan and Bissessar, 2011), the change in Ig prison was such that mentioning it seems more than appropriate.

Another direct result of the new approach was a distinctive change in the social climate of the institution. In Slovenia social climate in prison institutions has been measured at semi regular intervals since the early 1980s (Brinc, 1985; Brinc, 1995; Brinc and Petrovec, 2001; Brglez, 2006; Brinc, 2011), using the Moos questionnaire (Moos, 1968). By 1980, the staff in Ig prison enjoyed a higher standard of social climate than that experienced by prison workers in most Slovenian penal institutions, while the quality of social climate was far higher for inmates than in any other Slovenian prison institution. The positive changes were retained throughout the duration of the new practice.

Socio-therapy

The approach just described became known as socio-therapy, which avoided focusing purely on traditional psychiatric interventions or medical ideas in general. Socio-therapy focuses on the psycho-dynamic processes that occur within small groups and larger communities (termed therapeutic communities) and takes into account a number of external factors that influence the prisoner on release.

These external factors (family, friends, relatives, employment, etc.) were included in the so-called 'after care' from the very moment prisoners began serving their sentences, a liaison which continued well beyond the time a prisoner's release date (Petrovec and Muršič, 2011: 433).

The basic tenet of socio-therapy is granting as much freedom to the inmates as possible, not going against the law, but certainly going beyond the law, e.g. allowing inmates more day releases per month than legislation regulated or allowing them to co-operate in decisions that they (the inmates) felt important for their daily lives.

Such an approach demands direct communication and fair dialogue. If prison workers truly want to re-educate, to treat, to advise, they must get to know their wards and enter into meaningful relationships with them. For this to be possible, people in prison need to be allowed to behave freely. So, paradoxically, it may be said that control is best imposed by granting freedom.

The form of socio-therapy described granted such freedom under regulated yet sympathetic conditions, working on the basic principle that inappropriate behaviour should provoke a fair and proportionate response from a more equal level, rather than from an authoritarian 'up high' position (Petrovec and Muršič, 2011: 435).

The inclusion of the larger society

As prisoners were granted day release, it was necessary to prepare not only them but also their local community for their return. Support was given to their families, where many of their formative conflicts had arisen. Similarly for the prisoners' working environments, with the aim of allowing them to be accepted back into their former places of work. A clear message was thus conveyed to all parts of society, 'A prisoner is worthy of trust if he is granted free leave [day release], given a job outside prison, or conditionally released' (Petrovec and Muršič, 2011: 436).

When out in the community on day release, many prisoners came in contact with their victims. Contrary to what one might expect, in many cases, though obviously not in all, this led to constructive interpersonal relationship and resolution on both sides (Petrovec and Muršič, 2011).

Standard penal practice

After the success of the experiment in Ig prison the socio-therapy model became standard penal practice for many years in a small number of Slovenia's correctional institutions for both women and men. The model was introduced in Slovenska vas, Puščava and Radovljica. Unfortunately, the progressive regime has since been reversed in these prisons and also in Ig.

It is important to analysis why the socio-therapy model gained popularity and also the reasons behind its subsequent demise. Four conditions existed that were crucial to its success: Firstly, the scheme received the political support of the Ministry of Justice, the Ministry of Interior, and, later on, the Slovenian Parliament in adopting the basic principles of socio-therapy as an official penological concept within crime policy. Secondly, there was important support from the mass media in fostering a wider understanding of the rehabilitation of inmates and curiosity on the side of the public to see what would happen. Thirdly, there was strong support in the local communities where prisoners were released on leave (for work, family visits, medical treatment, etc.). Fourthly, there was institutional support from the prison service which expressed a positive attitude towards prisoners:

- To trust in what is good in a person and to support it

- To have courage to consider one's own strengths and weaknesses before treating prisoners

- To abstain from the use and abuse of power over inmates.

Treating people (as psychiatrists, psychotherapists, educators in prisons, etc) always brings about a strong temptation to abuse the power granted. In this respect, too many people are convinced about their moral integrity. There is a telling quotation in Tennessee Williams' *The Night of the Iguana*, in the movie adaptation of which Richard Burton describes the character of an honourable lady: 'She is a highly moral person. If she realised the truth about herself, it would destroy her!' In this context, all staff in the institutions that ascribed to the socio-therapy model underwent special sensitivity trainings in order to get an insight into their own behavioural practices.

In hindsight, this is one of the facets crucial to the success of the model. The strong support of the rehabilitative model among the employees and their willingness to give up some of the power normally retained by prison guards was also crucial to the success of the model. However, the socio-therapy model had not been institutionalised and relied on the support of the prison warden. This meant that when the warden retired the new warden, alien to the socio-therapy model, quickly parted from the philosophy which had been adhered to for 15 years, returning a closed carceral institution (Petrovec and Muršič, 2011; Brinc and Petrovec, 2001).

Yet the developments at Ig prison proved that it is not necessary to establish prison institutions which have predominantly severe regimes. While it is sadly necessary to keep some dangerous prisoners secure, the Slovenian experience identified that this would only represent 10 to 20 per cent of the overall prison population.[3]

---

[3] This figure might be higher in other settings and when the increase of prisoners with addiction problems is taken into account, but it is still not as high as our preconceptions might lead us to legislate for.

The limits of socio-therapy

While the Ig experiment was highly successful, there are some aspects that may make it less employable with certain groups of prisoners or in other settings.

Firstly, drugs are much more of an issue within prisons today than they were (in Slovenia) 30 or 40 years ago. The results socio-therapy achieves with people who have a drug addiction seem less clear. It is hard to imagine drug users in the chains of their addiction capable of the responsibility needed for the opening up of the prisons. Within the socio-therapeutic approach, as detailed above, prisoners are not merely passive recipients of more freedoms, but rather very active agents co-creating the prison institution. Another group that appears to be unresponsive to socio-therapy are prisoners with serious personality disorders and other serious mental health problems. These prisoners represent most of the ten to twenty percent of offenders who are unable to benefit from open regimes.

Other circumstances have changed also. The size of the prisons at present typically exceeds the desired size of open regime prisons and work groups (about a hundred prisoners in an institution/ about fifteen persons in each work group). There are differences across Europe, but typically the trend is going in the wrong direction of larger prisons, where it is more efficient to 'manage' prisoners, but much harder to establish meaningful relationships with them or conduct fruitful group or community meetings.

What has changed?

In Slovenia

The societal climate has changed dramatically in Slovenia, poor economic conditions have a very negative impact on the socio-therapy model. Work opportunities played an important role in the preparation of prisoners for life after prison. About 80 per cent of them were able to find work straight after leaving the prison and most of them had worked while still in prison (Petrovec and

Muršič, 2011). This was possible in a socialist system with virtually no unemployment, but is more problematic in the present pressing economic situation. Employment opportunities have become scarcer and are, if nothing else, of a much less stable nature than they used to be in 1980s Yugoslavia.

The socio-therapy model was established in several Slovenian prisons from the mid-seventies up until the early nineties and the advent of democracy after seceding Yugoslavia. Several things have changed since then. The political and societal context is entirely different, not always in ways we would have imagined or hoped for. The old Communist regime had sponsored and supported humanization of the prison system since the 1970s and had in fact used its authoritarian framework to reinforce the policy. Under communism, in short, it was socially and politically risky to display aggression toward prisoners on release or to voice intolerant or draconian ideas about them. Authoritarianism, that is to say, was helpful in discouraging authoritarian attitudes toward people who had been in prison.

Since independence in 1991, punitive appetites, now uninhibitedly expressed, have grown, much like elsewhere around the world (Pratt, 2007; Albrecht, 2001; Tonry, 2004; Meško and Jere, 2012; Petrovec and Muršič, 2011; Filipčič, 2009; Jager, 2009). A newly open mass media resulted in open and popular expressions of contempt and calls for harsh justice, to which elected officials everywhere seem willingly susceptible (Petrovec and Muršič, 2011; Meško and Jere, 2012). The result has been an increase in the maximum penalty from 20 to 30 years to life imprisonment without any real empirical or theoretical grounding. Imprisonment became a much more frequent sentencing option, while monetary penalties almost disappeared. The number of prisoners rose and had doubled in 2009 compared to 1995. Official attitudes changed accordingly: prisons no longer claim to be therapeutic or correctional facilities, but yielded into being containment facilities (Petrovec and Muršič, 2011).

Simultaneously, the legacy of socio-therapy was overestimated. Although successful, it was idealistic and all too easily substituted by a 'law and order' philosophy which spoke to more punitive instincts (Petrovec and Muršič, 2011).

Today's societal and political climate in regards to penal measures have become more and more restrictive and punitive (Flander and Meško, 2010). When first developed, the success or failure of socio-therapy was not impacted by this punitive discourse.

Nevertheless, the general attitude towards people who have committed a crime as well as marginal groups in general is far less progressive than in the past. It is very improbable to imagine the public being content with improvements in prison conditions or seeing politicians from either side of the spectrum openly endorsing progressive penal changes (Petrovec and Muršič, 2011; Ambrož and Šugman Stubbs, 2011). It is in fact often advanced in public discourse how Slovenian prisons are far above required civilised standards, with an implied sub tone of them being 'too good' for the 'criminals' they house.

The world

It is clear that the environment has not only changed in Slovenia, but elsewhere as well. Basic criminological and sociological truths keep being ignored by establishments across the world, such as groundbreaking research on inequality and its detrimental impact on society (Petrovec, 2000; Petrovec et al., 2007; Wilkinson and Pickett, 2009). The clear links between poverty and our response to crime seems irrelevant. What works is not even the important question anymore; it is what looks good and what seems to appeal to the public that gets ahead.

The results are here for all of us to see: mass incarceration across the globe, especially in the USA, overcrowding in prisons, overly punitive public rhetoric, the fear and hatred towards everyone and everything that seems different – be they immigrants, people of different religion or young people.

Human rights, which we once thought inalienable, have some-how muted to empty words that can be moulded to present needs. Torture, for example, that seemed to have finally been rejected as an instrument in seeking 'truth' in criminal proceedings, seems to have made an unexpected comeback.

This attitude that torture is acceptable in combating terrorists, in particular, in the 'ticking time bomb scenario' is argued by one of America's 'most distinguished (former) defenders of civil rights, Alan Dershowitz (Dershowitz, 2002).

Another example of our decaying standards which is difficult to believe is that of Prof. Igor Primorac, a prominent Croatian philos-opher now working in Australia. Primorac who has been regularly praised across the globe, has said that preventive ethnical cleans-ing could be a justifiable solution under certain circumstances (Petrovec, 2010b; Primorac, 2010).

In a similar tone, prison conditions seem to be rather irrele-vant in non-academic discussions. Without any substantive reac-tion, Mr Hammarberg, the former EU Commissioner for Human Rights, stated just a few years ago that prison conditions in France could be compared to those in Moldova. At the time, two prisoners per week committed suicide in French prisons (Petrovec, 2010a).

In another context, Pat Carlen was rightly appalled in the 1980s that in the UK women prisoners were forced to wear handcuffs while giving birth (Carlen, 1983). While the practice has largely stopped, more recently, the Home Office Minister did not oppose such treatment when confronted with it (Lonergan, 2007), while in the USA 33 states still continue with this practice (Costantini, 2012; Walshe, 2012). Politicians everywhere seem more than will-ing to look the other way when confronted with hard questions of dealing with marginal populations.

Conclusion

The crucial question seems to be, how can we expect to establish humane prison systems, when the protection of human rights in general has deteriorated to such a terrifying level. Doesn't it sound a bit like wanting to create a beautiful eco garden in the middle of Chernobil? Perhaps, yet we believe it is worth trying.

So why can't we simply 'copy and paste' the socio-therapy experiment, used in Ig and other prisons, into other contexts?

No impediment exists except the will of those who have power. That is why only a few Slovenian prison institution adopted the approach described, and why only one Grendon was established in England. There are so few similar examples around the world. The state authority tolerates only a limited quantity of freedom at the margin of society where the prison system operates. It is likely that such open institutions stand merely as exhibition pieces, isolated showcases for the liberties which democratic societies are willing to support in theory, at the level of a prototype, but not to render universal in the prison system. For anything surpassing this small quantity of freedom would decisively change the system itself and the balance of power it upholds.

Yet the models offered by socio-therapy and other pilot schemes stand freely available to all state polities: there is no copyright restricting its implementation. The greatest obstacle to applying it more generally lies within 'us', the law-abiding majority – as to make it work, we would have to accept that it could work. And to do this, we would have to address fundamental prejudices about the nature of 'criminal' persons, their rights, and their ability to handle freedom.

Bibliography

Albrecht, H. J. (2001) 'Post-Adjudication Dispositions in Comparative Perspective'. In: Tonry, M.H. And Frase, R.S. eds. *Sentencing and sanctions in western countries*. Oxford: Oxford University Press.

Ambrož, M. and Šugman Stubbs, K. (2011) 'Conditional Release (Parole) in Slovenia: Problems and Possible Solutions'. *The Prison Journal*, 91(4): 467–488.

Brglez, A. (2006) *Socialno vzdušje v zavodih za prestajanje kazni zapora in prevzgojnem domu leta 2005*. Ljubljana: Inštitut za civilizacijo in kulturo.

Brinc, F. (1985) 'Določitelji družbenega vzdušja v kazenskih zavodih v SR Sloveniji'. *Revija za kriminalistiko in kriminologijo*, 36: 304–316.

Brinc, F. (1995) *Družbeno vzdušje v zavodih za prestajanje kazni zapora v Republiki Sloveniji.* Ljubljana: Inštitut za kriminologijo pri Pravni fakulteti.

Brinc, F. (2011) *Družbeno vzdušje v zavodih za prestajanje kazni zapora in v prevzgojnem domu Radeče leta 2010.* Ljubljana: Inštitut za kriminologijo pri Pravni fakulteti.

Brinc, F. and Petrovec, D. (2001) *Družbeno vzdušje v zavodih za prestajanje kazni zapora v Republiki Sloveniji.* Ljubljana: Inštitut za kriminologijo pri Pravni fakulteti.

Carlen, P. (1983) *Women's Imprisonment: A Study In Social Control.* London: Routledge & Kegan Paul.

Costantini, C. (2012) 'Should Inmates Be Shackled While Giving Birth?' *ABC News*, 10 September. Available from http://abcnews. go.com/ABC_Univision/News/woman-shackled-giving-birth-states/ story?id=17436798 [29 October 2012]

Dershowitz, A.M. (2002) *The Case for Torture Warrants.* Available at: http://www.alandershowitz.com/publications/docs/torturewarrants. html (Accessed 20 October 2012).

Farabee, D. (2005) *Rethinking Rehabilitation: Why Can't We Reform Our Criminals?* Washington: Aei Press.

Fenton, N. (1965) *A Handbook on the Use of Group Counseling in Juvenile and Youth Correctional Institutions.* Sacramento: Institute for the Study of Crime and Delinquency.

Filipčič, K. (2009) 'La Slovénie'. *Déviance et Société*, 33(3): 367–382.

Filipčič, K. and Prelić, D. (2011) 'Deprivation of Liberty of Juvenile Offenders in Slovenia'. *The Prison Journal*, 91(4): 448-466.

Flander, B. and Meško, G. (2010) "Punitiveness' and Penal Trends in Slovenia: On the 'Shady Side of the Alps'?' In: Kury, H. and Shea, E., eds. *Punitivity. International Developments. Vol. 1: Punitiveness – A Global Phenomenon?* Bochum: Universitätsverlag Dr. Brockmeyer.

Jager, M. (2009) 'Slovenia: Crime Policy in Time of Change'. *9th Annual Conference of the European Society of Criminology.* 7 September. Ljubljana, Inštitut za Kriminologijo. Available at: http://videolectures. net/esc09_jager_cptc/ (Accessed 2 August 2012).

Loader, I. (2006) 'Fall of the 'Platonic Guardians': Liberalism, Criminology and Political Responses to Crime in England and Wales'. *Br J Criminol*, 46(4): 561–586.

Lonergan, J. (2007) 'Lecture on Women in Prisons'. *International conference: What Works With Women Offenders*. Monash University, 10-12 September. Prato, Italy: Monash University.

Maslow, A. H. (1954) *Motivation And Personality*. New York: Harper.

Meško, G., Fields, C. and Smole, T. (2011) 'A Concise Overview of Penology and Penal Practice in Slovenia: The Unchanged Capacity, New Standards, and Prison Overcrowding'. *The Prison Journal*, 91(4): 398–424.

Meško, G. and Jere, M. (2012) Crime, Criminal Justice and Criminology in Slovenia. *European Journal of Criminology*, 9(3): 323–334.

Moos, R. H. (1968) 'The Assessment of the Social Climates of Correctional Institutions'. *Journal of Research in Crime and Delinquency*, 5: 174–188.

Petrovec, D. (2010a) 'Odprava smrtne kazni: Ni razloga za veselje'. Available at: http://www.dnevnik.si/objektiv/vec-vsebin/1042340878 (Accessed 10 October 2012).

Petrovec, D. (2010b) *Lahkotnost ubijanja po Primorcu*. Available at: http://www.dnevnik.si/objektiv/vec-vsebin/1042369536 (Accessed 10 October 2012).

Petrovec, D. (2000) 'Poverty and Reaction to Crime: Freedom Without Responsibility'. *European journal of crime, criminal law and criminal justice*. 8(4): 377-389.

Petrovec, D. and Meško, G. (2007) 'Back to the Future: Slovenia's Penological Heritage'. *Varstvoslovje*, 8(3/4): 356–364.

Petrovec, D. and Muršič, M. (2011) 'Science Fiction: Opening Prison Institutions (The Slovenian Penological Heritage)'. *The Prison Journal*, 91(4): 425–447.

Petrovec, D., Tompa, G. and Šugman Stubbs, K. (2007) 'Poverty and Reaction to Crime: Irresponsibility Proven'. *Sociologija. Mintis ir veiksmas*. 20(2): 32-42.

Plesničar, M.M. (2012) 'Ženske in kriminaliteta'. In: Plesničar, M. M. ed. *Nežnejši spol? Ženske, nasilje in kazenskopravni sistem*. Ljubljana: Inštitut za kriminologijo pri Pravni fakulteti v Ljubljani.

Pratt, J. (2007) *Penal Populism*. London: Routledge.

Primorac, I. (2010) 'Upgrading Michael Waltzer's Theory on the 'Principle Of Civilian Immunity", *Peace Institute in Ljubljana lectures.* Ljubljana, 11 October.

Ramdhan, S. and Bissessar, L. (2011) *Recidivism.* Norderstedt: GRIN Verlag.

Rogers, C. (1961) *On Becoming a Person: A Therapist's View of Psychotherapy.* Boston: Houghton Mifflin.

Tonry, M.H. (2004) 'Why Aren't German Penal Policies Harsher and Imprisonment Rates Higher?' *German Law Journal*, 5(10): 1187-1206.

Vodopivec, K., Bergant, M., Kobal, M., Skaberne, V., Skalar, V. and Mlinarič, F. (1973) *Spreminjanje vzgojnih metod v vzgojnem zavodu v Logatcu.* Ljubljana: Inštitut za kriminologijo pri Pravni fakulteti.

Vodopivec, K., Bergant, M., Kobal, M., Mlinarič, F., Skaberne, B. and Skalar, V. (1974) *Eksperiment u Logatcu.* Beograd: Savez društava defektologa Jugoslavije.

Walmsley, R. (2011) *World Prison Population List (9th edition)*, London: International Centre for Prison Studies, King's College London.

Walshe, S. (2012) 'Women are born free in the US but everywhere give birth in chains'. *The Guardian,* 6 June. Available from: http://www.guardian.co.uk/commentisfree/2012/jun/06/women-born-free-give-birth-in-chains [29 October 2012]

Ward., T. and Maruna, S. (2007) *Rehabilitation.* Abingdon, New York: Routledge.

Wilkinson, R. G. and Pickett, K. (2009) *The Spirit Level: Why More Equal Societies Almost Always Do Better.* London: Allen Lane.

6

Can the Criminal Justice System Promote Desistance from Crime? Learning from Labelling

Shadd Maruna[1]

Introduction

The question of whether the justice system – our courts, prisons, probation and police – can facilitate desistance is a popular one these days. It is also an open question in many ways. The fact is that we know very little about how the criminal justice system impacts desistance from crime. As Farrall accurately summarises, 'Most of the research suggests that desistance 'occurs' away from the criminal justice system. That is to say that very few people actually desist as a result of intervention on the part of the criminal justice system or its representatives' (Farrall, 1995: 56). On the other hand, we know a great deal about how the criminal justice can impede desistance from crime, as frankly we have much more practice in that regard. Stigmatising, labelling, brutalising, institutionalising, excluding – these are things we have perfected in modern societies. In what follows I make the case that the dynamics of

[1]The author would like to thank Tom LeBel for his contributions to this work. Parts of this chapter have been previously published as Maruna, S. and LeBel, T. (2010). 'The Desistance Paradigm in Correctional Practice: From Programmes to Lives' (pp. 65-89) In McNeill, F. Raynor, P., & Trotter, C. (Eds.) *Offender Supervision: New Directions in Theory, Research and Practice.* Cullompton, UK: Willan. Reprinted with permission.

desistance are not all that distant from these dynamics of stigma and that advocates of rehabilitation can learn crucial lessons for effective reform by better understanding its polar opposite.

Learning from labelling

When agents of criminal justice and other experts on offender rehabilitation list the primary 'risk factors' predicting recidivism of prisoners, the focus is often on deficits in human capital (e.g., cognitive or educational shortcomings) or social capital (e.g., criminally minded associates or lack of prosocial social bonds), and occasionally even just plain old capital (e.g., poverty and lack of means of self-support). However, when ex-prisoners are asked about the biggest obstacles they face to leading a crime-free life, they will routinely list a factor that is routinely ignored by criminal justice agencies (for obvious reasons): the stigmatization of having been processed through the criminal justice system (see LeBel, 2008; 2012). According to one such individual:

> No matter how much time we do, everyone always thinks it's like once a criminal always a criminal and that is how people see me and it's very hard to deal with (Dodge and Pogrebin, 2001: 49).

Another former prisoner stated:

> You are labeled as a felon, and you're always gonna be assumed and known to have contact with that criminal activity and them ethics. And even when I get off parole, I'm still gonna have an 'F' on my record (Uggen et al., 2004: 283).

Moreover, formerly incarcerated persons often have multiple stigmatized identities and suffer from double or triple stigma as a former prisoner and because of their race (Pager, 2007), past substance use (van Olphen et al., 2009), or a mental disorder (Hartwell, 2004; Visher and Mallik-Kane, 2007). One formerly incarcerated person summarizes this bluntly in research by Wynn:

I am an outcast four times over. ... Ex-con, ex-junkie, black, and HIV-positive. I'd be lyin' if I told you I had any dreams (Wynn, 2001: 17).

Of course, the dangers of such self-fulfilling prophesies are at the heart of the labeling theory tradition in criminology (Becker, 1963; Lemert, 1951). Outlined eloquently by Frank Tannenbaum in 1938, the idea behind labelling theory is that:

> The process of making the criminal is a process of tagging, defining, identifying, segregating, describing, emphasising, making conscious and self-conscious; it becomes a way of stimulating, suggesting, emphasising and evoking the very traits that are complained of. ... He is made conscious of himself as a different human being than he was before his arrest. The person becomes the thing he is described as being (Tannenbaum, 1938: 19-20).

As original as this theory was at the time, it also corresponded with common sense. These are the words from the Governor of Sing Sing Prison in upstate New York that same year:

> We know now why men 'come back to prison a second, third or fourth time.' ... It is because the prisoner, on his discharge from prison, is conscious of invisible stripes fastened upon him by tradition and prejudice (Lawes, 1938: 298).

Despite some unfair criticism in the 1980s (see Paternoster and Iovanni, 1989; Petrunik, 1980), labeling theory has seen a resurgence in recent years both as a key element of important new theoretical developments (see e.g., Braithwaite, 1989; Bushway and Apel, 2012; Sampson and Laub, 1997) as its central premises have received substantial empirical support in recent research (e.g., Bales and Piquero, 2012; Fagan et al. 2003; Hagan and Palloni, 1990; McAra and McVie, 2011; Taxman and Piquero, 1998). For instance, in a study of 95,919 men and women who were either adjudicated or had adjudication withheld, Chiricos et al. (2007) found that those who were formally labeled were significantly more likely to recidivate within two years than those who were not.

In short, desisting from crime is a difficult process, especially for those who are deeply entrenched in criminal networks and living in disadvantaged circumstances. Successfully changing one's life in such circumstances requires a tremendous amount of self-belief, and this is made highly difficult, if not impossible, when those around a person believe the person will fail. Interviews with long-term, persistent offenders suggest many of these individuals develop a sense of hopelessness and despair, believing that all legitimate opportunities have been blocked for them (see Maruna, 2001).

What makes a conviction such a powerfully effective force? The formula is rather simple actually. First, of course, the conviction comes with a widely accepted credential (see Pinard, 2010). Drawing on Randall Collins (1979) classic, *The Credential Society*, Pager argues that the 'criminal credential constitutes a formal and enduring classification of social status, which can be used to regulate access and opportunity across numerous social, economic and political domains' and is therefore 'an official and legitimate means of evaluating and classifying individuals' (2007: 4, 5). Unfortunately, across the world, 'public policy seems to be moving inexorably toward making criminal records more widely available' (Jacobs, 2006: 419). In Germany, more than nine million disclosures are issued every year (Morgenstern, 2011). Criminal Records Bureau checks in the UK have soared from 1.4 million in 2002-2003 to over 3.8 million in 2008-2009 (Padfield, 2011). Applications for 'conduct certificates' in the Netherlands jumped from around 255,000 in 2005 to 460,000 in 2009 (Boone, 2011). In Australia, the national criminal record-providing agency processed around 2.7 million criminal history checks in 2009-2010 – 'a particularly striking number given that the total population of Australia is only around 20 million people' (Naylor, 2011). As Freeman argues, even with European privacy protections, once this information starts to be made available in this way, it may not be 'a genie that can be readily put back into Aladdin's lamp' (2008: 408).

Second, you get a name when you've got the credential. You become an 'offender.' Wonderfully, that name is ambiguous in regards to whether it refers to something you did in the past or something you are likely to do in the future; the implication is that it is about who you are. Other credentials work this way too. You pass your Ph.D. and you become a 'doctor' with all of the connotations of special insight and capability implicit with that title. Quickly, the person moves from something one has achieved (finished a big piece of research) to what someone is ('My son, the doctor').

Third, the criminal conviction is ritualized in the form of a degradation ceremony imbued with authority and legitimacy (Garfinkel, 1956), suggesting that a good signal is often performed in the form of ritual (see Maruna, 2011). It is no coincidence that the foremost sociological theorists of the 'credential' (e.g., Goffman, 1963; Collins, 1979) are also among our leading scholars of 'ritual.' Credentialism and performance go hand-in-hand (weddings and marriage certificates, graduations and diplomas, court trials and convictions) with the credential legitimizing the ritual and the ritual legitimizing the credential (Collins, 1979). As Kai Erikson pointed out half a century ago, a key feature of these degradation processes is that they 'are almost irreversible':

> [The individual] is ushered into the special position by a decisive and dramatic ceremony, yet is returned from it with hardly a word of public notice. ... From a ritual point of view, nothing has happened to cancel out the stigmas imposed upon him by earlier commitment ceremonies. ... A circularity is thus set into motion which has all of the earmarks of a 'self-fulfilling prophecy' (Erikson, 1961: 311).

Finally, individuals who have the stigmatising credential, name and ritual experience, also find themselves socially excluded from mainstream opportunities and marginalised into deviant subcultures (see Braithwaite, 1989). Individuals with criminal records can also be restricted from gaining licences for a remarkable range of jobs, including work as embalmers, billiard room employees, septic tank cleaners, plumbers, eyeglass dispensers, barbers and real estate agents (Pager, 2007). Discrimination against ex-prisoners is not only facilitated de facto but officially sanctioned, and these de jure consequences have increased 'in number scope and severity since the 1980s' (Pinard, 2010). Indeed, in the past three decades, the US Congress 'took collateral consequences to a new level of irrationality, making a single criminal conviction grounds for automatic exclusion from a whole range of welfare benefits' at the Federal level (Love, 2003: 112). American citizens with even a single conviction for drug offences and other charges can be denied housing assistance, food stamps, education loans, and the right to vote (see e.g., Allard, 2002). In such circumstances of exclusion, it is not difficult to imagine why individuals turn to deviant subcultures for acceptance and protection. Interestingly, in their study of labelling effects, Bernburg and Krohn and colleagues (2003) found that the process worked in much the same way as theorized by Braithwaite (1989) – intervention by the justice system predicted involvement with deviant gangs, which then led to increased offending.

Interestingly, this same formula – credentialism, re-naming, ritualising, and social marginalisation – is precisely the same formula that is used in the rites of passage involved in becoming a doctor, a priest, a soldier or an academic (see Maruna, 2011). As I have the most experience with the latter group, I can speak most directly to this. To become a university lecturer, one first must obtain a key credential: the Ph.D. This 'piece of paper' is a recognition that someone has achieved a piece of training – an original piece of guided research in the form of a dissertation – but it quickly becomes a 'signal' to employers of one's future potential. The credential also comes with a new name: One becomes 'a doctor.' (Although not a 'real doctor', as my children like to remind me, I still make them call me Dr. Maruna). Moreover, there are an inordinate series of rituals in this process of becoming a doctor, from the

Ph.D. 'viva voce' or oral defense to graduation ceremonies with all of their pomp and regalia. Finally, although academics are not formally excluded from mainstream society, there is no question that we become insular and marginalised in the so-called 'ivory tower.' Gradually, as one goes through this elaborate rite of passage to become an academic, one finds oneself increasingly set apart from the mainstream and preferring the company of fellow academics who better understand the work we do.

In summary, then, the process of labelling is based on a formula that works – a very sophisticated anthropological rite of passage that can almost ensure failure among ex-prisoners. Jacobs captures this nicely, when he writes:

> The criminal justice system feeds on itself. The more people who are arrested, prosecuted, convicted, and especially incarcerated, the larger is the criminally stigmatized underclass screened out of legitimate opportunities (2006: 387).

On the bright side of labelling

Promoting rehabilitation in such a climate may be nearly impossible. The challenge for those who support prisoner rehabilitation, then, is not just to devise ways of countering these predictable processes of stigmatisation, but to learn from them, mimic them and turn the same dynamics toward re-integrative ideals. In other words, desistance may be best facilitated when the desisting person's change in behaviour is recognized by others and reflected back to him in a 'de-labelling process' (Trice and Roman, 1970).

In previous work (Maruna et al., 2009), we draw upon Rosenthal's so-called 'Pygmalion Effects', from educational psychology, to argue that the high expectations of others can lead to greater self-belief (and subsequent performance) in individuals (Rosenthal and Jacobson, 1992). Here, the term Pygmalion derives from the Greek myth of the sculptor that falls in love with his statue, bringing it to life, and the subsequent George Bernard Shaw drama about a peasant girl transformed into a society lady. In *Pygmalion in the*

Classroom, Rosenthal and Jacobson (1992) describe Pygmalion effects as the influence of teachers' beliefs about a student's abilities on the student's self-beliefs and subsequent performance in the classroom. When teachers were made to believe their students could achieve great things, the students began to believe this, and their outcomes confirmed this optimism (see also McNatt, 2000).

We argue that personal transformation (or 'recovery' in the highly related arena of addiction treatment) also contains a looking-glass element. People start to believe that they can successfully change their lives when those around them start to believe they can. In other words, rehabilitation (or recovery) is a construct that is negotiated through interaction between an individual and significant others (Shover, 1996: 144). Not only must a person accept conventional society in order to go straight, but conventional society must accept that this person has changed as well.

There is scattered support for these sorts of Pygmalion Effects in the behavioral reform process. Maruna (2001), for example, found evidence of what he calls 'redemption rituals' in the life stories of successfully desisting ex-convicts. As with the 'degradation ceremony' (Garfinkel, 1956) through which wrongdoers are stigmatized, these de-labelling ceremonies are directed not at specific acts, but to the whole character of the person in question (Braithwaite and Braithwaite, 2001: 16). Although this research is retrospective in nature, it is supported by some experimental work inside and outside the laboratory. In one ingenious real-world experiment, for example, Leake and King (1977) informed treatment professionals that they had developed a scientific test to determine who among a group of patients were most likely to be successful in recovering from alcoholism. In reality, no such test had been developed. The patients identified as 'most likely to succeed' were picked purely at random. Still, the clients who were assigned this optimistic prophecy turned out to be far more likely to give up drinking than members of the control group. Apparently, they believed in their own ability to achieve sobriety because the professionals around them seemed to believe it so well (see also Miller, 1998).

Outside of criminological research, of course, hundreds of different studies have found confirmation for the idea that one person's expectations for the behavior of another can actually impact the other person's behavior. Meta-analyses of studies conducted both inside and outside the research laboratory suggest an average effect size or correlation (r) of over .30 in studies of interpersonal expectancy effects (Rosenthal, 2002; Kierein and Gold, 2000). In the most famous example, Rosenthal and Jacobson (1992) found that teacher expectancies of student performance were strongly predictive of student performance on standardized tests, and that manipulating these educator biases and beliefs could lead to substantial improvements in student outcomes (see also Miller et al., 1975). A nursing home study demonstrated that raising caretakers' expectations for residents' health outcomes led to a significant reduction in levels of depression among residents (Learman et al., 1990). Similar Pygmalion Effects and expectancy-linked outcomes have been found in courtroom studies, business schools, and numerous different workplaces (see Rosenthal, 2002 for a review).

Whether the same processes could be called into play in the rehabilitation process remains an open question. Performance on standardized tests or even in a factory setting is far different than criminal recidivism, as the latter is arguably impacted by a wider variety of influences. At the same time, criminal behaviour may involve a greater element of choice or agency than is involved in exam performance (Laub and Sampson, 2003). It might be, then, that Pygmalion processes could be more influential in criminology than in education.

Drawing on a winning formula

Achieving such re-labelling in practice may require advocates of rehabilitation to imitate the precise dynamics involved in the stigmatisation process: credentialism, ritual, re-naming, and social exclusion/inclusion. After all, the strongest form of symbolic de-labelling an offender could receive from the State is surely the chance to officially wipe the slate clean and move on from the stigma of one's criminal record. Research on desistance from crime refers to such a process as 'knifing off' one's criminal past whereby individuals sever themselves from past selves and personal entanglements by moving away, joining the military and starting over (Laub and Sampson, 2003; Maruna and Roy, 2007). The past cannot be taken away, of course, and nothing can undo the harm that has been done. Convictions, on the other hand, are merely labels given by the State in the name of punishment, and equally these can be taken away or sealed in the name of reintegration, along with a restoration of the full civil rights, liberties and duties that all of us share (Uggen et al., 2004). Such rewards provide an opportunity for qualified individuals with criminal records to demonstrate that they have paid their debt to society and earned the right to have statutory bars to jobs or other services lifted, as well as to have civil rights and public benefits reinstated (Choo, 2007).

The science of rehabilitation could also learn from research on the criminal credential by imagining means of accrediting desistance, such as the 'certificate of rehabilitation' intended to be a kind of 'letter of recommendation' (Lucken and Ponte, 2008) to employers. Love (2011: 775-776) argues that the formal pardon remains the 'gold standard' for 'confirming good character, so that an employer, landlord, or lending institution will have some level of comfort in dealing with an individual who has been deemed worthy of this high-level official forgiveness.' The primary problem with such policies is that they often involve a labyrinth of bureaucracy making them 'biased in favor of the wealthy and politically connected, and inaccessible as a practical matter to those without means' (Love, 2003: 116). President Bill Clinton's infamous pardon of the billionaire tax evader Marc Rich in his last days of office is an extreme example of the sorts of individuals most likely to receive such privileges at the Presidential level.

In Canada, former prisoners are eligible to apply for formal 'pardons' after remaining crime-free over a specified waiting period. Although almost all applicants are successful, only a tiny fraction actually apply. Ruddell and Winfree (2006) estimate the take-up at less than 5 per cent of those convicted between 1996 and 2002. Likewise, in the United States, 'certificates of good conduct' or 'certificates of rehabilitation' can be issued by state authorities (e.g. prisoner review boards) to law-abiding ex-prisoners, but these are currently used very sparingly and by only a handful of US states (Love and Frazier, 2006; Samuels and Mukamal, 2004).

The research on labelling and criminal careers would suggest that, to be useful, such opportunities might be made available earlier in the desistance process. Ex-prisoners, for example, might be allowed to 'earn' a pardon or 'certificate of rehabilitation' through doing volunteer work or making other efforts to make amends for what they have done (Maruna and LeBel, 2003). One advantage of this would be that individuals could earn a pardon after only a short time in the community or even during one's period of incarceration in some instances. Another advantage would be that this would make the rehabilitation process 'active' rather than 'passive'. That is, one would have to 'do something' to earn the right to be rehabilitated, rather than simply waiting for the passage of time (e.g. the usual five to seven years of crime-free behaviour that is currently required to prove one's reform).

The awarding of such certificates or pardons may provide an ideal opportunity to mimick or orchestrate the sorts of organic rituals of reintegration observed in studies of desistance (see Leong, 2006; Maruna, 2001). Indeed, this research suggests that delabelling might be most potent when coming from 'on high', particularly official sources like treatment professionals or teachers, rather than from family members or friends – where such acceptance can be taken for granted (Wexler, 2001). Moreover, if the delabelling were to be endorsed and supported by the same social control establishment involved in the 'status degradation' process of conviction and sentencing (e.g. judges or peer juries), this public redemption might carry considerable social and psychological weight for participants and observers (see Maruna and LeBel, 2003; Travis, 2005, for development of this idea).

In an early study of desistance, Meisenhelder advocated for what he calls a 'certification' stage of desistance, whereby 'some recognized member(s) of the conventional community must publicly announce and certify that the offender has changed and that he is now to be considered essentially noncriminal' (Meisenhelder, 1977: 329). This 'status elevation ceremony' would serve to 'publicly and formally to announce, sell and spread the fact of the Actor's new kind of being' (Lofland, 1969: 227), and effectively worked to counter the stigma of the person's criminal record. According to Makkai and Braithwaite, such recognition of efforts to reform can have 'cognitive effects on individuals through nurturing lawabiding identities, building cognitive commitments to try harder, encouraging individuals who face adversity not to give up ... and nurturing belief in oneself' (1993: 74).

Real-world opportunities for such reputational redemption can be found in the literature (see Maruna, 2011). In France, for instance, 'judicial rehabilitation' rituals take place in the same court rooms that sentence individuals to prison and (not coincidentally) 'resemble citizenship ceremonies' (Herzog-Evans, 2011; see also Maruna and LeBel, 2003). This 'judicial rehabilitation' benefits from 'a certain imprimatur of official respectability' (Love, 2003: 127) given 'the respectability that the judiciary enjoys in American society' (Love, 2011: 783). As Herzog-Evans (2011) astutely points out, courts have a distinct advantage over almost any other institution in society: 'they can state what the truth is.' This 'judicial truth' ('*vérité judiciaire*') or 'legal magic' carries real weight. Just as a degradation ceremony succeeds in condemning the whole self of the person (Garfinkel, 1956), the reintegration ritual acts to restore the person's reputation as ultimately good (Braithwaite and Mugford, 1994).

The solidification of such a reputation, however, will require thought about re-naming. Unfortunately, the issue of naming may be one of the most sensitive and least developed of the reintegrative dynamics. As Richards and Jones (2003), among others, have argued, once a person commits a crime, he or she becomes an 'offender' and that name seems to stick with the person throughout the punishment process and long after, suggesting that 'once an offender, always an offender' in many ways. Even commonly used names like reformed offender, former offender, and ex-offender all maintain the 'offender' root. 'Desister' of course is a terrible word, but creative work needs to be invested into trying to agree upon a better way of referring to individuals who have changed their lives for the better.

Likewise, although the issue of social exclusion and ex-prisoners is often discussed, more thought needs to be given to creating spaces for reformed former offenders (whatever they choose to call themselves) to support one another. In the book *Gangs, Rituals and Rites of Passage,* Pinnock and Douglas-Hamilton (1997) write:

> Research into gangs suggested a new, hard look at their rituals – which led to the conclusion that the best way to beat gangs might be to make better, richer, more ritual-filled, gang-like groups (Pinnock and Douglas-Hamilton, 1997: para. 13).

Likewise, Braithwaite calls for 'a culture, or rehabilitative subcultures as in Alcoholics Anonymous, where those who perform remarkable feats of rehabilitation are held up as role models' (1989: 163). Certainly, mutual aid organisations like Alcoholics Anonymous and Narcotics Anonymous have been enormously successful over the past decades. Indeed, rigorous studies of mutual-help groups, forty years hence, have found indeed that engaging in helping activities is related to better psychosocial adjustment and treatment outcomes (Zemore et al., 2004), and higher self-esteem and feelings of self-worth (Hutchinson et al., 2006; for reviews of the benefits of ex-prisoner mutual aid efforts, see LeBel, 2007).

This, of course, makes perfect sense. If the same dynamics can be used to turn ordinary people into academics, soldiers, priests, doctors, and even, bizarrely 'offenders', then this same formula should be able to produce desisters (or whatever they end up calling themselves).

Bibliography

Allard, P. (2002) *Life Sentences: Denying Welfare Benefits to Women Convicted of Drug Offenses*. Washington, DC: Sentencing Project.

Bales, W. D. and Piquero, A. R. (2012) 'Assessing the impact of imprisonment on recidivism'. *Journal of Experimental Criminology*, 8(1): 71-101.

Becker, H. (1963) *Outsiders*. New York: Free Press.

Bernburg, J.G. and Krohn, M.D. (2003) 'Labeling, life chances and adult crime: The direct and indirect effects of official intervention in adolescence on crime in early adulthood'. *Criminology*, 41: 12789-1318.

Boone, M. (2011) 'Judicial Rehabilitation in the Netherlands: Balancing between safety and privacy'. *European Journal of Probation*, 3(1): 63-78.

Braithwaite, J. (1989) *Crime, Shame and Reintegration*. Cambridge: Cambridge University Press.

Braithwaite, J. and Braithwaite, V. (2001) 'Part one'. In: Ahmed, E., Harris, N., Braithwaite J. and Braithwaite V. eds. *Shame Management Through Reintegration*. Cambridge: University of Cambridge Press, 3-69.

Braithwaite, J. and Mugford, S. (1994) 'Conditions of successful reintegration ceremonies: Dealing with juvenile offenders'. *British Journal of Criminology*, 34(2): 139–171.

Bushway, S. D. and Apel, R. (2012) 'A Signaling Perspective on Employment-Based Reentry Programming'. *Criminology & Public Policy*, 11(1): 21-50.

Chiricos, T., Barrick, K. and Bales, W. (2007) 'The labelling of convicted felons and its consequences for recidivism'. *Criminology*, 45(3): 547-81.

Choo, K. (2007) 'Run-on sentences: ABA, others focus on easing the added punishments for those convicted of crimes'. *ABA Journal*, January: 38.

Collins, R. (1979) *The Credential Society*. New York: Academic Press.

Dodge, M. and Pogrebin, M. R. (2001) 'Collateral Consequences of Imprisonment for Women: Complications of Reintegration'. *The Prison Journal*, 81: 42-54.

Erikson, K. T. (1961) 'Notes on the sociology of deviance'. *Social Problems*, 9: 307-314.

Fagan, J.A., Kupchick, A., and Liberman, A. (2003) *Be Careful What You Wish For: The Comparative Impacts of Juvenile Versus Criminal Court Sanctions on Recidivism among Adolescent Felony Offenders*. New York: Columbia Law School Public Law and Legal Theory Working Group.

Farrall, S. (1995) 'Why do people stop offending?' *Scottish Journal of Criminal Justice Studies*, 1: 51-59.

Freeman, R. (2008) 'Incarceration, criminal background checks, and employment in a low(er) crime society'. *Criminology & Public Policy*, 7(3): 405-412.

Garfinkel, H. (1956) 'Conditions of successful degradation ceremonies'. *American Journal of Sociology*, 61: 420–24.

Goffman, E. (1963) *Stigma: On the Management of Spoiled Identity*. Englewood Cliffs, NJ: Prentice-Hall.

Hagan, J. and Palloni, A. (1990) 'The social reproduction of a criminal class in working class London', *American Journal of Sociology*, 96: 265–99.

Hartwell, S. W. (2004) 'Comparison of Offenders with Mental Illness Only and Offenders with Dual Diagnoses'. *Psychiatric Services*, 55: 145-50.

Herzog-Evans, M. (2011) 'Judicial rehabilitation in France: Helping with the desisting process and acknowledging achieved desistance'. *European Journal of Probation*, 3(1): 4-19.

Hutchinson, D. S., Anthony, W. A., Ashcraft, L., Johnson, E., Dunn, E. C., Lyass, A. and Rogers, E. S. (2006) 'The personal and vocational impact of training and employing people with psychiatric disabilities as providers'. *Psychiatric Rehabilitation Journal*, 29(3): 205-13.

Jacobs, J. B. (2006) 'Mass incarceration and the proliferation of criminal records'. *University of St. Thomas Law Journal*, 3(3): 387-420.

Kierein, N. M. and Gold, M. A. (2000) 'Pygmalion in work organizations: A meta-analysis'. *Journal of Organizational Behavior*, 21: 913-28.

Laub, J. and Sampson, R. J. (2003) *Shared Beginnings, Divergent Lives*. Cambridge, MA: Harvard.

Lawes, L. E. (1938) *Invisible Stripes.* New York: Farrar and Rinehart, Inc.

Leake, G. J. and King, A. S. (1977) 'Effect of counselor expectations on alcoholic recovery'. *Alcohol Health and Research World*, 1(3): 16-22.

Learman, L. A., Avrorn, J., Everitt, D. E. and Rosenthal, R. (1990) 'Pygmalion in the nursing home: The effects of caregiver expectations on patient outcomes'. *Journal of the American Geriatrics Society*, 38: 797-803.

LeBel, T. P. (2008) 'Perceptions of and responses to stigma'. *Sociology Compass*, 2: 409–432.

LeBel, T. P. (2007) 'An Examination of the Impact of Formerly Incarcerated Persons Helping Others'. *Journal of Offender Rehabilitation*, 46(1/2): 1-24.

Lemert, E.M. (1951) *Social Pathology: Systematic Approaches to the Study of Sociopathic Behavior.* New York: McGraw-Hill.

Leong, N.(2006) *Felon reenfranchisement: Political implications and potential for individual rehabilitative benefits.* Stanford, California: California Sentencing & Corrections Policy Series, Stanford Criminal Justice Center Working Papers.

Lofland, J. (1969) *Deviance and Identity.* Englewood Cliffs, NJ: Prentice-Hall.

Love, M. C. (2011) 'Paying Their Debt to Society: Forgiveness, Redemption, and the Uniform Collateral Consequences of Conviction Act'. *Howard LJ*, 54: 753-788.

Love, M. C. (2003) 'Starting over with a Clean Slate: In Praise of a Forgotten Section of the Model Penal Code'. *Fordham Urban Law Journal*, 30: 101-136.

Love, M.C. and Frazier, A. (2006) 'Certificates of rehabilitation and other forms of relief from the collateral consequences of conviction: A survey of state laws'. In: ABA Commission on Effective Criminal Sanctions. ed. *Second Chances in the Criminal Justice System: Alternatives to Incarceration and Reentry Strategies.* Washington DC: American Bar Association.

Lucken, K. and Ponte, L. M. (2008) 'A just measure of forgiveness: Reforming occupational licensing regulations for ex-offenders using BFOQ Analysis'. *Law & Policy*, 30(1): 46-72.

Makkai, T. and Braithwaite, J. (1993) 'Praise, pride and corporate compliance', *International Journal of the Sociology of Law*, 21: 73-91.

Maruna, S. (2011) 'Reentry as a Rite of Passage'. *Punishment & Society*, 13(1): 3-28.

Maruna, S. (2001) *Making Good: How Ex-convicts Reform and Rebuild their Lives*. Washington, DC: American Psychological Association.

Maruna, S. and LeBel, T. P. (2003) 'Welcome home?: Examining the reentry court concept from a strengths-based perspective', *Western Criminology Review*, 4(2): 91-107.

Maruna, S. and Roy, K. (2007) 'Amputation or reconstruction? Notes on 'knifing off' and desistance from crime', *Journal of Contemporary Criminal Justice*, 23: 104-24.

Maruna, S., LeBel, T. P., Naples, M. and Mitchell, N. (2009) 'Looking-glass identity transformation: Pygmalion and Golem in the rehabilitation process'. In Veysey, B., Christian J. and Martinez D. J. (eds) *How Offenders Transform Their Lives*. Cullompton, UK: Willan.

McAra, L. and McVie, S. (2011). 'Youth justice? The impact of system contact on patterns of desistance'. In: Farrall, S., Hough, M., Sparks, R. and Maruna S. eds. *Escape Routes: Contemporary Perspectives on Life After Punishment*. London: Routledge.

McNatt, D.B. (2000) 'Ancient Pygmalion joins contemporary management: A meta-analysis of the result', *Journal of Applied Psychology*, 85(2): 314-22.

Meisenhelder, T. (1977) 'An exploratory study of exiting from criminal careers'. *Criminology*, 15: 319–34.

Miller, R. L., Brickman, P. and Bolen, D. (1975) 'Attribution versus persuasion as a means of modifying behavior'. *Journal of Personality and Social Psychology*, 31: 430-41.

Miller, W.R. (1998) 'Why do people change addictive behavior?', *Addiction*, 93: 163-72.

Morgenstern, C. (2011) 'Judicial rehabilitation in Germany – the use of criminal records and the removal of recorded convictions'. *European Journal of Probation*, 3(1): 20-35.

Naylor, B. (2011) 'Criminal Records and Rehabilitation in Australia'. *European Journal of Probation*, 3(1): 79-96.

Padfield, N. (2011) 'Judicial Rehabilitation? A view from England'. *European Journal of Probation*, 3(1): 36-49.

Pager, D. (2007) *Marked: Race, Crime, and Finding Work in an Era of Mass Incarceration*. Chicago, IL: University of Chicago Press.

Paternoster, R. and Iovanni, L. (1989) 'The labeling perspective and delinquency: An elaboration of the theory and an assessment of the evidence'. *Justice Quarterly*, 6: 359-94.

Petrunik, M. (1980) 'The rise and fall of 'labelling theory': The construction and destruction of a sociological strawman', *Canadian Journal of Sociology*, 5: 213-33.

Pinard, M. (2010) 'Collateral consequences of Criminal Convictions: Confronting Issues of Race and Dignity'. *New York University Law Review*, 85(2): 457-534.

Pinnock, D. and Douglas-Hamilton, M. (1997) *Gangs, Rituals & Rites of Passage*. Cape Town: African Sun Press.

Richards, S. C. and R. S. Jones. (2004) 'Beating the Perpetual Incarceration Machine: Overcoming Structural Impediments to Re-entry'. In: Maruna, S. and Immarigeon, R. eds. *After Crime and Punishment: Pathways to Offender Reintegration*. Cullompton: Willan.

Rosenthal, R. (2002) 'Covert communication in classrooms, clinics, courtrooms, and cubicles', *American Psychologist*, 57: 839-49.

Rosenthal, R. and Jacobson, L. (1992) *Pygmalion in the Classroom (expanded ed.)*. New York: Irvington.

Ruddell, R. and Winfree Jr., T. (2006) 'Setting aside criminal convictions in Canada: A successful approach to offender reintegration'. *The Prison Journal*, 86: 452-469.

Sampson, R. J. and Laub, J. (1997) 'A life-course theory of cumulative disadvantage and the stability of delinquency'. In: Thornberry, T. P. ed. *Advances in Criminological Theory: Vol. 6, Developmental Theories of Crime and Delinquency*. New Brunswick, NJ: Transaction.

Samuels, P. and Mukamal, D. (2004) *After Prison: Roadblocks to Reentry*. New York: Legal Action Center.

Shover, N. (1996) *Great Pretenders: Pursuits and Careers of Persistent Thieves*. Boulder, CO: Westview Press.

Tannenbaum, F. (1938). *Crime and the community*. Boston: Ginn.

Taxman, F. S. and Piquero, A. (1998) 'On preventing drunk driving recidivism: An examination of rehabilitation and punishment approaches', *Journal of Criminal Justice*, 26: 129–43.

Travis, J. (2005) *But They All Come Back: Facing the Challenges of Prisoner Reentry*. New York: Urban Institute.

Trice, H. M. and Roman, P. M. (1970) 'Delabeling, relabeling and Alcoholics Anonymous', *Social Problems*, 17: 538–46.

Uggen, C., Manza, J. and Behrens, A. (2004). 'Less than the average citizen: stigma, role transition and the civic reintegration of convicted felons'. In: Maruna, S. and Immarigeon, R. eds. *After Crime and Punishment: Pathways to Offender Reintegration*. Cullompton: Willan.

van Olphen, J., Eliason, M. J., Freudenberg, N. and Barnes, M. (2009) 'Nowhere to Go: How Stigma Limits the Options of Female Drug Users after Release from Jail'. *Substance Abuse Treatment, Prevention, & Policy*, 4: 1-10.

Visher, C. and Mallik-Kane, K. (2007) 'Reentry experiences of men with health problems'. In: Greifinger, R. ed. *Public Health is Public Safety: Improving Public Health through Correctional Health Care*. London: Springer-Verlag.

Wexler, D. B. (2001) 'Robes and rehabilitation: How judges can help offenders 'make good'', *Court Review*, 38: 18-23.

Wynn, J. (2001). *Inside Rikers: Stories from the World's Largest Penal Colony*. New York: St. Martin's Press.

Zemore, S. E., Kaskutas, L. A. and Ammon, L.N. (2004) 'In 12-step groups, helping helps the helper'. *Addiction*, 99(8): 1015-23.

7

Women and Prison: Is There a Need for a Different Approach?

Jean Corston

Introduction

The Irish Prison Service (IPS) *Annual Report 2011* (2012) revealed that the number of women committed to prison had doubled in the last six years. In 2011 the number of men sent to prison stabilised, while the number of women imprisoned, within a 12 month period, rose by 10 per cent. In 2006, 960 women were sent to prison, representing 10 per cent of the persons committed to prison (IPS, 2007). By 2011 the number of women committed had risen dramatically to 1,902, comprising 16 per cent of those sent to prison (IPS, 2012). It may be that this alarming increase is consequent on the nature of austerity programmes faced by countries in the European Union, involving often drastic cuts in public expenditure and the inevitable decline in public services, on which women are more likely to rely.

However, these figures mirror almost exactly the situation which faced me when I was commissioned by the British Government to conduct a *Review of Women with Particular Vulnerabilities in the Criminal Justice System* (Corston, 2007). In the decade ending in 2006, the women's prison population in England and Wales rose by 94 per cent; the corresponding rise for men was 38 per cent. The reason was quite simple, courts were using custody more frequently for women for less serious offences.

Reflecting on the rationale for the Corston Report

My report arose from circumstances surrounding the self inflicted deaths of 14 women in prisons in England and Wales in 2003, followed in 2004 by a total of 13. In 2006, there were on average 4,447 women in our prisons, and 73,680 men (United Kingdom. Berman and Dar, 2013). It was immediately obvious that women were being shoe-horned into a system designed for and largely run by men. Women and men are equal but different. Women in our prisons were treated in exactly the same way as men, leading to a high prevalence of institutional misunderstanding within the criminal justice system of the things that matter to women and the high level of unmet need. The outcome was anything but equality.

Indeed, when I came to Ireland in May 2008, I visited the Dóchas Centre in Dublin, which I considered provided a model for the way in which these women should be treated. I spoke to a young woman who was near the end of her sentence. She had her youngest child, a baby, with her. I asked if she had been in prison before and she said, 'Yes, in Limerick'. Limerick is essentially a men's prison with a section for women. I asked whether there was any difference between the two places, and she replied that Dóchas was much better, 'because in Limerick they treat us the way they treat the men. In here, we are treated as women'.

Homes and children define many women's lives, so to take this away from them causes huge damage to them and their family. It is estimated that more than 17,240 children were separated from their mothers by imprisonment in England and Wales in 2010 (BBC News UK, 2011). And of course, because there are relatively few women in prison, (there are only 13 women's prisons in England and Wales), they are inevitably held far from home, with little chance of family visits. This break in contact between mother and child can be catastrophic.

What I discovered (Corston, 2007) was that three-quarters of women sentenced to custody were there for less than twelve months. Only 3.2 per cent of the total female prison population are assessed as presenting a high or very high risk of serious harm to others in the community. Forty-five per cent of women remanded into custody went on to receive a custodial sentence. They were generally on remand for 28 days which was long enough to lose both home and children, with little chance of getting either back. Only 5 per cent of children remained in the family home when their mother is imprisoned, so they were invariably taken into care. Upon release, the women were treated as single for housing purposes, because they did not have their children with them, and they were not allowed to take their children out of care because they did not have suitable family accommodation – a tragic Catch-22.

Women with histories of being victims of violence and abuse are over represented in the criminal justice system. Up to 50 per cent of women in prison actually report having experienced violence at home; one in three have suffered sexual abuse. It is shocking how often it is childhood sexual abuse, which has left them feeling not only a total lack of self confidence, but a lack of self worth. Because of course, like many victims, they blame themselves.

Nearly 80 per cent of these women have mental health problems. At least half of them were a suicide risk before they went into prison, and on release, they are 23 times more likely than women in the general population to commit suicide.

Three-quarters of them are drug dependent, and not just on Class A drugs; some women entering prison can have a poly-drug misuse of prescription and illegal drugs, and alcohol.

And the self-harm statistics are grim to say the least. In 2010 there were 26,893 incidents of self-harm in our prisons (United Kingdom. Ministry of Justice, 2011a). Women accounted for 47 per cent of all incidents of self-harm, despite representing only 5 per cent of the prison population. Much of this self-harm is too shocking to describe, yet women will assert that it is their way of blocking out memories of an intolerable past. As Rachel Holford, director of the campaign group Women in Prison, put it:

> They have no power, which mirrors their previous experi-
> ence of abuse and neglect. As a woman in prison told us,
> 'Putting the blade in and watching the blood come down is
> the only time I can control something that's happening in
> here and stop the pain' (Townsend, 2012a).

The following describes a typical ten-day period in a women's local prison:

- A woman had to be operated on because she had pushed a cross-stitch needle deep into a self inflicted wound.

- A woman in the segregation unit with mental health problems had embarked on a dirty protest.

- A pregnant woman was taken to hospital to have early induced labour over concerns about her addicted unborn child. She went into labour knowing that the Social Services would take the baby away shortly after birth.

- A young woman with a long history of self-harm continued to open old wounds to the extent that she lost dangerous amounts of blood. She refused to engage with staff.

- A woman was remanded into custody for strangling her six-year old child. She was in a state of shock.

- A woman set fire to herself and her bedding.

- The in-reach team concluded that there was a woman, in psychosis, who was extremely dangerous and had to be placed in the segregation unit for the safety of the other women until alternative arrangements could be made.

- A crack cocaine addict who displayed disturbing and paranoid behaviour (but who had not been diagnosed with any illness) was released. She refused all offers of help to be put in touch with community workers.

Significantly, the overwhelming majority of the women I spoke to had limited life skills. The things that we all take for granted, which we assume to be part of the human condition, are, by and large, things which we learn. For example: how to hold a conversation, how to take turns, how to make a persuasive phone call, how to work with and cooperate with others and how to clean a toilet.

Finally, the women are in prison for short periods of time which does not facilitate meaningful intervention. Upon release, their biggest challenge is not employability – the holy grail of most prison regimes – but accommodation. Time and again I heard the heartbreaking lament, 'I just want somewhere for me and my kids'.

It will surprise no one to learn that I concluded in my report that these women were, by and large, troubled rather than troublesome. And please do not run away with the notion that these statistics, personal stories and circumstances are confined to England and Wales. I have been struck by how many people from all over the world who have read my report on the web and who assert that I must have visited their country, because it is just the same. It is, by and large, just the same the world over.

Impact of the Corston Report

As to my conclusions and recommendations, I first considered the nature of these women's vulnerabilities, which seemed to me to fall into three categories. First: domestic circumstances and problems such as domestic violence, child care problems, being a single parent and debt. Second: personal circumstances such as mental illness, low self-esteem, eating disorders, substance misuse and low educational attainment. Third: most significantly, socio-economic factors such as poverty, isolation and unemployment. When women are experiencing a combination of factors from each of these three categories of vulnerabilities, it is likely to lead to a crisis point that ultimately leads to prison.

I made 43 recommendations in all; 41 of them were accepted, some with qualification. I had concluded that as women and men are obviously different, there ought to be a prison regime tailored to women's needs. The dominant culture was if considered appropriate for men – namely extreme security and constant searching – it was appropriate for women. I considered that this flew in the face of the Gender Equality Duty, which was to come into force in April 2008 (United Kingdom, Equal Opportunities Commission, 2007). Subsequently, when the Ministry of Justice assumed responsibility for the prison estate, a Gender Equality Scheme was published (United Kingdom, National Offender Management Service, 2009).

I found that there was no one person or distinct body with overall responsibility for women's prisons. They were an afterthought on any agenda, so I called for an Inter Departmental Ministerial Group for women who offend or are at risk of offending.

While I have never argued that no woman should ever be sent to prison, I concluded that prison was an entirely inappropriate place for turning round the lives of the vast majority of the women we locked up. I called for a network of women's centres, to be used for referrals by the courts and other public bodies and individuals, like family doctors and teachers, who often can identify a chaotic lifestyle which could lead to offending. I visited such centres, run by extraordinary and pioneering women, in Halifax, Worcester and Glasgow, and saw for myself that by taking a woman centred approach, lives can be turned around. Issues like mental ill health, debt, life skills, parenting, diet and accommodation can all be dealt with under one roof by qualified professionals. This approach is far more effective than making dozens of appointments with different organisations, especially for women whose lives are so chaotic that a failure to keep an appointment is almost a foregone conclusion. I met a woman in one of these centres who had been in and out of prison since she was fifteen, always for very short periods and for petty offences. She had three children, the eldest had been put up for adoption without her consent and the second was in care, with little chance of being reunited. She was waiting to move into a flat with her third child. I asked why she was at the centre and she told me that a magistrate had sent her there, because prison had clearly not had any positive influence on her life. I asked what had been the outcome for her coming to the centre and she said:

> When I have been in prison, there was always someone else I could blame. 'If my step-dad hadn't done that to me', 'If my mother had protected me'. 'If I had not been abused', 'If I hadn't got pregnant', 'If I hadn't been introduced to crack cocaine', 'If I hadn't been coerced into prostitution because I was poor', It was always someone else's fault. Now, I am 41, and this is the first time someone has sat down with me and asked, 'What is your responsibility for being in this situation?' And she added, 'Actually, it's much harder than being in prison, but I do really feel I am turning my life around'.

I asked her the question I often ask people in prison, 'Do you like yourself?', she said she was beginning to do so. It is my contention that this is the foundation of self-esteem and self-confidence. When I was working on my report, I was told that the total cost of keeping a woman in prison for a year was £70,000. The cost of a place at the centre in Worcester at that time was £750. I know which I think is the better value for money on every count.

Another recommendation which was dear to my heart was that the strip searching regime should be radically changed. Women were repeatedly and routinely strip searched; for example, before going to court and on return to prison, even though they had been under supervision throughout. Prison governors to whom I spoke told me that they never found anything during these searches. I considered these searches to be a waste of staff time, and a terrible thing to do to women who had been victims of abuse. I am proud to tell you that, following a pilot project in four women's prisons, routine strip searching was abolished in the women's estate on 1 April 2009.

It is impossible to list progress on all my recommendation in the time available but I want to call attention to some more. In 2008, Maria Eagle, then a Home Office Minister, provided the visible leadership. I had been calling for a Ministerial champion for women in the criminal justice system. She announced the start of a 'long-term sustainable strategy' to implement the 'Corston blueprint for change' and to cut the numbers of women in prison (Eagle, 2008: 3). She also committed to regular reporting to Parliament on progress made, a promise that was kept. The infrastructure to drive the necessary integrated approach and joined up work across departments was put in place when an Inter Ministerial Group for Women Offenders and Women at Risk of Offending was established as well as a cross-department Criminal Justice Women's Strategy Team.

Despite huge economic problems, the government at the time had the foresight to invest £15.6 million in 2008/10 to develop and expand the network of women's centres and projects. In 2008, I was approached by representatives of 22 Charitable Trusts and Foundations which had been involved in the criminal justice system, who after reading my report, concluded that they had been putting money and resource into a failing culture. They came together as the Corston Independent Funders' Coalition, to press for the full implementation of the report's recommendations. The Coalition developed a ground-breaking partnership with the Ministry of Justice with match-funding from the Women's Diversionary Fund, providing further investment of over £5 million in 2010 and 2011 to sustain the network of 39 projects. The coalition also established a new 'umbrella' organisation, Women's Breakout, an important infrastructure organisation needed so as to work on future sustainability, quality standards and evidencing success.

Following my report I called for the government to announce within six months a clear strategy to replace existing women's prisons with suitable, geographically dispersed, small, multi-functional custodial centres within ten years. I was subsequently told that the conclusions of research on this proposal were that women themselves were hostile to the notion. I have no way of knowing the nature of the research.

A National Service Framework for Women Offenders has been issued, as has an Offender Management Guide to Working with Women, so as to improve the probation response to working with women, and a set of gender specific standards for women's prisons was established (United Kingdom, National Offender Management Service, 2008).

The National Offender Management Service (NOMS) has developed a Women Awareness Staff Programme, a course for all staff and volunteers working with women. This was crucial because the majority of prison staff had no idea of how to respond to the complex needs of women in prison. Indeed, in early 2012, Clive Chatterton, the last Governor of Styal Prison in Cheshire, one of the largest women's prisons in England, expressed his shock at working in a women's prison. While Chatterton had over 30 years of experience in the prison service, always in the male estate, he said he was still haunted by the sights and sounds from his time as governor in Styal. He admitted being scarred by the experience (Townsend, 2012b). He is now, in retirement, a dedicated campaigner for the cause of women in prison.

It probably goes without saying that many of the women who end up in prison are sex workers. A new training programme for staff, 'Sex Workers in Prison', has been developed, enabling women to discuss their experiences and receive support whilst in prison to assist them in leaving sex work. This work is not for the faint-hearted. The northern area manager for the organisation Women in Prison described a 22-year-old inmate, as 'very typical' – frequent, short jail terms, suffered parental neglect and was coerced into prostitution from the age of 12, where she was raped by ten men a day 'before tea time', as she put it (Townsend, 2012a).

There has been other progress made since the Corston Report, though it is taking longer to achieve than I had hoped. The number of women on remand in England and Wales fell by 12 per cent in the year to 31 March 2012, to 689 (United Kingdom, Ministry of Justice, 2012). As I noted earlier, there were on average 4,447 women in prison in 2006 (United Kingdom, Berman and Dar, 2013). By June 2010, the number was 4,267 (United Kingdom, Ministry of Justice, 2010) and on 30 June 2011 there were 4,185 (United Kingdom, Ministry of Justice, 2011b), a reduction of 300 in five and a half years. Given the effect of the global recession and the trends in other countries, the fact that there is a reduction at all is, I suppose, a cause for celebration.

There is also a lot of work needed in persuading sentencers of the efficacy of alternatives to custody. In some areas, there are new and enlightened in-court schemes for diverting women from custody, including in Bristol, the city I was proud to represent in the House of Commons for 13 years. Ten Women in Focus events were held across England and Wales, to increase awareness of the gender equality duty and to engage the judiciary in the agenda for women.

Some role back in implementing recommendations, but pressure remains

I would like to report that the modest progress I have described has been maintained, but it is not the case. Some of the good progress in implementing recommendations has been lost under the 2010 Conservative/Liberal Democrat government. The concept of a 'Champion' and clear leadership for the needs of women in prison has been somewhat lost. Infrastructure that had been put in place to secure an integrated approach across government for women offenders and those at risk of offending – the Inter-Ministerial Group and the cross-departmental Criminal Justice Women's Strategy Team – have now been dismantled. There is now no written, joined-up, cross-government strategy to reduce the numbers of women in custody, and no reporting to Parliament, so it is difficult to see how momentum on progress can be maintained and evidenced.

But the pressure for change will not diminish. There is a strong body of organisations and individuals whose determination, commitment and capacity to influence has a powerful and broad reach, for example, the Prison Reform Trust, the Howard League for Penal Reform, the 21 organisations in the Corston Independent Funders' Coalition, leading academics in the field, like Loraine Gelsthorpe and Carol Hedderman, and practitioners across the women's voluntary sector agencies. Thank goodness that the women's community projects and centres continue to work so hard and with such enthusiasm to engage with and work with these women.

The Review by Dame Anne Owers et al. into the Northern Ireland Prison Service in October 2011 and its call for small custodial units for women (2011), and the recent positive response to Dame Eilish Angiolini's Commission on Women Offenders in Scotland (2012), both maintain the pressure for change, and point in broadly the same direction as my report.

There are also wider levers for change at a national and international level relating to equality and human rights issues. These are being looked at closely by campaigners and practitioners in their efforts to secure change for women and their children caught up in the criminal justice system – women who can still risk being 'dismissed' as a minority. The Gender Duty (United Kingdom, Equal Opportunities Commission, 2007), the European Convention on Human Rights (Article 3) (Council of Europe, 1953), the UN convention on the rights of the child (UN General Assembly, 1989), the UN General Assembly Bangkok Rules in December 2010 (UN General Assembly, 2010) and CEDAW – the Convention on the Elimination of Discrimination Against Women (United Nations Entity for Gender Equality and the Empowerment of Women, 1979), all these together present a powerful rationale for change.

A few years ago, I was doing some ironing on a winter Saturday afternoon and was surprised to hear reference to both my name and my report. It was a programme about two women who had been through the women's centre regime I had recommended. They had, on reception, been asked to fill in assessment forms, with questions like, 'what had you wanted to be when you grew up?', 'what do you think you could achieve now?', 'Are your children proud of you?' They said that they had thought these forms were rubbish, but had stuck with the process because it was better than being in prison. A few years on, they were in work or further education and had their own accommodation together with their children. Their children were proud of them. They were asked what had become of those assessment forms which had been so ridiculed. One said hers was on her bedroom wall; the other had put hers on the fridge.

For me, that says it all.

Bibliography

Angiolini, E. (2012) *Commission on Women Offenders*. Glasgow: Scottish Government. Available at: http://www.scotland.gov.uk/Resource/0039/00391828.pdf (Accessed 30 January 2014).

BBC News UK (2011) 'Howard League says jailing mothers damages children'. BBC News UK, 30 September. Available from http://www.bbc.co.uk/news/uk-15122495 [30 January 2014]

Corston, J. (2007) *The Corston Report*. London: Home Office.

Council of Europe (1953) *European Convention of Human Rights*. Available at: http://www.echr.coe.int/Documents/Convention_ENG.pdf (Accessed 30 January 2014).

Eagle, M. (2008) *Delivering the Government Response to the Corston Report*. London: Ministry of Justice.

Irish Prison Service. (2012) *Annual Report 2011*. Longford: Irish Prison Service Print Unit.

Irish Prison Service. (2007) *Annual Report 2006*. Longford: Irish Prison Service Print Unit.

Owers, A., Leighton, P., McGrory, C., McNeill, F. and Wheatley, P. (2011) *Review of the Northern Ireland Prison Service: Conditions, management and oversight of all prisons*. Belfast: Department of Justice Northern Ireland. Available at: http://www.dojni.gov.uk/index/ni-prison-service/ nips-publications/reports-reviews-nips/owers-review-of-the-northern-ireland-prison-service.pdf (Accessed 30 January 2014).

Townsend, M. (2012a) 'Women prisoners: self-harm, suicide attempts and the struggle for survival'. *The Observer,* 11 February. Available from: http://www.theguardian.com/society/2012/feb/11/women-prisoners-suffering-mental-health [29 January 2014]

Townsend, M. (2012b) 'Women's prisons in desperate need of reform, says former governmor'. *The Observer,* 11 February. Available from: http://www.theguardian.com/society/2012/feb/11/women-prisons-urgent-reform-needed [29 January 2014]

United Kingdom, Berman, G. and Dar, A. (2013) *Prison Population Statistics*. London: House of Commons Library.

United Kingdom, Equal Opportunities Commission. (2007) *Gender Equality Duty Code of Practice England and Wales.* London: Equal Opportunities Commission.

United Kingdom, Ministry of Justice (2012) *Offender Management Statistics Quarterly Bulletin: January to March 2012, England and Wales.* London: Ministry of Justice.

United Kingdom, Ministry of Justice. (2011a) *Safety in Custody 2010 England and Wales.* London: Ministry for Justice. Available at: https:// www.gov.uk/government/uploads/system/uploads/attachment_data/ file/218397/safety-custody-2010.pdf (Accessed 29 January 2014).

United Kingdom, Ministry of Justice (2011b) *Offender Management Statistics Quarterly Bulletin: April to June 2011, England and Wales.* London: Ministry of Justice.

United Kingdom, Ministry of Justice (2010) *Offender Management Statistics Quarterly Bulletin: April to June 2010, England and Wales.* London: Ministry of Justice.

United Kingdom, National Offender Management Service. (2009) *Promoting Equality in Prisons and Probation: The National Offender Management Service Single Equality Scheme 2009-2012.* London: Race and Equalities Action Group. Available at: http://www.justice.gov.uk/ downloads/publications/noms/2009/noms-single-equality-scheme.pdf (Accessed 29 January 2014).

United Kingdom, National Offender Management Service. (2008) *National Service Framework: Improving Services to Women Offenders*. London: Ministry for Justice. Available at: http://webarchive.nationalarchives. gov.uk/20100303141250/http://noms.justice.gov.uk/news-publications-events/publications/strategy/NSF-Women-08?view=Binary (Accessed 29 January 2014).

United Nations Entity for Gender Equality and the Empowerment of Women (1979) *Convention on the Elimination of all Forms of Discrimination against Women*. Available at: http://www.un.org/ womenwatch/daw/cedaw/cedaw.htm (Accessed 30 January 2014).

United Nations General Assembly (1989) *Convention on the Rights of the Child*. Available at: http://www.childrensrights.ie/sites/default/files/ UNCRCEnglish.pdf (Accessed 30 January 2014).

United Nations General Assembly (2010) *United Nations Rules for the Treatment of Women Prisoners and Non-custodial Measures for Women Offenders*. Available at: http://www.un.org/en/ecosoc/docs/2010/res%20 2010-16.pdf (Accessed 30 January 2014).

8

The Social and Economic Costs of Female Imprisonment: The Prisoners' Point of View

Rafaela Granja, Manuela P. da Cunha and Helena Machado

Introduction

Recent prison studies emphasise the need to abandon views of offenders as socially isolated members of society, as such views fail to recognise that families and communities are also affected by penal policies (Pattillo et al., 2004). Some studies have therefore begun to raise questions about the unintended consequences (Clear, 1996) or collateral costs of imprisonment (Cunha, 2008; Hagan and Dinovitzer, 1999; Mauer and Chesney-Lind, 2002; Travis and Waul, 2003). Recognising the multiple facets of prisoners' identities – as fathers and mothers, sons and daughters, partners, local residents, workers and, indeed, citizens – means highlighting the ways in which people in prison continue to count for their families and communities (Western, Patillo and Weiman, 2004: 11-12).

A substantial body of interdisciplinary literature has been produced on the hidden costs of imprisonment (Braman, 2002; Comfort, 2008; Ferraro et al., 1983). In particular, the impact of incarceration on families ranges from financial hardship, emotional issues, feelings of shame and social stigma and the experience of being involved with prison routines (through visits and other ways of maintaining contact), to reconfigurations of family roles and responsibilities in the household (Arditti, 2005; Comfort, 2007; Hagan and Dinovitzer, 1999; Hairston, 2002; Light and Campbell, 2006). Among the multiple collateral consequences of imprisonment (Mauer and Chesney-Lind, 2002; Pattillo et al., 2004), this chapter intends to assess the social and economic cost of women's imprisonment from the women's point of view, by considering their own perceptions of the roles they formerly played in family life and support networks prior to imprisonment.

Drawing on doctoral research conducted by the authors (Granja et al., ongoing), this chapter explores the impact of imprisonment on women and their families in Portugal.

The selectivity of the penal system and its impact on low-income communities

Prisoners tend to be disproportionately drawn from poor and minority communities (Wacquant, 2000). Although imprisonment affects all social groups and can occur in any neighbourhood, it is more prevalent among deprived groups in poor urban communities. Therefore, the collateral effects of imprisonment tend to have a more intensive impact on these communities (Clear, 2002: 184). The unintended consequences of imprisonment may be extensive, damaging social and financial capital, overburdening and eroding informal support networks (Cunha, 2002; 2008; Pattillo et al., 2004), destabilising marital dynamics and child care arrangements (Granja et al., 2012a; 2012b) and affecting informal social control (Lynch and Sabol, 2004).

Since the prison system has a significant influence on poor and minority urban neighbourhoods, imprisonment is an increasingly normal event in the lives of members of such neighbourhoods, often affecting a wide range of family and community networks (Cunha, 2002). The spatial centralisation of incarceration disrupts social networks based on kinship and friendship, since it depletes human, social and economic resources, and increasingly overburdens those who remain available to help (Cunha, 2013). Thus, the concentrated expansion of the penal system challenges family and community 'elasticity', a concept developed by Sandra Enos which she defines as 'the ability of family units to accommodate additional members and responsibilities during times of crisis' (Enos, 1998: 61).

As Cunha has noted in the Portuguese context, in the face of insufficient public services or social policies designed to reduce the impact of imprisonment, the 'welfare society' (see Santos, 1993) – in other words, family and community resources and support – assumes the role designed for state welfare and acts as 'a "pillow" that ... softens the harshness of a life that would otherwise benefit from little (formal) protection in crucial aspects, especially among the poor' (Cunha, 2013: 82).

This process is highly gendered, since the welfare society acts mainly through kinship ties and especially women. As Sílvia Portugal points out, 'what is mobilised is not exactly the family, but the women of the family' (2008: 32). In the Portuguese context, women are central to creating and maintaining community support networks, given that they are mainly responsible for providing assistance to the elderly and to dependent relatives, (Portugal, 1995; Torres, 2002) and financial and emotional support for relatives serving prison sentences (Condry, 2007; Cunha, 2002). Therefore, female solidarity is central to the maintenance and activation of informal support, and the costs of the 'welfare society' are borne mainly by women, thus revealing gender inequalities (Portugal, 1995; 2008; Santos, 1993).

The already overburdened role of women as 'family and community caregivers' in low-income families and neighbourhoods is further complicated by the constant threat of possible arrest and detention faced by women themselves and/or their family members (Richie, 2002: 145-46). Family arrangements always face the potential erosion of human (and economic) resources due to the actions of the penal system, which leads to fewer adults remaining available to assume care and financial responsibilities during imprisonment (Cunha, 2002).

Thus the penal system, in absorbing and overloading the few available support networks in deprived communities, may be contributing towards increasing poverty and social vulnerability, both for prisoners (Marchetti, 2002) and their families (Hanlon et al., 2007).

The family: A gendered institution

In recent years a wealth of interdisciplinary literature has sought to explore the profound changes that have challenged the traditional notion of the family as anchored in the institution of (heterosexual) marriage or cohabitation. The changes are varied, complex and constrained by historical, economic, political and cultural factors, and by individual trajectories permeated by gender, social class, race and stage of life (Collier and Sheldon, 2008).

In general terms, the decline of the male breadwinner, coupled with the large number of women entering the labour market as well as their continuing involvement in waged labour after they have had children, have been recurring themes in this literature (Collier and Sheldon, 2008; Torres, 2004). Other key interlinking themes include the diversity and heterogeneity of parental 'family practices', the rising divorce rate, the dissociation between conjugality and parenting – corroborated by the growing importance of single parent households (Wall and Lobo, 1999) – and the decreasing size of families. Together these dynamic processes and multiple reconfigurations have contributed towards a significant shift in our understanding of what constitutes a family, and have highlighted the need to move away from the notion of the family as a 'given' and towards an increasingly fluid and diverse institution (Smart and Neale, 1999).

With regard to the social and economic costs of female imprisonment, the focus of this chapter lies in understanding the logic that surrounds the 'performance' of family life during periods of enforced change, including an appreciation of the fluidity and diversity of different family forms and connections. This approach resists the concept of the family which characterises most prison studies literature – namely heterosexual couples with children – and acknowledges the complexity and diversity of family practices and composition (Almond, 2006; Smart and Neale, 1999).

A gender-sensitive approach is also crucial to assessing women's experiences, perceptions and representations. Studies in Portugal on the role of women in the family (Torres, 2002), women's experiences of transgression (Duarte, 2011) and victimisation (Alves and Maia, 2010), and their contact with the justice (Beleza, 1990; Machado, 2004) and prison system (Cunha, 1994; 2002) have demonstrated the importance of addressing women's experiences from a gender perspective in order to portray and understand the specific features that surround and embody women's lives (Matos and Machado, 2007).

As in other countries, the male prison population in Portugal is disproportionately higher than female prison population (94 per cent versus 6 per cent) (Direção-Geral de Reinserção e Serviços Prisionais, 2014). Despite the growing importance assigned to a gender perspective, most of the literature on the social impacts of incarceration has typically considered the consequences of male imprisonment, meaning that very little of the debate focuses specifically on the collateral effects of female incarceration(but see Cunha, forthcoming). Framing this debate so narrowly in male-centred terms ignores the gendered consequences of imprisonment and the central role of women in community and family dynamics (Richie, 2002).

The family is a highly gendered institution and men and women experience family life, parenting and romantic relationships in different ways and play different roles in the organisation of the household (Aboim, 2006; Portugal, 1995; Torres, 2002). Therefore, as prison studies literature has shown, an imposed separation from family life has different consequences for women and men (Sharp et al., 1998; Tasca et al., 2011), particularly in terms of childcare (Cunha and Granja, forthcoming; Ferraro and Moe, 2003; Johnson and Waldfogel, 2004), but also due the central role that women play as economic and care providers (European Commission, 2005). In fact, the majority of prisoners who are mothers are generally the primary carers of children prior to imprisonment (Ferraro and Moe, 2003; Hairston, 1991). They also tend to be the sole or main source of household income, as the fathers are already either in prison or absent (Greene et al, 2000; Henriques, 1996). If sent to prison, many mothers cannot therefore entrust their children to the care of their fathers, whereas the reverse rarely occurs: when the father is imprisoned, the children usually stay together with the mother under the same roof. When the mother is imprisoned, the children often end up separated from both parents as well as from brothers and sisters, since siblings are distributed among other relatives, neighbours or institutions (Cunha, 2002; 2013; Palomar Verea, 2007).

Given that most women, prior to imprisonment, play an active part in the maintenance and structure of their families, imprisonment highlights the realignment and reconfigurations that occur in family roles, responsibilities and relationships when a woman is sent to prison. It is, therefore, a phenomenon that invites reflection on the gendered consequences of women's imprisonment, including an assessment of the fluidity and diversity of family forms and connections.

Methodology

The social and economic cost of women's imprisonment was explored from the point of view of women themselves, drawing on interviews with twenty inmates of a women's prison in Portugal and considering their perceptions of the role they had played in family life prior to imprisonment The interviews took place between April and September 2011 and had an average duration of one hour and forty minutes.

The women interviewed were serving sentences mainly for drug trafficking and property offences. The sentences ranged from two years and seven months to 25 years, with 18 women serving sentences of more than four and a half years. The majority of the interviewees came from precarious economic, social and cultural backgrounds, reflecting the trends shown in other national and international studies on female inmates (European Commission, 2005; Cunha, 2002). The women had very low levels of educational and social capital: most women only completed six years of school-ing and, prior to imprisonment, the majority had been dependent on the welfare system due to low incomes and high rates of un-employment. All the women interviewed were mothers, with an average of three children each, and their ages ranged from 20 to 52 years old. In terms of family composition, fourteen of the women had lived in a household consisting of their children and partner (not necessarily the father of the children) prior to their arrest.

Results

Drawing on the prisoners' narratives, four scenarios emerged re-garding the prevailing role of women in the family unit prior to im-prisonment. The scenarios are not mutually exclusive and they all describe the following significant dimensions: the roles played by women in family life prior to imprisonment, the reconfiguration and realignment of family roles and responsibilities following im-prisonment, the logic surrounding the activation of support net-works, and the limitations and consequences of women's impris-onment for the family. The four scenarios are: i) women as single mothers, ii) women as lone mothers: family situations mediated by prison, iii) women as daughters, and iv) women as wives.

Women as single mothers

In the period prior to imprisonment several women were the main or sole providers and carers for their children (Ferraro and Moe, 2003; Hairston, 1991). The fathers usually played a peripheral role in education and child support, or were completely absent from their children's lives, exonerating themselves from any financial and emotional responsibility for their offspring (Machado and Granja, 2013). Some disadvantaged women who find it more difficult to meet the challenges of single parenthood (Faria, 2011; McCormack, 2005), resort to family support (cohabitation, informal care) to help reconcile timetables and the financial difficulties of single parenthood, and also to compensate for inadequate family policies in this area (Wall et al., 2002).

Rita, aged 28, single and sentenced to five years for drug trafficking, has three children from different relationships. Before she went to prison Rita was the only care provider:

> There was one time I called him to say I needed money for my kid. I needed to go to the chemist's and I didn't have the money. ... The more I said I didn't want a relationship with him, the more he hated my daughter. ... He only recently began giving money for my daughter after I took him to court. ... Until then he never, never, never, never, gave anything, not even a loaf of bread.

When Rita was sent to prison she was unable to leave the children in the care of their respective fathers since they were always absent. Rita's mother, a 65-year-old cleaning lady living in an economically deprived neighbourhood in very vulnerable financial circumstances was therefore the only person available for childcare. However, she was reluctant to care for her three grandchildren due to the strain of living on a very low income:

> [During the trial] I knew I would go to prison and my mum had always told me 'if you're arrested I'll take care of the older children but I won't take care of the youngest' and I didn't know what would happen to my youngest daughter.

However, after Rita went to prison her mother became responsible for her three grandchildren, aged 13, 8 and 3.

Maria, aged 35 and sentenced to six years for attempted murder, was given custody of her daughter after her divorce. Before she went to prison she had started living with her boyfriend and her daughter. After the divorce, the father played a more peripheral role in the child's life, both emotionally – with fortnightly visits – and financially – partly contributing to the child's upkeep. When Maria was sent to prison she left her daughter in the care of an aunt and her child's father continued to play a secondary role in the life of his daughter: 'When I came here I had to leave my daughter safe somewhere, and the only thing I could do was leave her with her aunt.'

When women are sent to prison, the role of the fathers remains the same, characterised by total absence or intermittent presence. Conversely, family members – such as grandparents or aunts – who have already given the mother informal support, assume full custody, albeit temporarily, even if this increases the social vulnerability of some families.

Women as lone mothers: Family situations mediated by prison

Sometimes the imprisonment of a family member creates a temporary, involuntary, single parent household (Arditti, 2005). In this study, 12 of the women interviewed had, at some point in their lives, had partners serving prison sentences. Some, but not all, of these women maintained relationships with their imprisoned partners for long periods of time, thus creating an involuntary single parent household. Another element that also characterised romantic relationships for most of these women was drug addiction or alcoholism in their partners. In some cases, the same relationship involved both imprisonment and addiction issues (see Comfort, 2008; Granja et al., 2012a).

In this family configuration, domestic groups centre on the mother, since the man is often absent due to imprisonment, or plays a passive role, being dependent on the woman's wages as a result of drug addiction or alcoholism and tending to drain rather than contribute to the family budget (Comfort, 2008; European Commission, 2005: 36).

In these situations women assume a central place in the family as the only breadwinner in the house, supporting their husbands – as prisoners or drug addicts – as well as their dependent children. This was the case with Claudia, aged 35 and serving a sentence of four years and eight months for drug trafficking, who has one 11-year-old daughter. Despite a marriage which lasted 12 years, she only lived with her husband for a short period of time:

> I was with him for 12 years, but to tell you the truth I only lived with him for two and a half years. Because he was always in prison. ... He lived with the girl for a year and a half.

During the time he spent in prison, Claudia visited her husband regularly and provided him with emotional and financial support – which can be a very heavy burden for low-income families (see Christian, 2005).

During the short periods of time that Claudia's husband was at home:

> I was working, he wasn't. ... I was the one who covered all the expenses for the house and children. ... He spent all his money on drugs, more than he earned.

In addition to imprisoned partners, many women may have other family members also serving time in prison. Claudia, now in prison, is doing time together with her husband and two siblings. Thus, after Claudia's imprisonment, her parents – who are 60 and 56 years old – became mainly responsible for supporting all the members of the family who were in prison (in two different prisons) and caring for two grandchildren (Claudia's daughter and nephew):

> My parents don't have much money, with us all in prison and them taking care of two grandchildren. ... My mother still says it was robbery. My mother says that the police

robbed her, stole her two daughters. And she feels helpless ...; all of my parents' children are in prison and they have two grandchildren to take care of on the outside.

Sometimes the erosion of support networks is so great that no one on the outside is able to support both imprisoned relatives and dependent family members. Isabel, aged 32 and serving a five-year sentence for drug trafficking, has three children. When she went to prison most of her family (her parents, several siblings, and partner) were already doing time, and her only option was to leave her children, aged 14, 8 and 6, in foster care:

Everybody was in prison, I had no support from anyone. ... So I chose to give them [the children] to those gentlemen [a social institution] so they could take care of them.

Prior to imprisonment, the women bore extensive and heavy responsibilities for raising children and taking care of the family. After they were sent to prison, these roles were either assumed by social institutions or transferred to other family members, who subsequently had to divide their time and resources between multiple family members in need of assistance – adult sons and daughters in prison and dependent grandchildren – in order to visit family members in prison, care for children (see also Cunha, 2008: 339) and reconcile these responsibilities with work.

Women as daughters

Before they were sent to prison, the lifestyles of some had been mainly characterised by continuous drug abuse, drifting between the labour market and criminal activity. Despite their drug addiction, which had multiple personal and family consequences (Gonçalves and Pereira, 1982; Pires, 2004), some women maintained strong ties with family members, especially with their mothers and siblings, financially and emotionally supporting and being supported by them.

They maintained precarious relationships with their offspring, since the accumulated problems that marked their lives (lack of resources and suitable housing, drug addiction, alcoholism, crime) had led to the termination of parental rights when the children were young or even newborn (Granja et al., 2012b). In some cases the mothers had taken this decision to ensure the children had a more secure and stable environment than they could provide for them; in other cases it was the child welfare system or family intervention that had removed the children from the woman's care, even if the mother wanted to raise them herself. Generally, in both scenarios, family members assumed responsibility for child care, but when they were unable to provide care, the children were placed in foster homes. When the women were sent to prison, the children therefore remained in the same environment, not experiencing direct consequences of imprisonment, although other relatives – such as parents and siblings – generally experienced some impacts.

Sandra, aged 25 and sentenced to seven years for theft, lived with her mother, father and brothers and contributed significantly to the household income. 'We didn't have a good standard of living at home but with my job we always had a little something to eat, and we could pay our bills'. In the years that followed she became a drug addict but continued to contribute to the family income. After she was sent to prison, the loss of Sandra's income left the family, especially her mother who is 64 years old and retired due to disability, in poverty:

> In my head I was responsible for my family's misfortunes. The troubles that my mother started to have after I was sent down, starving, not having this, not having that ... I was to blame for that. That's what I thought. ... My mother told me she had got so behind with the rent that she had been sent a letter saying that if she didn't pay at least one or two instalments by a certain date, she would be evicted.

Before she went to prison, Madalena, aged 36 and a drug addict sentenced to four years and six months for drug trafficking, took care of her dependent mother, aged 65, on a daily basis. After she was sentenced, her mother became dependent on some neighbours helping sporadically, and also on assistance from charity institutions. However, most of the time Madalena's mother is alone at home, which exacerbates Madalena's concerns:

> I went to my mother's house every day. I worked till seven, eight pm and then I went to my mother's, no matter what time of day it was. ... My mother needs me for everything. She is disabled ... she wears diapers, she needs me to dress her, feed her, get her up, take her to the bathroom, everything. ... Now a neighbour is taking care of her. ... The Santa Casa da Misericórdia [a charity institution] also goes there but if you don't take her off the wheelchair, she doesn't eat. She is completely dependent. She is shut up at home, alone, during the night. The neighbour walks away and locks the door – what if something happens?

Unlike other women, these prisoners *are somewhat more* peripheral to childcare, although they are involved in complex arrangements for shared household resources and care which are interrupted when they are sent to prison. Their absence often places the family itself in jeopardy, leaving dependent people with limited or no care and financial support.

Women as wives

One last family configuration concerns female prisoners formerly living in households consisting of a partner present in daily family life, dependent children and sometimes dependent elderly parents or other relatives. These women were usually active in the labour market, and their income, together with that of their partner, constituted the household budget. Yet, the women were mainly responsible for household chores, childcare and helping the elderly and other dependents (Portugal, 2008; Torres, 2004).

In this sample, ten of the women interviewed were serving prison sentences as well as their partners – due to the fact that they were both involved in the same case – (Granja et al., 2012a) and most had been living with their partners and other relatives prior to imprisonment. These dual sentences entail the removal of both members of the couple from households where both had been responsible for dependent children and elderly people. Maria Luísa, aged 44, was sentenced to five years for fraud and forgery, together with her husband. Before she was sent to prison she had been taking care of her 15-year-old son and 73-year-old father 'after my mother died, my father ate at my house, and I took care of his needs'.

After the couple were sentenced, Maria Luisa's father became responsible for his grandson and the family income consisted only of his meagre retirement pension:

> My life totally fell apart. Out there I worked, and my husband did too and my son had a happy childhood, he didn't miss out on anything. The day I came here my kid missed everything. He missed his mother, his father ... I mean, now my father has to pay for the water, electricity and all the regular household bills. And he has to feed my son....

This situation, in addition to restricting the lives of the elderly – who have to adapt to full-time care, nurturing, and protection of children (Landry-Meyer and Newman, 2004) – also entails adjusting to a meagre family budget. These reconfigurations generate a greater vulnerability to unforeseen events, which create concerns for parents in prison due to the likelihood of elderly people falling ill. This is exemplified by the case of Natalie, aged 32, serving a 14 year sentence for an aggravated offence resulting in death, together with her husband. Natalie is concerned about her father-in-law's health, since he is 65 years old and is taking care of her three children, aged 16, 13 and 9:

> I am worried, ... if anything happens, what's going to happen to my children? Who will take care of them? I'm here,

and their father is in prison too. I pray to God every day to give my father-in-law good health. Every day I worry about it, every day, because my children have no one else except my father-in-law. He's the only person they have out there.

The resources that women can draw on to provide financial support and care for their children and other dependent relatives while they are in prison vary widely. When families are doubly or triply affected by prison sentences the collateral consequences of imprisonment are even greater. Usually elderly grandparents, both men and women, formerly dependent on the care of others, reverse their position and become the ones mainly responsible for the care of dependent children. Women's imprisonment generally leads to a very depleted family network mainly affecting children and the elderly who, as dependents, are in a socially vulnerable position with fewer opportunities for improving their situation.

Conclusion

In line with the growing recognition that the effects of imprisonment extend far beyond prisoners and significantly impact on their social networks, the aim of this chapter has been to focus on the consequences of women's imprisonment for their relatives on the outside. According to the women's narratives, for the majority of families, women's imprisonment compounds social and economic disadvantage. This disadvantage mostly affects children and the elderly.

Despite the fluidity of family arrangements, most of the women's narratives highlighted the fact that they played an active part in the maintenance and structure of their family, being the central providers of care and economic resources prior to imprisonment.

Imprisonment of these women triggers a reconfiguration affecting their most intimate family environment and becomes increasingly serious when it affects poor families and communities. The reconfigurations of the household, even if temporary, become an ongoing process, forcing family members to reposition themselves in relation to unexpected life changes and leading to financial hardship and emotional issues.

In general, the people available to assume the roles played by women prior to imprisonment are their parents, who are also socially and economically deprived, and usually elderly. Assuming new responsibilities in addition to their existing ones often triggers a 'domino effect of social exclusion' for families (European Commission, 2005: 7), exacerbating their financially vulnerable situation. Older people tend to reverse their position within the family from that of a dependent to someone in charge of child care. In other situations, elderly people lose the person mainly responsible for their care and become dependent on informal community support.

Children are also in a vulnerable situation, since they generally lose their main or only carer, are usually deprived of both parents, and risk entering into an unstable cycle of child care placements, combining family, community and foster care (see Cunha, 2013; Palomar, 2007). Children also face a clear reduction in the family budget since, in most cases; an important share of the household income is lost. This is consistent with research showing that imprisonment can significantly increase levels of child poverty (De-Fina and Hannon, 2010).

Bibliography

Aboim, S. (2006) 'Conjugalidade, Afectos e Formas de Autonomia Individual'. *Análise Social*, XLI(180): 801-825.

Almond, B. (2006) *The Fragmenting Family*. Oxford: Clarendon Press.

Alves, J. and Maia, Â. (2010) 'Experiências Adversas Durante a Infância e Comportamentos de Risco para a Saúde em Mulheres Reclusas'. *Psicologia, Saúde e Doenças*, 11(1): 151-171.

Arditti, J. A. (2005) 'Families and Incarceration: An Ecological Approach'. *Families in Society: The Journal of Contemporary Social Services*, 86(2): 251-260.

Beleza, M. (1990) *Mulheres, Direito, Crime ou A Perplexidade de Cassandra*. PhD Thesis. University of Lisbon.

Braman, D. (2002) 'Families and Incarceration'. In: Mauer, M. and Chesney-Lind, M. eds. *Invisible Punishment: The Collateral Consequences of Mass Imprisonment.* New York City: New Press.

Christian, J. (2005) 'Riding the Bus: Barriers to Prison Visitation and Family Management Strategies'. *Journal of Contemporary Criminal Justice,* 21(1): 31-48.

Clear, T. R. (1996) Backfire: When Incarceration Increases Crime. *Journal of the Oklahoma Criminal Justice Research Consortium,* 3(2): 1-10.

Clear, T.R. (2002) 'The Problem with "Addition by Subtraction": The Prison-Crime Relationship in Low-Income Communities'. In: Mauer, M. and Chesney-Lind, M. eds. *Invisible Punishment: The Collateral Consequences of Mass Imprisonment.* New York City: New Press.

Collier, R. and Sheldon, S. (2008) *Fragmenting Fatherhood: A Socio-Legal Study.* Oregon: Hart Publishing.

Comfort, M. (2008) *Doing Time Together: Love and Family in the Shadow of the Prison.* Chicago: The University of Chicago Press.

Comfort, M. (2007) 'Punishment Beyond the Legal Offender'. *Annual Review of Law and Social Science,* 3(1): 12.1–12.26.

Condry, R. (2007) 'Families Outside: The Difficulties Faced by Relatives of Serious Offenders'. *Prison Service Journal,* 174: 3-10.

Cunha, M.I. (2013) 'The Changing Scale of Imprisonment and the Transformation of Care: The Erosion of the "Welfare Society" by the "Penal State" in Contemporary Portugal'. In: Fletcher, M. and Fleischer, F. eds. *Careful Encounters: Ethnographies of Support.* Palgrave MacMillan.

Cunha, M.I. (2008) 'Closed Circuits: Kinship, Neighborhood and Incarceration in Urban Portugal'. *Ethnography,* 9 (3): 325-350.

Cunha, M.I. (2002) *Entre o Bairro e a Prisão: Tráfico e Trajectos.* Lisbon: Fim de Século.

Cunha, M.I. (1994) *Malhas que a Reclusão Tece. Questões de Identidade numa Prisão Feminina.* Lisbon: Centro de Estudos Judiciários.

Cunha, M. I. and Granja, R. (forthcoming) 'Gender Asymmetries, Parenthood and Confinement in Two Portuguese Prisons'. *Champ Pénal/ Penal Field.*

DeFina, R. H. and Hannon, L. (2010) 'The Impact of Adult Incarceration on Child Poverty: A County-Level Analysis, 1995-2007'. *The Prison Journal,* 90(4): 377-396.

Direção-Geral de Reinserção e Serviços Prisionais (2013) Estatísticas 2014. Available at: http://www.dgsp.mj.pt (5 March 2014).

Duarte, V. (2011) *Quantos Caminhos em Alice do Outro Lado do Espelho? Experiências, Discursos e Percursos de Raparigas em Conflito com a Lei.* PhD Thesis. University of Minho.

Enos, S. (1998) 'Managing Motherhood in Prison: The Impact of Race and Ethnicity on Child Placements'. *Women and Therapy*, 20(4): 57-73.

European Commission (2005) *Women, Integration and Prison: An Analysis of the Processes of Socio-labour Integration of Women Prisoners in Europe. MIP Project, Final Report. Barcelona*: European Commission. Available at: http://ec.europa.eu/research/social-sciences/pdf/mip_en.pdf (Accessed 16 February 2012).

Faria, A. (2011) *'E Sempre Sou Eu o Pai e a Mãe...' A Monoparentalidade Feminina Empobrecida, o Gênero e a 'Autonomia Vulnerável'.* Msc Thesis, University of Minho.

Ferraro, K. J. and Moe, A. M. (2003) 'Mothering, Crime, and Incarceration'. *Journal of Contemporary Ethnography*, 32(1): 9-40.

Ferraro, K. J., Johson, J. M., Jorgensen, S. R. and Bolton, F. G. (1983) 'Problems of Prisoners' Families: The Hidden Costs of Imprisonment'. *Journal of Family Issues*, 4(4): 575-591.

Gonçalves, A. M. and Pereira, M. G. (1982). 'Variáveis Familiares e Toxicodependência'. *Revista da SBPH*, 14(2): 228-251. Available from: http://pepsic.bvsalud.org/scielo.php?pid=S1516-08582011000200014 andscript=sci_arttext (Accessed 20 June 2012).

Granja, R., Cunha, M. P. and Machado, H. (ongoing) 'Representations about the social and family impacts of prison: male and female views', ref SFRH/BD/73214/2010.

Granja, R., Cunha, M. P. and Machado, H. (2012a). 'Children on the Outside: The Experience of Mothering Among Female Inmates'. *3rd Global Conference Experiencing Prison*. Prague, May.

Granja, R., Cunha, M. P. and Machado, H. (2012b). 'Intimidades em (Des) Conexão com a Prisão: As Relações Amorosas de Mulheres Antes e Durante a Reclusão'. *VII Congresso Português de Sociologia Sociedade: Crise e Reconfigurações*. Oporto, June.

Greene, S., Haney, C. and Hurtado, A. (2000) Cycles of Pain: Risk Factors in the Lives of Incarcerated Mothers and Their Children. *The Prison Journal*, 80(1): 3-23.

Hagan, J. and Dinovitzer, R. (1999). 'Collateral Consequences of Imprisonment for Children, Communities, and Prisoners'. *Crime and Justice*, 26: 121-143.

Hairston, C. (1991) 'Mothers in Jail: Parent-Child Separation and Jail Visitation'. *Affilia*, 6(2): 9-27.

Hairston, J. (2002) 'Prisoners and Families: Parenting Issues During Incarceration'. *From Prisons to Home Conference*. National Institutes of Health, January.

Hanlon, T. E., Carswell, S. B. and Rose, M. (2007) 'Research on the Caretaking of Children of Incarcerated Parents: Findings and Their Service Delivery Implications'. *Child Youth Serv Rev*, 29(3): 384-362.

Henriques, Z. (1996) 'Imprisoned Mothers and Their Children'. *Women and Criminal Justice*, 8(1): 77-95.

Johnson, E. I. and Waldfogel, J. (2004) 'Children of Incarcerated Parents: Multiple Risks and Children's Living Arrangements'. In: Pattillo, M., Western, B. and Weiman, D. eds. *Imprisoning America: The Social Effects of Mass Incarceration*. New York: Russel Sage Foundation.

Landry-Meyer, L. and Newman, B. M. (2004) 'An Exploration of the Grandparent Caregiver Role'. *Journal of Family Issues*, 25(8): 1005-1025.

Light, R. and Campbell, B. (2006) 'Prisoners' Families: Still Forgotten Victims?' *Journal of Social Welfare and Family Law*, 28(3): 297-308.

Lynch, J. P. and Sabol, W. J. (2004) 'Effects of Incarceration on Informal Social Control in Communities'. In: Pattillo, M., Western, B. and Weiman, D. eds. *Imprisoning America: The Social Effects of Mass Incarceration*. New York: Russel Sage Foundation.

Machado, H. (2004) 'Cidadania Polifónica e a (In)Justiça para as Mulheres'. *Ex-Aequo: Revista da Associação Portuguesa de Estudos sobre as Mulheres,* 11: 13-26.

Machado, H. and Granja, R. (2013) 'Paternidades fragmentadas. Género, emoções e (des) conexões biogenéticas e prisionais'. *Análise Social*, 208, XLVIII(3): 552-571.

Marchetti, A.M. (2002) 'Carceral Impoverishment: Class Inequality in the French Penitentiary'. *Ethnography*, 3(4): 416-434.

Matos, R. and Machado, C. (2007) 'Reclusão e Laços Sociais: Discursos no Feminino'. *Análise Social,* XLII(185): 1041-1054.

Mauer, M. and Chesney-Lind, M. (Eds.). (2002) *Invisible Punishment: The Collateral Consequences of Mass Imprisonment.* New York City: New Press.

McCormack, K. (2005) 'Stratified Reproduction and Poor Women's Resistance'. *Gender and Society,* 19(5): 660-679.

Palomar Verea, C. (2007) *Maternidad en Prisión.* Guadalajara: Universidad de Guadalajara.

Pattillo, M., Weiman, D. and Western, B. (Eds.). (2004) *Imprisoning America: The Social Effects of Mass Incarceration.* New York: Russel Sage Foundation.

Pires, P. (2004) 'A Arte de Negociar (Estudo de Caso do GAT do Montijo)'. *V Congresso Português de Sociologia.* Braga.

Portugal, S. (1995) 'As Mãos que Embalam o Berço. *Revista Crítica de Ciências Sociais,* 42: 155-178.

Portugal, S. (2008) 'As Mulheres e a Produção de Bem-Estar em Portugal'. *Oficina do CES,* 319: 1-40.

Richie, B. E. (2002) 'The Social Impact of Mass Incarceration on Women'. In: Pattillo, M., Western, B. and Weiman, D. eds. *Imprisoning America: The Social Effects of Mass Incarceration.* New York: Russel Sage Foundation.

Santos, B. D. S. (1993) 'O Estado, as Relações Salariais e o Bem-Estar Social na Semi-Periferia: O Caso Português'. In: Santos, B. S. ed. *Portugal: Um Retrato Singular.* Oporto: Afrontamento.

Sharp, B. S. F., Marcus-Mendoza, S. T., Bentley, R. G., Simpson, D. B. and Love, S. R. (1997/1998) 'Gender Differences in the Impact of Incarceration on the Children and Families of Drug Offenders'. *Journal of the Oklahoma Criminal Justice Research Consortium,* 4: 1-30.

Smart, C. and Neale, B. (1999) *Family Fragements*? Cambridge: Polity.

Tasca, M., Rodriguez, N. and Zatz, M. S. (2011) 'Family and Residential Instability in the Context of Paternal and Maternal Incarceration'. *Criminal Justice and Behavior,* 38(3): 231 – 247.

Torres, A. (2002) 'Casamento: Conversa a Duas vozes e em Três Andamentos'. *Análise Social,* XXXVII(163): 569-602.

Torres, A. (2004) *Vida Conjugal e Trabalho: Uma Perspectiva Sociológica.* Oeiras: Celta.

Travis, J. and Waul, M. (Eds.). (2003) *Prisoners Once Removed: The Impact of Incarceration and Reentry on Children, Families, and Communities.* Washington DC: Urban Institute Press.

Wacquant, L. (2000) *As Prisões da Miséria.* Oeiras: Celta Editora.

Wall, K., Correia, S. V. and José, J. S. (2002) 'Mães Sós e Cuidados às Crianças'. *Análise Social*, XXXVII(163): 631-663.

Wall, K. and Lobo, C. (1999) 'Famílias Monoparentais em Portugal'. *Análise Social*, XXXIV(150): 123-145.

9

Retribution or Restorative Justice:
A False Dichotomy

Patrick Riordan

Introduction

An image which has remained with me is that of Pope John Paul II visiting his failed assassin Mehmet Ali Agca in prison. It was reproduced on the cover of *Time* magazine (Morrow, 1984), and included the caption 'The Pope Pardons the Gunman'. The victim of a very public assault went to the convicted criminal and offered a very public gesture of forgiveness. And yet, despite the forgiveness, the assassin remained in prison. If he was forgiven, should he not be released?

Would repentance on the part of the convict make a difference? Or should it? In practice we know that many who have repented, and shown remorse for their crime, and at the same time have been forgiven by their victims, remain in prison until their term is up, or there are grounds of administrative efficiency for releasing them, at least into a more open form of detention. On the other hand, many are released at the end of their prison sentence, who have neither repented, nor been forgiven.

This lack of fit between the dynamics of punishment and the dynamics of forgiveness provokes several questions. Does punishment have its own rationale which is not reducible to the rationale of reconciliation? Is that rationale which may operate in practice intellectually defensible, or should it be critiqued and possibly abandoned? Is the appropriate stance for that critique the moral concern with the dynamics of repentance, forgiveness and reconciliation?

The growing interest in and commitment to restorative justice can be situated in this tension. Those who wish to promote the vision of restorative justice tell the stories of successful encounter between perpetrator and victim leading to reconciliation, or at least acceptance, and understanding. It often serves their purpose of highlighting the benefits of restorative justice to contrast these with the vindictiveness and ineffectiveness of retributive punishment.

In entering this debate, this chapter draws on the work of Charles Barton (1999; 2003), who has been involved in the restorative justice movement in Australia, and has written 'how to do it' books to assist the movement. However, he also embraces a strong retributive position, and refuses to accept that the choice is a simple either-or between retribution and restoration.

Barton's model

It is helpful to begin with the position Barton advocates, which he labels 'the empowerment model'. Despite the accusations made against the inherited penal system, that it is punitive and vindictive, he argues that the main fault of our dominant model in punishment is that it does not empower the principal people who are concerned in the event. With this focus in mind, Barton can with considerable fairness maintain that the failure of many attempts at restorative justice is due to the disempowerment of the principal persons concerned. Hence his very practical focus on 'how-to' procedures and checklists, since the professionals of restorative justice can be as much in danger of disempowering people as the traditional professionals. Barton argues:

> ... the problem is that the status quo *disempowers* the primary stakeholders in the conflict. Typically it silences and marginalises them. The primary stakeholders are the victim, the offender, and their primary circles/communities

of influence and care – typically their respective families, friends, peers and colleagues. Their disempowerment is the single most significant reason why the criminal justice system so often fails to achieve justice for those on the receiving end of the criminal justice response, including victims and the general community, who continue to suffer the consequences of the system's inability to prevent re-offending and crime (Barton, 2003: 15).

This line of thought leads us to reflect on one of those very prevalent assumptions which sustains common life. It is simply taken for granted that clients are benefited by the services of professionals. The patient benefits from the attention of dentist or doctor, the plaintiff or defendant benefits from the professional advice and representation by lawyers, society benefits from the work of competent and qualified public officers in various roles of public service, from prosecutor to warden to judge. This assumption was copper-fastened in the history of philosophy by Socrates' use of it in his famous craft analogy, arguing that virtues were like crafts or professions, whose exercise benefited a client. But maybe it is the case that the power which accrues to the professional by virtue of their expertise also serves to disempower the clients who may benefit in one sense, but significantly lose out on another level. They are marginalised, left to one side, in the handling of the cases in which they are involved. Barton puts it strongly:

> In their purported mission to protect the innocent and punish the guilty, contemporary criminal justice systems marginalize and disempower the very people who have most at stake in particular criminal justice interventions. Most significantly, victims and accused alike are discouraged and denied real opportunities to take an active role in the legal processing and resolution of their cases. In effect, they are reduced to the status of idle bystanders in what, after all, is *their* conflict (Barton, 2003: 26-7).

Barton advances various arguments to counter the suggestion that reliance on retributivism is the cause of the failure of the status quo. In particular he looks at the absence of any serious adoption of retributivism in public policy, and the reliance instead in public declarations of purpose in the penal system on consequentialist reasoning, in terms of deterrence, social defence, incapacitation and also rehabilitation or reform. But his principal focus is on the disempowerment of people as the basic reason why the penal system including the prison system is not working. The reliance on professionals is a key reason for this failure, he suggests:

> The experts and officers of bureaucratic authorities tend to have their own priorities which inevitably play a role in decisions, but those priorities seldom reflect the interests of the principal parties in criminal cases (Barton, 2003: 27).

As noted, he warns that the professionals of restorative justice are equally in danger of making the same mistake in thinking that they know better, and so disempowering the people 'whose case it is': '... not unlike the legal professionals they so readily criticise, restorative justice administrators and practitioners are as susceptible as anybody else to seek the comfort of the familiar...'. They are just as likely to '... equate the concept of good practice with whatever they happen to have become familiar and comfortable with' (Barton, 2003, footnote 25, p. 31).

Barton's work is based on experience in Australia where restorative justice has already found some institutional expression. His basic point is reinforced from Canadian experience. A philosopher, Keneth Melchin, and a criminologist, Cheryl Picard (2008), ask the searching question: who does the learning in conflict mediation and restorative justice? Reviewing the literature in this field they ask about the intended subject of learning in the processes of managing conflict. This is the most radical element in the book, asking about institutions and structures of adjudication and mediation: Who does the learning? Who comes up with the solutions? Insofar as the professional mediators or the social scientific observers acquire knowledge in the processes and then apply that knowledge to managing the conflict, there can be progress towards resolution. But it remains fragile and in danger of reversal so long as the parties in conflict themselves have not undergone change through learning about themselves and each other.

Melchin and Picard apply their ideas to two case studies, located in the context of alternative justice processes. These exemplify the point about the participants in conflict themselves rather than the professional practitioners undergoing transformative learning. However, as seen in one of case studies – which involved citizens and the wider community participating in a sentencing circle which led to the imposition of a sentence on an offender and proved a genuine source of change – the judge in court had to first acknowledge the failure of standard penal responses and second, be willing to try a different approach. The other case study was of a victim-offender mediation, in which the perpetrator and victim of an armed robbery were brought together, and the resultant process of discovery led to significant change, including a healing of the victim's persistent trauma from the event, and a growth in the offender's awareness of the harm he had inflicted. The study maps the progress of learning in each case, both individual and communal, and draws attention to the roles played by feelings and values, direct and inverse insights, and the dynamism of testing.

Melchin and Picard's conclusion that justice systems can learn from this experience coheres with the growing movement of restorative justice. But in particular it underlines that the guiding question for justice has to focus, not so much on 'who is guilty', but what is to be done. The prevailing assumption that enough is done when the guilty party is punished in conventional ways short-circuits a process which could require much more. As the authors conclude, 'for democratic life to thrive requires that citizens be willing and prepared to do the hard work of learning in conflict' (Melchin and Picard, 2008: 128).

A defence of retribution

Barton conveniently summarises his argument about the compatibility of restoration with retribution in four steps:

> 1. The status quo is not solely interested in retribution.
>
> 2. The problem with the status quo is not that it is based on retribution but rather that it disempowers primary stakeholders.
>
> 3. Restorative justice is quite compatible with retribution.
>
> 4. Restorative justice is superior to the status quo because restorative justice approaches have the potential to empower primary stakeholders to deal with matters the way it is right for *them* (Barton, 2003: 16).

Empowerment of primary stakeholders is his focus; the failure to do it is the main weakness of the status quo, and its greater capacity to achieve empowerment is the great advantage which restorative justice has over the status quo.

This chapter will now concentrate on the third step in Barton's argument: *restorative justice is quite compatible with retribution.* The argument needs to go beyond merely rejecting the view that the status quo in punishment is handicapped by its reliance on retributivism. The argument has to make a case for retribution as an integral part of punishment which is compatible with restorative justice.

Retribution names a reason for punishment, not a particular form or method of punishment. Deterrence or social protection might name other reasons, and there is no reason why only one reason should be in play in any case or system of punishment. John Tasioulas (2006) advocates a pluralist approach to the justification of punishment, which is prepared to incorporate themes from the various theories, including retributivism. Discussion of retribution as a reason for punishment is often confused by people using the term in a casual or colloquial sense, not to name a kind of reason, but to point to the painful manner of punishment, or the vindictiveness with which it is carried out. Insofar as an element of reason remains in this popular usage, it is the notion of revenge, and punishment based on retribution is held to be indefensible because it merely institutionalises revenge, which is assumed to be unjustified and so immoral. Some of these themes will be returned to later in the chapter. For now the task is to clarify what is the positive or defensible meaning of retribution as a reason for punishment.

At the heart of the notion of retribution are two ideas: the first is that of desert, that the one punished gets what s/he deserves; and the second is that of rebalancing, that the punishment is a paying-back, or getting even. Barton writes:

> The *just deserts* conception of retribution is defined by reference to a specific type of reason or rationale that is behind the imposition of the punishment, namely the offender's ill-desert, and which is satisfied through some sort of negative repayment, or pay-back, which is the punishment (Barton, 2003: 16).

This is simplifying to some extent: there are several discussions of retribution which find a more complex classification of versions (Cottingham, 1979).

It is difficult to make sense of the idea of desert, what is deserved, in relation to punishment. This is because people spontaneously identify deserts with positives, such as rewards. The negative content of punishment makes it more difficult to associate punishment with the idea of desert, even though popular expressions such as 'he brought it on himself', 'she had it coming', 'he has only himself to blame' capture the common sense idea involved, as something owed, or due, on the basis of personal prior wrongdoing. The idea of pay-back or balance is more easily appreciated. Here the point of punishment is seen as re-establishing a balance or equality between parties which had been disrupted by wrongful action by one party. Restoring relationships of fairness temporarily disrupted by the unfairness of one party is pithily captured in the phrase 'getting even'. Barton finds in the aboriginal practices of punishment in traditional cultures precisely this idea of getting even, and cites the use of the term 'pay-back' in their preferred translation of their practice into English (Barton, 2003: 23-4).

In his earlier study Barton offers the following clarification in combining the two elements of retribution: 'While *repayment* indicates the nature of the activity we call retribution, *desert* indicates the nature of the justification for that activity' (Barton, 1999: 44). In punishment as just and fair retribution there is a pay-back to those convicted of wrong doing, and those people are punished *because* they deserve it.

Barton's (1999) title for the earlier study, *Getting Even*, is also the title of a work by Jeffrie Murphy (2003), although the books are distinguishable by their subtitles. Both are concerned with a defence of retribution, although in different contexts. Murphy investigates themes of forgiveness and mercy. This had been the topic of an earlier joint book with Jean Hampton, *Forgiveness and Mercy* (1988). In his later book Murphy argues that the case for retribution in punishment remains even where there is forgiveness.

Barton examines revenge and asks whether, as commonly thought, revenge is simply reprehensible. He follows a line of thought in an opposite direction to the one usually taken. Instead of arguing that since retribution is akin to revenge, and revenge is morally indefensible, retribution is to be rejected, he finds a core of defensible rationality in revenge, and the same rational core persists in forms of retributive punishment which have replaced revenge. This goes against a common theme in philosophical discussion that punishment and revenge are to be distinguished. Robert Nozick (1981) most famously drew the distinction and listed five characteristics on which revenge and punishment might be distinguished. However, challenges such as that by Leo Zaibert (2006), examining each of the elements in turn, have called in question the adequacy of the asserted clear distinction.

Barton's solution to this problem of the distinction is to find the rational core of both revenge and punishment, and to identify the differences in other aspects. The rational core is found in the idea of paying back, or getting even. But in neither case is it to be assumed that the taking of revenge or the imposition of punishment in order to get even is automatically justified. There can be unjust imposition of punishment, just as revenge can be unjust. Principles of justice specify the constraints on getting even, and if these principles are violated in the activity, it fails to be just. Among the examples of unjust retribution Barton mentions getting the wrong person, or in reaction to actions which are not actual crimes or instances of wrong doing, such as happens in reprisals against whistle-blowers (Barton, 1999). These examples illustrate some of the six constraining principles of justice identified by Barton.

What about the very personal and emotional aspect which is said to characterise revenge? Barton concedes that 'revenge is personal in a way that other forms of retributivism need not be...' (Barton, 1999: 69). He defines revenge as 'personal retribution which is typically accompanied by feelings of indignation, anger and resentment for wrongs suffered in one's personal domain of concern' (Barton, 1999: 70). Note that the core of the definition points to retribution, qualified as personal. The role of feelings is that they are typically present, but not relied upon for the essential definition. Zaibert among others point out that the feelings of hatred or anger can be present too in the case of institutionalised criminal punishment, and they can be a source of injustice there, but no less so in the case of revenge (2006).

According to Barton's proposed understanding, 'retribution can be personal or non-personal; it can be institutionalized or not' (Barton, 1999: 79). This provides a matrix, in which personal non-institutionalised retribution is commonly identified as revenge.

On the other hand, our systems of legal criminal punishment aim to be non-personal institutionalised retribution. A third case of institutionalised but personal retribution is conceivable, when officers of the law courts take it upon themselves to give vent to personal feelings but within institutional forms and so their acts of revenge are hidden. The fourth possibility of non-personal, non-institutionalised retribution is the kind of scenario imagined by John Locke (1970) in his state of nature, in which everyone has the right to punish any transgression of the law of nature, whether or not they are personally affected by the wrongdoing.

Barton's clarifications and distinctions set up the problem he still has to solve: how to justify retribution. He needs to show that retribution is a legitimate and morally acceptable reason for punishment, assuming it is constrained by the principles of justice. Retribution holds that punishment of wrongdoing is good in itself, not merely because of possible desirable effects (1999). Barton notes:

> The core retributivist idea that there is an intrinsic moral connection between wrongdoing and liability for punishment is not supported by justifications which make only a consequentialist or functionalist link between the two (1999: 90).

So the challenge for the theorist is to show that the 'moral responsibility borne by people for their wrongful actions is itself a *prima facie* good reason for justly punishing them.'

The path Barton follows for his attempted justification is a form of transcendental argument. He argues from the essential sociality of humans: a society of mature morally responsible individuals would have to hold one another accountable for wrongs to fellow members and to the common good. Unless one accepts this burden of responsibility, and so liability to blame and punishment for one's wrongful deeds, one misses the possibility of moral maturity. And so the conclusion follows, which may have a stronger or weaker version:

Since individual flourishing and the achievement of one's full humanity, including moral maturity, are good things worthy of being pursued, retributive punishment within the limits set by the principles of justice is also a morally good thing which may be pursued and, unless contra-indicated by countervailing instrumental and functionalist considerations, or by the appropriateness of mercy and forgiveness, ought to be pursued' (Barton, 1999: 93). ... Were a society not to hold its members responsible for their wrongful actions, it would amount to treating those members as something other than adults, mature developed human beings (Barton, 1999: 97).

Needless to say, this kind of argument summarised here requires a more extensive elaboration. It is highly normative, relying as it does on a view of what would be essential for human fulfilment and moral completion. That extended argument will not be given here. But it should be noted that his argument does not rely on any appeal to the satisfaction of desires which victims or others may have to see wrongdoers punished. That kind of retributivism would be a form of consequentialism, in which the consequences to be pursued are the gratification of the aggrieved, as Cottingham (1979) has pointed out (Barton, 1999).

Such feelings of grievance, resentment and anger following wrongdoing, in particular where one is victim of the misdeed, provide Murphy (2003) with his focus in the discussion of forgiveness, revenge and retribution. Murphy understands forgiveness,

as the overcoming, on moral grounds, of ... the *vindictive passions* – the passions of anger, resentment, and even hatred that are often occasioned when one has been deeply wronged by another. These are passions that often prompt acts of vengeance or revenge, but one can have the passions without acting on them... (Barton, 2003, p. 16).

While these passions or feelings are potentially destructive and dangerous, he argues against a totally negative view of them. Much of his analysis depends on understanding the positive and morally valuable role these passions can play in human psychology and human relations.

Murphy acknowledges the influence of Bishop Joseph Butler in his analysis of the psychology of the passions. With Butler he considers that the danger of resentment is not so much that one has these feelings after suffering wrongdoing, but that one becomes so dominated and possessed by them that balance and rationality are jeopardised. These passions have a positive role to play in reaction to wrongs. Murphy argues that resentment is a good thing to the extent that it is tied to self-respect and self-defence:

> As the initial response to being wronged, however, the passion stands in defence of important values – values that might be compromised by immediate and uncritical forgiveness of wrongs (Murphy, 2003: 19).

Although his topic is forgiveness he does not advocate it as the appropriate response to wrongdoing. The values of self-defence and self-respect, and also respect for the moral order, require attention to what is due to the wrongdoer for her misdeeds, and the immediate response of resentment points to this requirement. To that extent it is positive and serves a valuable function, not just in relation to the individual victim, but also in relation to the social order. Murphy affirms that '[w]e all have a duty to support – both intellectually and emotionally – the moral order, an order represented by clear understandings of what constitutes unacceptable treatment of one human being by another' (2003: 20).

Where the passions of resentment and anger are allowed dominate a person's response to wrongdoing he or she might demand imposition of a punishment with the desire to see the culprit suffer. This would be vengeance, the infliction of suffering in order to satisfy vindictive emotions. Murphy explains, 'the goal of vengeance is simply to provide vindictive satisfaction to victims, and victims may require for their satisfaction something other than what is necessary to control crime or what wrongdoers deserve'

(2003: 17). For this reason he is wary of victim impact statements because they can allow vindictive passions to find legal expression (Murphy, 2003). In a concluding chapter he defends his philosophical views on forgiveness and retribution as consistent with what he takes to be the Christian stance:

> Kant's point – a point that would, I think, be embraced as quite orthodox by most Christians – is that love does not forbid punishment. What it forbids is *punishment out of hatred* (Murphy, 2003: 102).

There are major points of agreement between Barton and Murphy. Both of them see something positive and not only negative in the emotions of resentment and anger which can be at play in both revenge and punishment. Both emphasise that people are linked in a shared moral order which needs to be upheld so that individuals can flourish. Upholding that order requires a punitive response to wrongdoing, so that those who violate the moral order are given the punishment that they deserve.

Restorative justice can include a retributive element

This chapter now returns to the question of the compatibility of retribution and restorative justice. Barton undertook a defence of retribution in his first book, and in the second he argued that restorative justice would not involve an elimination of retribution, but that some punitive retributive measure could be part of the outcome of a restorative conference between primary agents of perpetrator and victim and their respective families and support groups. In part his argument relies on the well entrenched expectation that wrongdoers will get a punishment that they deserve. There are deep-rooted passions and feelings associated with this expectation, but as argued, it is not the satisfaction of the desires linked to these feelings which is demanded. Instead it is retributive justice:

That wrongdoing deserves punishment is a fundamental aspect of our reality, even if that reality is, in part, socially constructed. Our liability to punishment is part of what defines us as mature and responsible members of the moral community and as such cannot be eliminated. As a result, in many cases of serious victimisation, no amount of therapy, or indeed conference discussion, may replace a victim's and the community's need to know that wrongdoing is punished, that justice, including justice in the retributive *just deserts* sense, is done (Barton, 2003: 22).

Because of the rootedness of retributive justice Barton is convinced that it needs to be included in the proposals of restorative justice. If what is at stake in restorative justice is the empowerment of all primary stakeholders, then the exclusion of every and all retributive elements would disempower those victims of crime and other members of society who have a valid reasonable expectation that crime be punished. And so Barton concludes:

... it is a mistake to think that punitive elements of an agreement automatically undermine or weaken its restorative potential. Quite the contrary. Some appropriate level and form of punitiveness will enhance the effectiveness of the restorative justice response, and will often have to form part of agreements to be acceptable to the relevant parties (Barton, 2003: 22).

The combination with retribution will be essential for the public acceptability of restorative justice as the normal response to crime:

Indeed it is difficult to see how restorative justice processes could become a widely accepted, let alone the preferred, response to crime, unless they were either complemented by punitive responses through other forums, such as the courts, or allowed direct incorporation of punitive elements in restorative justice outcomes and resolutions, as in fact they do (Barton, 2003: 21).

Conclusion

This chapter began with an image from the cover of *Time* magazine, showing a famous victim supposedly forgiving his failed assassin. The literature surveyed in this chapter provides analysis for understanding that forgiveness is not incompatible with retributive punishment, i.e. punishment that is deserved by the wrongdoer. We have also seen that retribution is not justified in terms of satisfying the desires of those who experience resentment and anger in response to wrongdoing. Those passions point to relevant values, of self-respect and respect for the shared moral order, and the worth of the victim as well as the goodness of the moral order being upheld. The wrongdoer in his action showed disrespect for the victim and for the shared social order. By being punished – as he deserves – a balance is restored in that the victim and the moral order are given their due. Restorative justice measures, inviting a conference of primary agents and their supports, will also have to respect these requirements of retributive justice.

Bibliography

Barton, C. K. B. (2003) *Restorative Justice: The Empowerment Model.* Sydney: Hawkins Press.

Barton, C. K. B. (1999) *Getting Even. Revenge as a Form of Justice.* Chicago and La Salle: Open Court Publishing.

Cottingham, J. (1979) Varieties of Retribution. *Philosophical Quarterly,* 29: 238-46.

Finnis, J. (1999) Retribution: Punishment's Formative Aim. *American Journal of Jurisprudence.* 44: 91-103.

Locke, J. (1970) *Two Treatises on Government.* Cambridge: Cambridge University Press.

Melchin, K. R. and Picard, C. A. (2008) *Transforming Conflict through Insight.* Toronto: University of Toronto Press.

Morrow, L. (1984) 'Why Forgive? The Pope Pardons the Gunman' (Cover). *Time Magazine,* 8 January, p. 1.

Murphy, J. G. (2003) *Getting Even: Forgiveness and its Limits*. Oxford: Oxford University Press.

Murphy, J. G. and Hampton, J. (1988) *Forgiveness and Mercy*. Cambridge: Cambridge University Press.

Nozick, R. (1981) *Philosophical Explanations*. Cambridge, Mass: Harvard University Press.

Tasioulas, J. (2006) Punishment and Repentance. *Philosophy*, 81(316): 279-322.

Zaibert, L. (2006) Punishment and Revenge. *Law and Philosophy*, 25: 81-118.

10

Managing the Reintegration of Prisoners in Belgium from a Prisoners' and a Probation Officers' Perspective

Rudy Machiels and Aline Bauwens

Introduction

This chapter intends to begin to fill the (Belgian) research gap by exploring how the process of reintegration is understood by prisoners and probation officers. It is based on two PhD's involving empirical research conducted with each of these groups. The Belgian reintegration approach is a combination of preparing a 'social reintegration plan' while in prison and showing compliance with the imposed conditions while on release.

We argue that the way to a renewed citizenship as the main goal of reintegration starts in prison and continues outside prison. The move from prison to the outside world means a transfer from a prisoner identity to a new citizen identity. This process can be simplified or restricted by actors involved in this transformation process. Whilst we acknowledge that there are many actors involved who might have an impact on the identity change of prisoners (e.g. family, partner, children, Psychosocial Service, Sentence Implementation Courts, welfare organisations, etc.), we focus in this chapter on the perspective of the prisoner (in prison) and the probation officer (outside prison). The two actors both work with 'official tools'. Prisoners have to instigate the release procedure, including the preparation of their social reintegration plan. Probation officers have a role assisting in the development of a release identity, based upon the imposed conditions. The social reintegration plan and the conditions imposed upon the offender combine to form the prisoners' 'release identity'.

After a short introduction to the conditional release system in Belgium and an explanation of the social reintegration plan, we look at the 'release (or parole) identity' from two different points of view. Firstly, we seek to examine the prisoners' perspective on his release identity. We argue that the plan is a collection of release identities that has to fit into a 'normalised' frame. Secondly, we analyse the probation officers' perspective when they have to work with the release conditions imposed upon the ex-prisoner. We show that there is some elasticity in working with release conditions as their 'working tool', as long as offenders remain within the boundaries of acceptable conduct. In our concluding discussion, we question whether the social reintegration plan and the conditions imposed give the released prisoner enough space to experiment with different 'provisional selves', which serve as probationary identities in a trial and error process of refining and improving their skills and behaviours (Ibarra, 1999).

Parole in the Belgian context

Following the Dutroux case in 1996, the Belgian parole system was thoroughly reformed in 1998 and 2006. Decision-making was transferred from the Minister of Justice to multidisciplinary 'Sentence Implementation Courts'; supervision and follow up of conditionally released prisoners was tightened and the proportion of recalls increased. Legislation was provided under two new Acts of 17 May 2006 (Government of Belgium, 2006). The first Act resulted in nine multidisciplinary Sentence Implementation Courts, each presided over by a judge with two assessors (one specialised in social reintegration, the other specialised in prison matters), have replaced the former 'Parole Commissions', which had been established in 1998). The new Sentence Implementation Courts were established to increase the legitimacy of release procedures by 'fostering their independence, professionalism and transparency' (Snacken et al., 2010: 99). Although this Act was supposed to be applicable to all prisoners considered for conditional release, its application has for practical reasons been temporarily limited to prisoners serving sentences of more than three years. Prisoners serving less than three years imprisonment are eligible to *provisional release,* which is still decided by the prison administration.

The second Act (specifically Art 47, 1) of 17 May 2006 concerning the legal position of convicted persons sentenced to deprivation of freedom, and the rights accorded to the victim, now meant that conditional release *must* be granted when the minimum term has been served (one-third of the sentence, two-thirds of the sentence for legal recidivists), provided there are no counter-indications which might entail a serious risk for the community or could reasonably be thought to hinder the social reintegration of the offenders (Government of Belgium, 2006). These counter-indications relate to: (1) the absence of opportunities for social reintegration, (2) a risk of new serious offences, (3) a risk that the offender would cause further distress to the victim, and (4) the attitude of the convicted person towards the victim(s) of the crime(s) that have led to his/her conviction. (For more detailed information about early release from prison in Belgium, see Snacken et al., 2010).

The Belgian 'social reintegration plan'

As mentioned above, and according to the 2006 Belgian legislation, every prisoner admissible to conditional release has to present a 'social reintegration plan' showing his/her willingness to reintegrate in the community and outlining the efforts already produced in this regard.

The prisoner has to take the initiative for the preparation of this plan and is assisted by the competent services, the Psychosocial Service in prison and the relevant 'forensic welfare' services in the community. Since 1998 the Psychosocial Service is available in every prison, and responsible for evaluating the possibilities for the social reintegration of the prisoner, his attitude towards the victims and his risk of recidivism. According to the Act, the prisoner can make use of two 'tools' to prepare his reintegration: day leave and the systematic prison leave, both still decided by the prison administration.

It is interesting to note that the law does not prescribe the content of the social reintegration plan. The Ministerial Circular (N° 1695 of 26 February 1999), however, indicates that the social reintegration plan should include the following elements: (1) his activities and steps taken during detention (employment, education, treatment, taking responsibility, assistance provided to his family, ...); (2) his address and his social environment; (3) his financial resources (income, fees ...); (4) his planned activities (work, leisure ...); (5) his anticipated medical and/or psychosocial support; (6) his attitude and commitment to his victims and (7) any conditions that can facilitate his reintegration opportunities.

Prisoners' perspective

The first part of this chapter will focus on the prisoners' perspectives in relation to their possible return to society. The prisoners' perspective is not meant to be a profile of prisoners nor an evaluation of their efforts to get released. We focus on what kind of stories they told us regarding their prison experience and their preparation of a possible return to society.

In his seminal work, Goffman (1961) described in detail the 'entrance script' for the inmates. Since then, much research has dealt with how prisoners cope with doing time in prison. As part of an ongoing research by one of the authors (Machiels and Snacken, forthcoming), the focus here will be on the 'exit script' of some (potentially) to-be-released prisoners. This study aims to explore

163

and explain the process of reintegration from the prisoners' perspective. The research design includes a longitudinal approach starting in prison and ending one year after release, and focuses on the identity work of (to-be) released prisoners who spent at least five years in prison.

This chapter draws on in-depth interviews with eight prisoners while they were still in prison and will present the preliminary results from a narrative analysis of the prisoners' perspectives on re-entry and reintegration. The respondents had on average exceeded their eligibility date for parole by almost two years. A first reading of the transcripts looked for the overarching narrative. A second reading focused on the different storylines within the overarching narrative. At a further level of analysis, we engaged in identifying the similarities and differences in the stories.

Core narratives

In his study of illness narratives, Frank (1995) identified three core narratives: restitution (illness, treatment, and restoration), chaos (multiple problems, world collapsing, and no resolution) and quest narratives (journey, wisdom, and transformation). In his seminal work on desistance *Making Good*, Maruna (2001) describes the 'condemnation' script (blocked opportunities, insurmountable obstacles, hopelessness) versus the 'redemption' script (transformation).

Referring to Frank (1995) and Maruna (2001), we noticed two core narratives: one perspective envisaging re-entry (quest, redemption), having one foot out ('out narratives'); and one perspective that does not envisage re-entry (chaos, condemnation), still having two feet in ('in narratives'). The distinction, however, is not that straightforward: the same storylines expressed by prisoners occurred in different core narratives (indicating that storylines are dynamic and time-related). Furthermore, these narratives can also be analysed through the positions taken up by the prisoners: the positioning of the prisoner (e.g. as victim, underdog) is of great importance and restricts the use of certain storylines.

The 'out narratives' are mainly structured around the 'I' person (internal attribution), progress, future orientation and looking forward (focus on the outside world), while the 'in narratives' are full of 'They' sentences (external attribution), standstill, fear, lack of support and no future (focus on now, coping with prison life).

We want to stress that the interviews took place in prison at the time that all respondents were already involved in their release planning, and some had already received one or more negative decisions of the Sentence Implementation Court. The scripts are clearly a 'snapshot' and these scripts can change over time, as certainly some of the storylines will. It seems that the prisoners using the in narrative still have to 'choose', they seem to be still functioning in 'prison mode'. The two narratives can also be interpreted as release scripts, albeit that the 'in script' is not readily followed by a release, nor is the 'out script'!

The 'out narrative' can be interpreted as the 'end' narrative before leaving prison, while the 'in narrative' represents the struggle which can lead to the 'out narrative', or even a different script (suicide, end of sentence).

These two core narratives are made up of different storylines. In the following section we present a few storylines present in the core narratives.

Prison experience

Talking about their prison experience prisoners showed multiple identities. The prisoner storyline speaks of 24/7 performances, refers to the rules that have to be followed, and doing what you are told. The prisoner identity puts a pressure on their behaviour; they are expected to be 'perfect', otherwise sanctions can follow. Being a prisoner is something you cannot wash off, it is an everlasting mark, although there are different accents noticeable. Some refer to themselves as criminals, a bit criminal or not criminal at all.

Prisoners with certain jobs or educational activities feel the ascribed prisoner identity less.

This prisoner identity is neither their 'real' nor their 'own' identity. Every prisoner storyline is filled with the dramaturgical metaphor of the mask. They all wear masks, do window dressing, hide their real selves and play the game, play comedy. The prisoners state that they have to be macho; they cannot show emotions and frustration, they prefer to stay out of trouble. Being a prisoner means having a low profile identity. One gets used to prison life and being a prisoner, nevertheless wearing a mask gets more difficult with the passing years. This is described as a learning process, getting tougher as time goes on. Emotions are expressed between the safe walls of the prison cell. Most prisoners express the feeling that they can only be their real selves when the cell doors are closed. They give voice to their need for a space where they can 'belong to themselves'. Those prisoners who have already been outside talk about the button that has to be turned off when walking through the prison door.

Part of the prisoner storyline deals with their relationships inside the prison. The contacts with other prisoners or staff members are mostly superficial. They have a close relationship with one or two prisoners, often based on selectivity (hobby, crime, religion). They talk about a lack of trust in general, the gossip, and the strange mentality in prison (referring to drugs).

While the focus of the prisoner identity remains the inside, some prisoners simultaneously develop a semi-citizen identity. They are partially occupied with the outside world, trying to re-establish certain social roles, re-arranging their world for the future and have concerns about the people outside.

Prisoners often use a 'good boy' storyline, referring to their helping capacities in prison. These storylines always involve other people. A similar storyline is that of transformation, the story of being a changed person, having another view of life, talking about the virtue of their detention. Prisoners describe discovering positive elements, being proud of themselves and receiving positive feedback from staff and family acknowledging the transformation. Some respondents described their prison sentence as a 'good thing' that happened to them. It was an opportunity to change, to break with the past. These storylines are person-oriented. The transformation storyline is also used in a different way. Prisoners feel broken, are letting themselves go, are giving up or don't care any longer. This 'negative' transformation gives rise to a search for alternative 'escape routes' from prison, be it ending their life or end of sentence.

Talking about the release procedure

The primary actors are the Psychosocial Service in prison, especially social workers and psychologists, supported by members of the Flemish community (relating to welfare issues) and family members (if available). The Psychosocial Service decides when to start the release procedure and how to go about it.

This start can be described as one big problem storyline. Most of the time the procedure starts late, the service has a waiting list, is slow moving, the prisoners are not well informed, there is miscommunication, responsibilities are misunderstood or the procedure seems too complex. Prisoners stress that it is not up to them to take the initiative, nevertheless they have to do it all by themselves. Depending on the evolution of the interpersonal relationship between the prisoner and the Psychosocial Service the focus stays on the struggle towards mutual cooperative work. This struggle is translated into a reproachful articulation of the 'work' of the Psychosocial Service, using expressions like 'it's a disgrace' or being 'treated unfair', sometimes leading to the discontinuation of the procedure.

The compliance storyline is mainly used by prisoners who act against the proposals of the Psychosocial Service. One prisoner described his visits to the Psychosocial Service as 'a lot of head nodding and saying 'yes'. Others are less compliant and express their feelings of receiving no support from the services, being blocked in trying to change their lives, since they are opposing their future professional reintegration (e.g. exclusion from certain professional activities, such as being the owner of a combat sports school, or being a relationship counsellor). Although the services often stress the 'fear' of relapse, the prisoners try to minimize or even ridicule these risk factors (e.g. 'I love combat sports, so I am a dangerous person').

The delay storyline deals with the prisoners' interpretation of being postponed. Dealing with a delay is stressful for every prisoner and might impact on motivation. Prisoners stress the sometimes absurd arguments used by decision makers. They feel evaluated and judged in a negative way. Reintegration plans have to be modified to meet the arguments. Delay can therefore be interpreted as a rejection of their future identities, meaning a prolonged stay in prison.

Delay in procedure is not always interpreted in a negative way. Some prisoners showed an insight and understanding of delays in the procedure. Part of this storyline is the prisoners' views on the timing and expectations of the procedure. Some prisoners have a realistic view of their release date, adding some years after their date of eligibility following comparison with similar cases. Many prisoners do not have high expectations, protecting themselves against negative decisions. Their expectations can be summarised as 'approaching 1/3 is difficult because hope gets alive, and mostly disappointments follow'. Feelings of hope and uncertainty arise at the start of the procedure. The disappointments refer to the lack of support, the lack of hope. Many prisoners had expected an engagement from day one, criticize the lack of help and ask themselves why all this has to happen at the end of their sentence (referring to 1/3).

Meaning of reintegration

Asked about their expectations of the reintegration process, the prisoners used several metaphors.

The chapter storyline describes leaving prison as a chapter that will be closed, the start of a new life, focusing on re-discovering life, and being part of the hectic life on the outside. There is a clean break between present and future, between prison and life after prison.

The minimal (conforming) storyline stresses the 'expected' topics like working, saving money, renewal of family ties and being a good husband and father. Prisoners speak of being happy with less than before. One prisoner said: 'reintegration means having a place of my own, where I can cope with my prison experience'.

The struggle storyline focuses on the fight (against) or the support (from) others. Reintegration is described as a fight for their place, a fight for acceptance. Prisoners express their fear of the unknown, the fear of being rejected by society.

The support storyline is a cry for help, often followed by serious doubts. Prisoners say they have nothing to look forward to and ask themselves if it possibly can end in a positive way.

Possible identities

The storylines concerning their future life have been split into their hoped-for identities and feared identities. The hoped-for identities talk about work, family, relationship, a good life, and getting support, while the feared identities relate to stigmatisation, being rejected, family issues, surviving financially, relapse and receiving no support on the outside. These storylines are not intertwined with references to their past or present life. It seems as if the future stands on its own. These storylines are a reflection of what is expected of prisoners by society (dominant cultural script) and acknowledge the topics mentioned in their reintegration plans.

Probation officers' perspective

Whilst we have seen the prisoners' perspective in the first part of this chapter, the second part will focus on the probation officers' perspective. We will focus on the management of parole conditions, related to the 'follow-up' of released prisoners in the community from the perspective of the probation officer.[1] Accurate insights into probation practice and the role of the supervising probation officer remain largely underexplored in Belgium as well as in other jurisdictions (see, for instance, Werth, forthcoming: 14). So there is a lack of research insights into *how* probation officers actually operate within the criminal justice system, including how the management of parole conditions related to the 'follow-up' of released prisoners in the community takes place. In this part, therefore, we explore the focus of Belgian supervision practice and how practitioners approach their tasks.

Recent research by one of the authors (Bauwens, 2011) highlights a complex process through which not only offenders, but also probation officers have to construct a conception of parole and parole conditions. For the probation officers, this implies the use of release conditions as their 'working tool', and a high level of professional discretion necessary for the management of released prisoners whilst retaining a commitment and being accountable to the Probation Service as well as the Sentence Implementation Courts. The research was undertaken between 2007 and 2011. Framed by Garland's *The Culture of Control* (2001), the study aimed (1) to examine the extent to which developments in probation policy in two jurisdictions (England and Wales, and Belgium) are consistent with his account of penal transformation, and (2) to ask the same question of probation practice. The analysis of practice was narrowed down to the probation officers' interactions with offenders, who were given a probation or conditional release order. The research design combined a content analysis of policy documents and ethnographies of practice in both jurisdictions. The fieldwork made use of method triangulation (i.e. file analyses, informal talks, interviews, and, to a more limited extent, observations of probation 23 probation officers

---

[1] In 1999 probation officers became officially 'justice assistants'. This name change was the result of a reorganisation of the probation agencies and the establishment of 'Houses of Justice' in each jurisdiction.

over three probation areas took part in the research. All 23 probation officers had fieldwork roles; they had at least three years' work experience, and all had experience in penal matters and had worked mainly with offenders who had been given probation orders or conditional release orders.

We begin with a brief examination of the aims of release conditions in the Belgian probation context, moving on to consider the difficulties probation officers may encounter with regard to these release conditions.

Release conditions in the Belgian probation context

The primary intended outcomes of 'offender guidance' identified in the National Standards underline the tasks of the probation officer. These are: '(1) to prevent recidivism; (2) to limit the damage caused by judicial intervention towards the offender; and (3) to aim for the restoration of social networks' (Directorate General of the Houses of Justice, 2008, own translation). In addition, the National Standards require the probation officer to supervise the offender's compliance with the requirements of the conditional release order, and to provide advice, guidance and assistance so that the offender may comply with his/her conditions. The conditions imposed upon the ex-prisoner, in his/her conditional release order, are the legal constraints on the offender's freedom, entailing a variety of detailed prescriptions and proscriptions. Except for information about sentences for a new offence or police reports, all other indicators for recall will usually involve reporting by the probation officer involved in the supervision, thus making them an important actor in recall procedures.[2]

Belgian policy documents refer explicitly to release conditions as 'means, 'tools' or instruments to foster a learning process for the offender to encourage him/her to adopt a certain type of behaviour, which will no longer provoke judicial interference' (Di-

---

[2] For more detailed information about how Belgian reforms have impacted recall, see Bauwens et al., 2012.

rectorate General of the Houses of Justice, 2010: 2, own translation). Thus, the use of release conditions in the probation service is just a means to an end. At the same time, the release conditions are of pivotal importance to build a relationship of mutual trust between the probation officer and the offender. Through this relationship of trust, the areas of work the probation officer may focus on are *exclusively areas linked to the release conditions* that have been imposed. As mentioned above, one core principle of the vision statement that has been identified as underpinning 'offender guidance' also reads 'to limit the damage caused by judicial interference towards the offender'. This implies that Belgian policy and practice strongly emphasize that the principles of proportionality and 'minimal intervention' need to be respected.

The difficulties with release conditions experienced by probation officers

But how well does the 'working tool' of release conditions translate into supervision practice? The research findings indicate two different kinds of difficulties probation officers may encounter.

A first difficulty is noticed when the instructions by means of release conditions, offered by the Sentence Implementation Court, are inadequate. A non-exhaustive list of examples of inadequate conditions obtained from the study is provided below:

• Instructions that are too vague: e.g. 'to attend at appointments with a psychologist *as long as necessary*'. Is 'as long as necessary' to be understood in the eyes of the psychologist, the probation officer or the offender?

• Contradictory instructions: e.g. a requirement to 'avoid a particular city', when the office of the probation service is located in the centre of that city.

• Instructions that are not verifiable: e.g. to continue attending A.A. (Alcoholics Anonymous) meetings.

- Irrelevant instructions: e.g. a condition prohibiting the consumption of alcohol, when there is no mention of an alcohol problem in the case file nor was the consumption of alcohol related to the offence.

- The 'to be of good behaviour instruction': this instruction has been referred to as the 'catch-all formula' (Perriëns, 2001: 22). Probation officers see this release condition as conflicting with the principles of proportionality and minimum intrusion, as well as involving normative judgement.

- Too many instructions: Data from the case file analysis indicate that conditions ranged from a low of five to a high of seventeen conditions, with an average of nine conditions imposed. Probation officers confirmed that, without any doubt, the more conditions are imposed, the more likely it is that the offender will be found in breach of those conditions.

Given that the release conditions are the working tool of the probation officer as well as the exclusive areas the probation officer may focus on, inadequate conditions can jeopardise the objectives of offender guidance (see above) and hamper the building of a trusting relationship between the probation officer and the offender.

A second difficulty arises when the working tool is not used as a means to an end by the probation officers in their decision-making processes, but is dealt with as an end goal.

All the probation officers in the study accepted accountability for implementing the rules and guidelines of the Probation Service as well the Sentence Implementation Courts. There was, however, a notable difference in the extent to which they saw themselves bound to work with and interpret the 'working tool' of release conditions. There were two broad views amongst the practitioners. One group, comprising many (senior) practitioners, emphasised the 'outcome' of offender guidance; the other group, comprising fewer and often junior practitioners, emphasised a strict use of the 'working tool' and procedural fairness.

Working with numerous conditions gave rise, for instance, to different views as to how to work with the release conditions. While the first group interpreted and gave priority to certain conditions, the second group queried this approach and stressed the equal importance of all conditions, regardless of the number of conditions imposed. The former explained the different emphasis that was put on certain conditions as a 'common sense' way of working, not as a 'pick and mix' approach. Another example relates to the transition from prison into the community, which all probation officers recognised as challenging. In their experience, the first months following release from prison are for many very critical months, as many released prisoners have difficulties adjusting to life outside of prison. While, for instance, the requirements of residency and employment were set out as conditions in the social reintegration plan and the release conditions, once in the community ex-prisoners had to deal with and manage their real-life issues. For instance, an employer may have already hired someone else to do the job, or the requirement to reside permanently with a family member may not work out.

On several occasions probation officers pointed out that 'returning the offender to court' after a breach of one of his/her conditions was not difficult; the challenge was to successfully engage with, and to remain engaged with, the person.

> Offender guidance is a process. You can never see offender guidance as 'a straight line', I mean: they come to us, and all of a sudden everything will work out just fine. ... Relapse is unfortunately very common. Our task is to support the offender's change processes ... and I always tell offenders on my caseload that the issue is not that one or more conditions have not been respected, but to know and to find out why these conditions have not been respected, and how we can resolve it (Resp. 4).

174

One of the key points in our analysis is clearly that of elasticity in the use of the working tool. While some emphasised a stricter use of the tool, which reduces (but does not necessarily eliminate) the use of professional discretion, others focused on the tool as a means to an end, requiring wide-ranging discretion. They used the working tool as a way of achieving or at least moving towards longer-term compliance, rather than short-term rule compliance, in ways that are reflected in the Belgian policy documents. (See also Bottoms, 2001; Robinson and McNeill, 2008).

A topic for future research could be to analyse the use of professional discretion and the educational background and skills of the probation officer, given that since 1999 there has been an increase in educational qualifications (i.e. no longer a social work degree only) as the entry route into Belgian probation work.

Discussion and conclusion

While the Psychosocial Service assumes responsibility for the preparations of release forms within the correctional system, the Probation Service takes on the task of implementing them. It is clear that the reintegration approach used by both services is based on a dynamic concept using instruments (reintegration plan, gradual release, release conditions) to control, monitor and manage the return to society. In general, Belgian criminal justice policies, both within as well as outside prison, refer to need/support-based models of offender rehabilitation. However, release from prison and conditional release orders equally rely on elements of control/risk-based models (Bauwens, 2011).

Every actor involved in the release process and follow-up of the release makes their own risk assessment, albeit with a different focus. For the Psychosocial Service (and Sentence Implementation Court) there exists a fear of releasing the person too early. For the prisoner there is the fear as to whether 'society will give me another chance', and for the probation officer there is the fear as to how lenient they can (or have to) be with the interpretation of the parole conditions, including the initiation of breach proceedings.

Whatever model of offender rehabilitation is currently used, all of these models presuppose *normative judgements* concerning what is beneficial to the community and to society as well as to the offender. Becoming and being a prisoner gives the prisoner an ascribed identity, a cultural stereotype, with several attributes and a certain profile. But prisoners are not a homogeneous group and differences between prisoners can lead to different approaches to reintegration. Nevertheless, they all have to 'fit into' a normalized discourse, moving from prisoner to law-abiding citizen. The attributes of the prisoner have to be replaced by the attributes of a law-abiding citizen. This cultural expectation includes work, housing and relations, leading to a mainstreamed identity that can be easily managed. All kinds of 'marginal' identities (e.g. homelessness) are not tolerated (at first). Since the prisoner has no right to make certain choices on his own (acknowledging his identity), the mainstream identity becomes imposed. The moment they are working on their reintegration plan, they are forced to choose 'new identities'. Their new identities are put to the test, first by the Psychosocial Service and the Sentence Implementation Court, later by the Probation Service. They have to be the 'acceptable' identities.

Ibarra (1999) describes how people purposely seek out and experiment with different 'provisional selves', which serve as probationary identities in a trial and error process of refining and improving skills and behaviours. Prisoners have several identities in prison. In their reintegration plan they 'try out' certain identities on paper, after release they have to try them out in real life.

We agree with Turnbull and Hannah-Moffat, who note that parole conditions are designed to help prepare prisoners for 'freedom' by mobilising particular techniques of self-governance, while simultaneously operating as modes of surveillance that police the boundaries of acceptable conduct' (2009: 533). In this sense, parole conditions are techniques that target need/risk factors and promote normative lifestyles. They reflect both productive as well as repressive forms of penal power.

But what are 'normative lifestyles'? What is 'acceptable conduct'? If one's identities have to be in a range of acceptability, if they are evaluated and judged, can one then still talk about one's own identities? Does the social reintegration plan (and/or the probation officer) leave enough space for the trial and error process as described by Ibarra (1999)? Is Belgian offender reintegration truly client-oriented, if different actors in the criminal justice system hand over lists of requirements and restrictions?

Although the 2006 Act states that a prisoner who fulfils the conditions must be released, it becomes increasingly difficult for prisoners to fulfil the conditions imposed upon them, leading to an increasing number of prisoners who prefer the certainty of the prison term over the uncertainties of working out a social reintegration plan, the uncertainties of the parole decision-making and the risk of recall.

Bibliography

Bauwens, A. (2011). *The Transformation of Offender Rehabilitation.* Unpublished PhD diss. Unpublished thesis, Department of Criminology, Vrije Universiteit Brussel.

Bauwens, A., Robert, L. and Snacken, S. (2012). 'Conditional Release in Belgium: How Reforms Have Impacted Recall'. *European Journal of Probation*, 4(1): 19-33.

Bottoms, A. (2001). Compliance with Community Penalities. In: Bottoms, A., Gelsthorpe, L. and Rex, S. eds. *Community Penalties: Change and Challenges* (pp. 87-116). Cullompton: Willan.

Directorate General of the Houses of Justice. (2008). *National Standards*, internal document.

Directorate General of the Houses of Justice. (2010). Vision Statement of 'Offender Guidance', internal document.

Frank, A. (1995). *The Wounded Storyteller: Body, Illness, and Ethics.* Chicago: University of Chicago Press.

Garland, D. (2001). *The Culture of Control: Crime and Social Order in Contemporary Society.* Oxford: Oxford University Press.

Goffman, E. (1961). *Asylums: Essays on the Social Situation of Mental Patients and Other Inmates.* London: Penguin Books.

Government of Belgium *Act of 17 May 2006 on the External Legal Position of Prisoners and the Rights of Victims.* (2006) Brussels: Government of Belgium (Beligum).

Ibarra, H. (1999). 'Provisional Selves: Experimenting with Image and Identity in Professional Adaptation.' *Administrative Science Quarterly,* 44: 764-791.

Machiels, R. and Snacken, S. (forthcoming). 'On Parole: Living with an Imposed Mainstreamed Identity'.

Maruna, S. (2001). *Making Good: How Ex-convicts Reform and Rebuild their Lives.* Washington, DC: American Psychological Association.

Perriëns, R. (2001, November). 'Conditio sine qua nonsense'. Paper presented at the Conference '*Op weg naar een communicatieve en participatieve justitie'.*, met de steun van de Koning Boudewijnstichting, Provinciehuis Antwerpen, November.

Robinson, G. and McNeill, F. (2008). 'Exploring the Dynamics of Compliance with Community Penalties'. *Theoretical Criminology,* 12(4):, 431-449.

Snacken, S., Beyens, K. and Beernaert, M. A. (2010). 'Belgium'. In: Padfield, N., van Zyl Smit, D. and Dünkel, F. eds. *Release from Prison – Converging European Practices?* Cullompton: Willan Publishing.

Turnbull, S. and Hannah-Moffat, K. (2009). 'Under These Conditions. Gender, Parole and the Governance of Reintegration'. *British Journal of Criminology,* 49 (4): 532-531.

Werth, R. (forthcoming). 'I Do What I'm Told, Sort of: Reformed Subjects, Unruly Citizens, and Parole'. *Theoretical Criminology,* first published online on 24 October 2011, 1-18.

11

Desistance, Restorative Practices and the Role of the Prison Officer

Tim Chapman and Hugh Campbell

Introduction

Emerging from the Northern Irish conflict the Northern Ireland Prison Service is in a process of transition and reform. This chapter will discuss the challenges facing the Prison Service in re-imagining its purpose in a modern society. The Prison Review report (Owers et al., 2011) recommended that prisons should make more use of research into offending and theories of desistance. This will require a major rethinking of the ways prisoners are managed, rehabilitated and reintegrated into the community on release. There is a perception that prisons should be places where prisoners learn civic responsibility, but too often in reality they learn to be more problematic criminals.

This chapter will argue that a restorative approach offers the values, processes and practices needed to support prisoners along the way to successful reintegration and desistance from further harmful behaviour. Practices based upon restorative justice contribute to the creation of a safe, respectful and just environment in which prisoners may learn to be respectful and responsible and to restore relationships with people whom they have hurt, with their community and with their families.

Generally such learning is more effectively attained through daily interaction with other prisoners and staff than through education and programmes (though both have a critical contribution to make). Consequently, we believe that the prison officer is the most important professional in the prison system. The chapter will outline how the role of the prison officer should be enhanced.

This chapter is based upon our work within the University of Ulster's Restorative Practices Programme. Through this programme we have provided accredited training to over 30 prison officers, facilitated strategic discussions among senior prison managers, conducted research into the role of the prison officer, made submissions to the Prison Review Team and facilitated group work based upon desistance theory and restorative practices with prisoners serving long term sentences.

Northern Ireland Prison Service in transition

Between the years of 1969, when civil conflict escalated into politically motivated violence and the Good Friday Agreement in 1998, prisons were one of the sites where the Northern Irish 'Troubles' were most intensely enacted. During that time it has been estimated that up to 25,000 republicans and loyalists were imprisoned (Shirlow and McEvoy, 2008). Various conflicts were fought between prisoners and the government – internment without trial, strip searching, and the prisoners' struggle for special status, which escalated from the 'blanket protest' through the 'dirty protest' to the hunger strikes in which 10 prisoners died. Throughout this period prison officers were given the task of maintaining security and control. During that period 30 prison staff were murdered because of their employment, and many others, including their families, were seriously injured or were subject to prolonged physical, verbal and psychological intimidation and abuse. Prison officers adapted to this environment and learnt to distance themselves from the prisoners to avoid being 'conditioned' or intimidated.

It would not be surprising that prison officers have a deeply in-grained security mindset based upon the potential risks prisoners pose to them. While this made sense during the 'troubles', this set of attitudes has led to severe criticism in recent years. A key aspect of the peace process has been to increase the level of monitoring, accountability and inspection of public services, particularly those in the criminal justice system.

Since 2002, there have been over 40 reports or reviews on various issues in the Northern Ireland Prison Service. They have tended to repeat overarching themes:

- Safer custody, particularly in relation to suicide;

- Security breaches;

- Daily activities not including sufficient education and rehabilitation;

- Health and well-being of prisoners (especially women and juveniles) not being given priority;

- Staffing and management being unprepared to change;

- Diversity and equality not being rigorously observed.

In 2011 the Northern Ireland Prison Service had 27 live action plans and approximately 1,200 recommendations arising from the inspections and enquiries.

The Hillsborough Agreement in 2010 led to the devolution of policing and justice powers to the Northern Ireland Assembly and its Ministers. A Prison Review was established to address these aforementioned issues and to recommend how the Northern Ireland Prison Service could be reformed according to international obligations and best practice. The Prison Review Team published its findings in 2011. Their report was comprehensive and detailed. A key theme running through it was that the purpose of prisons must be aligned to the development of a safer society and that it can provide opportunities for prisoners to change. Research into desistance from offending and the importance of the quality of relationships between prisoners and staff were seen as key components of an improved approach to the rehabilitation and resettlement of prisoners (Owers et al., 2011).

The change process has commenced. This has involved a change management programme (Strategic Efficiency and Effectiveness), a redundancy package and a recruitment drive to introduce fresh staff, and a new training programme for both recruits and experienced staff.

The purpose of prisons in modern society

The Northern Ireland Prison Service has adopted as its purpose: 'improving public safety by reducing the risk of reoffending through the management and rehabilitation of offenders in custody'. Argyris and Schon (1974) distinguished between 'espoused theories' and 'theories in use'. This was based on their studies of organisations which espoused a positive purpose. Yet, when their practice was scrutinized it bore little relation to this purpose. The actual practices were their theories in use. Prison systems usually espouse the value rehabilitation yet it is clear that the priority of the system in its daily routines is to maintain security and order. This priority is based upon the premise that prisoners will get up to no good if left to their own devices and that a coercive approach will give them pause for thought.

The indignities that this approach causes have resulted in an inmate culture of resistance (Clemmer, 1958; Sykes, 1958). The inmate culture offers a range of coping mechanisms. The prisoner's macho image of toughness and the threat of violence create respect. Solidarity among groups of prisoners reduces the sense of isolation. Resistance to authority, along with various illegal activities, reassert a sense of agency and control. This culture reinforces the regime's distrust of prisoners which in turn is perceived as institutional disrespect. In such a vicious circle prison regimes actually reinforce criminality (Haney, 2005) rather than transform it. Current ideas in prison reform attempt to neutralise the negative effects of this culture through the concepts of legitimacy and moral performance. This requires prison officers to treat prisoners with a basic decency. Rehabilitation is delegated to specialist professionals in offending programmes.

Crewe's study of HMP Wellingborough (2005) has demonstrated that such a culture of resistance, while still retaining a currency among prisoners, is often not observed in practice and has declined in importance. Improved conditions such as in-cell television have reduced solidarity. Similarly hard drug use and dealing has weakened inmate solidarity. The incentives and earned privileges scheme give prisoners a stake in conforming to what authority expects of them. Loyalties to ethnic groups or localities often outweigh solidarity with all prisoners. Even 'grassing' was justified in certain circumstances, for example, in cases of bullying. These factors all contributed to more courteous relationships between prisoners and officers. Liebling (1999) has documented the competence that officers employ in this 'peace keeping' role. These skills were referred to as 'gaol craft' in our research.

We believe that this approach of keeping the peace, while valuable lacks real ambition regarding the outcomes of imprisonment. Treating prisoners decently is, of course the right thing to do. But it is still a way of managing the negative effects of inmate culture rather than a means of transforming it. It also retains elements of professionals treating prisoners as 'objects' to be managed (Duguid, 2000). The delivery of programmes to reduce the risk of offending is based upon a 'medical model' of assessment, sentence planning and the correct 'dosage' of programmes. This is based in turn upon the premise that criminality owes its origins in the predispositions of the criminal rather than the context in which he or she must live and make choices. There are several reasons why the medical model on its own is limited in its effectiveness:

- It is difficult to deliver to the majority of prisoners who repeatedly serve short term sentences

- It is difficult to deliver in conditions of overcrowding

- It struggles with engaging the motivation of the prisoner

- It can become part of a game a prisoner is playing to gain early release

- Its influence is weak compared to the daily influence of the inmate culture.

Fundamental reform of the prison system requires a new context in which prison officers and prisoners work together to create the conditions in which strong pro-social relationships, responsibility and respect can be generated within the prison as a means of preparing prisoners to have a good life and live safely in the community.

Restorative practices and desistance from offending

Offender management including risk management, programme delivery, and resettlement arrangements driven by a performance management system, all have their part to play in a modern prison service. However, experience has demonstrated that you cannot manage and problem-solve your way to a vision of a safer society. The fundamental reform of the Northern Ireland Prison Service (NIPS) needs to take into account the complexity and relational nature of the problem of crime and the harm it causes.

A prison must sustain a culture which meets the needs of victims and communities affected by crime as well as supporting progress towards desistance from offending. This requires restorative principles and practices informed by research into desistance.

Maruna (2000) outlines three theories emerging from the research into desistance:

- Maturational reform theory based upon the statistical reality that the vast majority of people who offend eventually desist

- Social Bonds theory based upon relationships as a vehicle of informal social control and upon social capital as a critical resource supporting a life free of crime

- Narrative theory based upon a process of transforming one's identity, one's possibilities and one's relationship with society.

Such perspectives value the individual's motivation, choices, and agency. The individual's strengths and capabilities (human capital) and their access to support and resources (social capital) are critical to their success in overcoming obstacles to desistance and to a better life. This model places the actions of the offender at the centre of the process of change and as such challenges the prevailing perception of effective practice as dependent upon the actions and knowledge of experts. This is not to say that trained staff are redundant. Their skills and knowledge are needed to facilitate, support and unblock processes of change rather than drive and control them. Desistance is closer to a public health model rather than medical model.

A clear, evidence based desistance practice model has yet to fully emerge though elements of it can be identified in the practices of restorative justice. There is a body of international and local research supporting the effectiveness of restorative justice in reducing offending (Robinson and Shapland, 2008).

Practices designed to support desistance cannot simply be captured in programme manuals or standards of practice. They must be brought alive by the intelligence, energy, skills and commitment of staff through positive relationships with prisoners. Restorative justice provides the moral energy which animates practices based upon desistance research. It is founded upon the premise that to be found to have harmed people and society creates a set of obligations:

- To be accountable to your victim

- To repair the damage as far as you can

- To take steps to desist from offending

- To learn other ways of meeting your needs

- To contribute to society as an active citizen.

What should be expected of prisoners?

> *To address the consequences of the actions that brought them to prison*

↓

> *To understand the obstacles to their desistance*

↓

> *To develop the human and social capital to overcome the obstacles*

↓

> *To have in place a plan for reintegration and desistance.*

If a prison sentence could engage prisoners in fulfilling these obligations, victims, local communities and the general public would feel that their needs for safety, justice and social control were being met.

A culture, which reinforces desistance, must be designed to accomplish two outcomes:

1. That prisoners repeatedly practice specified behaviours likely to become useful habits when they are released.

2. That the regime makes it easier for prisoners to practice these behaviours than to do nothing or to continue to behave in ways that reinforce their criminality.

This philosophy treats prisoners as moral agents, subjects in their own lives rather than objects subject to the control of others. Such an approach transforms a sentence from passive 'doing time' to the possibility of actively investing your time. It also alters the mindset of intervention from correcting deficits to restoring what is required for a good, law-abiding life. In this way the prison culture could be designed to restore safety, justice, dignity, decency, loss, physical and mental health, damaged relationships, community, empathy, responsibility, respect, and citizenship.

Zehr (2009) identifies three core values underpinning restorative justice: respect, responsibility and relationships. These values can be connected to the three theories of desistance. The narrative theory expounded by Maruna (2001) contrasts the condemnation script of the persister with the redemption script of the desister. Underlying the redemption script are issues of respect and self-respect. Social bonds theory is based upon the value of pro-social relationships. Maturation theory is essentially about developing the ability to take responsibility for one's actions and their consequences. Restorative practices enable offenders to take responsibility for the harmful consequences of their actions, to make amends and repair relationships and to develop respect for themselves and others. The best opportunities for such practices are in the daily interactions among prisoners and staff on the wings.

Such a learning model would involve prison officers actively modelling and reinforcing specific behaviours consistently on a daily basis. Conflicts and breaches of disciplines become opportunities to learn the importance of relationship, respect and responsibility through restorative processes. In this way the inmate subculture would be challenged and prisoners would be engaged in transforming themselves and each other.

In most regimes the management of harmful behaviour is separated from offending behaviour, educational and vocational programmes. In restorative justice the management of harmful behaviour becomes both an accountability and a learning process about the value of responsibility, respect and relationship. In this way the restorative approach offers a different perspective; the process of rule enforcement can be rehabilitative.

Restorative processes address harmful acts, conflict and breaches of rules far more rigorously than legalistic procedures. They require the person how has offended to consciously take responsibility for their actions and to actively take steps to repair the harm they have caused. In doing so, they satisfy the needs of those who have been harmed and restore good relations. These can be practised formally and informally within prisons and with victims, families and communities outside the prison. Such practices would not only develop a community of care on the landings but would also bring victims, families and community into the rehabilitation and resettlement processes.

Cullen et al. (2001) developed the idea of the virtuous prison, one in which restorative justice and rehabilitation would be combined to 'foster virtue in inmates'. We were interested in the idea of the prison officer as a person of virtue, someone who modelled pro-social behaviour, treating people with fairness and respect, who saw a larger purpose to his or her work than safe confinement and who had the capacity to use his or her relationships as part of a change process. What we also knew was the service had many officers who were disenchanted, cynical or worn out and in some cases unfit for the job. To better understand the officer role and mindset we were granted permission to meet focus groups of officers across all prison establishments, male and female, many of whom were veterans.

The importance of the Prison Officer

There is a key judgement to be made on the role of the prison officer. Given the criticism by a succession of reports on the prison service in Northern Ireland, it would be tempting to prescribe detailed standards of practice, rigorous procedures for managing prisoners and challenging targets. This approach would require a high level of performance management – monitoring, auditing, inspection and enforcement to achieve compliance.

This strategy was employed to modernise the police and probation in Britain over the past ten years. It resulted in a loss in confidence in the judgement of officers, a reduction in professional decision making, an inward looking perspective detached from the needs of victims, offenders and communities. Consequences included the needless criminalisation of many young people. It is now being reversed. Bureaucracy is being reduced and officers are being trained and encouraged to use discretion once again.

A new culture requires leadership at all levels including prison officer level. This should be supported by clear high level standards and values to inform discretion and accredited training to build competence and provide recognition of professionalism. With this in mind we conducted research into the role of the prison officer by conducting six focus groups, two from each prison in Northern Ireland.

We found that Prison Officers were extremely frustrated and negative about their work and the way they were managed and demonised by external reports. However, this frustration was caused by their wish to do their job professionally and to be valued by their families, the wider community and their managers. The officers we met talked about their wish to maintain high standards and they held positive values about the potential of rehabilitation. Collectively they articulated a sophisticated account of the prison officer's role. They were aware of the importance of protecting the public as well as providing opportunities for prisoners to desist from further offending and to find productive ways to contribute to society on their return. Yet they felt marginalised from rehabilitation and resettlement despite being at the centre of prisoners' daily lives. We met a group of people who have been rigorously inspected and investigated, but rarely listened to.

They described a 'blame culture' rather than a 'taking responsibility culture' in the prisons. Staff feel insecure and fear that they will be subject to allegations and discipline. They cope through avoiding risks, watching each other's backs, developing a collective cynicism and resistance towards the authority of managers. These are echoes of Reiner's (1992) work in police culture where he saw its main constituents as pessimism, suspiciousness, solidarity mixed with social isolation, strong internal cohesiveness, conservatism, machismo, and pragmatism – getting from here to tomorrow (or the next hour) safely and with the least fuss and paperwork. Interestingly the prison officer staff culture bore many similarities to inmate culture suggesting that they reinforced rather than challenged each other. What we found was that the identity of a prison officer in Northern Ireland is 'spoiled'. They feel despised by inspections, elements of their own management and media depictions of their service.

In spite of this, the majority of staff across all groups described their role as involving skills and values beyond that of a 'turnkey'. The term 'gaol craft' was frequently used to describe what it meant when an officer was really doing their job well. Skills included assessing and defusing potentially violent situations, communication skills, and teamwork. This is confirmed by Hemmens and Stohr (2000) 'There is reason to believe that the correctional role is much more demanding, broad and rich than is generally believed – correctional staff are engaged in guiding, mentoring, facilitating and developing prisoners. If a prisoner needs assistance with a job, getting along with others, interacting with staff, then officers are therefore likely resources given proximity and frequency of contact'.

Their intelligence and skill were demonstrated directly to us through the performance of 30 officers who enrolled on the University of Ulster Certificate in Restorative Practices course. All passed and about half of them were awarded commendations.

The need to professionalise the role of the Prison Officer

If prisons are to become environments where people learn to live in community, to meet their needs and to resolve conflict without recourse to harming others, we believe that the role of the prison officer is critical. If this is true the prison officer should be seen as a professional of at least equal value to the other professionals such as psychologists, probation officers, medical staff and teachers. This belief has driven our work at the university over the past five years.

It began when we met a prison governor who was personally interested in restorative justice. He became an important catalyst. He facilitated the recruitment of 18 staff from across the service to participate in our Certificate in Restorative Practices. This gave us a concrete way of engaging with a service that was beleaguered. We began a training programme with this group in 2008 and the course stretched over 18 months.

Our approach was to regard the prison officer, the man or woman on the landing as a cultural vehicle for the prison. We set out to affirm their sense of agency and to understand and support their sense of vocation. Of course we also knew we were getting students who were motivated to learn as they had been handpicked for our training. They completed the programme successfully and a further course was commissioned. This time there was an open training and not a selection process.

Our participants came to the university campus to attend classes. In time, many of them discussed how significant this was. In their eyes it elevated the experience above the norm. They described satisfaction and pride at becoming university students. Key elements in our approach to creating the learning experience included:

- Promoting reflection and discussion which honoured and challenged individual experience

- Developing a culture around reading, reflecting and writing

- Allowing space for officers to share their doubts, cynicism and concerns about the state of their service without descending into a state of permanent pessimism or powerlessness.

We believe that the success of this course influenced the Prison Review to recommend that prison officers engage in training delivered by external bodies which could award accreditation. For the first time new recruits and experienced officers will participate in comprehensive training in all aspects of their role with an emphasis on respectful relationships, communications skills and knowledge on how prisons can be supported to desist from crime.

Parallel to this training we embarked on a series of meetings with significant stakeholders. The purpose of these meetings was to learn about the challenges facing the prison service, to build relationships and to offer our support. We met the Director General, senior managers and the Prison Officers Association. In 2010 we extended this by holding discussions with representatives of all the political parties. As a result of the trust we developed, we were asked to facilitate a sensitive management workshop and approached to consider an engagement with a group of prisoners who had 'separated' status within the prison.

Our direct work with a high risk group of prisoners has convinced us that the principles and practices of restorative justice complement the insights that research into desistance has generated. We are now working on how this model can be made available to more prisoners.

Through both these meetings and delivering this course we aspired to a relationship between the university and the Prison Service which was both critical and supportive, a 'critical friend'. We were and remain curious about and open to forging a relationship that would be characterised by openness, trust and practical value to the reform of the Prison Service.

Conclusion

The prison system as it operates at present contributes more to the reinforcement and support of criminality than it does to support pathways to desistance. This is primarily due to the powerful influence of the inmate culture and the resignation of the authorities in the face of it. If the prison system is serious in its intention to contribute to a safer society it needs to generate and sustain a culture of respect which nurtures pro-social relationships and which supports prisoners to become responsible citizens. Restorative justice provides a framework of values, principles and practices which if consistently implemented can support such a culture. Prison officers are the professionals that spend most time with prisoners and as such they are best placed to engage prisoners on a daily basis in restorative practices.

Bibliography

Argyris, C. and Schon, D. (1974) *Theory in Practice*. San Francisco: Jossey-Bass.

Clemmer, D. (1958) *The Prison Community*. New York: Rinehart.

Crewe, B. (2005) 'Codes and Conventions: The Terms and Conditions of Contemporary Inmate Values'. In Liebling, A. and Maruna, S. (Eds.). *The Effects of Imprisonment*. Cullompton: Willan.

Cullen, F.T., Sundt, J.L. and Wozniak, J.F. (2001) 'Virtuous Prison: Toward a Restorative Rehabilitation'. In Pontell, H.N. and Shichor, D. (Eds.). *Contemporary Issues in Crime and Criminal Justice: Essays in Honor of Gilbert Geis*. Upper Saddle River: Prentice Hall.

Duguid, S. (2000) *Can Prisons Work? The prisoner as object and subject in modern corrections*. Toronto: University of Toronto Press.

Haney, C. (2005) 'The contextual revolution in psychology and the question of prison effects'. In Liebling, A. and Maruna, S. (Eds.). *The Effects of Imprisonment*. Cullompton: Willan.

Hemmens, C. and Stohr, M. K. (2000) 'RSAT in Idaho'. *American Society of Criminology Conference*. San Francisco, 14-18 November.

Liebling, A. (1999) 'Prison Suicide and Prisoner Coping'. In Tonry, M. and Petersilia, J. (Eds.). *Prisons, Crime and Justice: A Review of Research*. Chicago: The University of Chicago Press.

Maruna, S. (2001) *Making Good*. Washington, DC: American Psychological Association.

Maruna, S. (2000) 'Desistance From Crime and Offender Rehabilitation: A Tale of Two Research Literatures'. *Offender Programs Report*, 4(1): 1-13.

Owers, A., Leighton, P., McGrory, C., McNeill, F. and Wheatley, P. (2011) *Review of the Northern Ireland Prison Service: Conditions, management and oversight of all prisons*. Belfast: Department of Justice Northern Ireland.

Reiner, R. (1992) *The Politics of Police, Second Edition*. Toronto: University of Toronto Press.

Robinson, G. and Shapland, J. (2008) 'Reducing Recidivism: A Task for Restorative Justice?' *The British Journal of Criminology*, 48: 337-358.

Shirlow, P. and McEvoy, K. (2008) *Beyond the Wire: Former Prisoners and Conflict Transformation in Northern Ireland*. London: Pluto Press.

Sykes, G. (1958) *The Society of Captives*. Princeton: Princeton University Press.

Zehr, H. (2009) *Restorative Justice and Peacebuilding. Available at:* http://emu.edu/now/restorative-justice/2009/04/20/restorative-justice-and-peacebuilding/ (Accessed 20 February 2014).

12

Prisoner/Patient: Prisons as Mental Health Institutions

Bronwyn Naylor[1]

Introduction

The de-institutionalisation movement of the 1960s and failure of governments to adequately support people with mental illness and intellectual disabilities, coupled with heightened risk aversion in the community, has meant that many are ultimately left to be 'managed' in the criminal justice system (Priebe et al., 2005). Today, it is widely recognised that the numbers of people with mental illness (and intellectual disabilities) in the prison system is both significant, and increasing.

As a consequence there will be increasing numbers of prisoners who are difficult to manage, difficult to communicate with, and at greater risk of harm to themselves and others. At the same time, prisons are notoriously under-resourced, with mental health and related services in prisons particularly poorly supported in many jurisdictions, and pressure on these limited resources will only increase.

This chapter raises serious concerns about the incarceration of people with mental illness and the need to balance rights/

---

[1] This chapter will draw on a major research project on Implementing Human Rights in Closed Environments to make a comparative evaluation of three potential drivers for change, in Europe and more widely: rights-focused litigation; mental health-focused reforms; and monitoring for protection of rights.

autonomy with treatment/ safety issues; the use of segregation, seclusion and disciplinary proceedings as management tools; access to medical treatment; and resource allocation for psychiatric facilities inside and outside prisons. Examined in the chapter is the importance of human rights litigation, governmental and regional reforms, and international monitoring in creating positive change for people with mental illness in the criminal justice system.

The problem

There are different definitions of mental illness (and intellectual disability) and different points at which this data is recorded, and the sets of data are therefore difficult to compare. The following statistics at least illustrate the potential breadth of the problem.

According to the World Health Organisation (WHO), of the 2 million prisoners in Europe, at least 400,000 suffer from a significant mental disorder, and more suffer from common mental health problems such as depression and anxiety (WHO, 2012). Personality disorders are the most common form of mental health problem in prisons, but the WHO reports that 'a substantial part of the remaining prison population suffers from psychosis-related problems'. Women prisoners have very high levels of mental illness; the WHO reports that '80% of women in prison have an identifiable mental illness' (WHO, 2012). Mental health is also put at risk in prisons from factors such as overcrowding, bullying, marginalisation and discrimination (WHO, 2012).

In England and Wales, with 86,821 people held in prisons as at August 2011,

> Up to 90% of prisoners have some form of mental health problem (including addictions and personality disorder ...) and 10% of male and 30% of female prisoners have previously experienced a psychiatric acute admission to hospital (Centre for Mental Health, 2011: 2).

Statistics for the prevalence of mental health problems in prison and in the general community reported by the Centre for Mental Health showed, for example, 0.5% of the general population experiencing psychosis compared with 8% of the prison population, and 13.8% of the general population suffering depression or anxiety compared with 45% of the prison population (2011).

People with mental impairments who commit criminal offences can be held in secure psychiatric facilities if found not guilty on the basis of their mental illness. In 2009 there were 4,258 restricted patients in secure hospitals in England and Wales (Centre for Mental Health, 2011: 5). Other people may become mentally ill once in prison. It has long been recognised that prisons also *produce* (or at least exacerbate) mental illnesses (Edgar and Rickford, 2009). If the illness is severe enough they should then be transferred to a psychiatric facility. Transfers from prison to a secure hospital depends on the availability of beds, and can often involve long delays (Council of Europe, 2012; Bradley, 2009).

The US and Australia experience similar issues; indeed it is reported that in the US there are 'three times as many mentally ill people in prisons than in mental health hospitals, and the rate of mental illness in prisons is two to four times greater than in the general public' (Fellner, 2006: 392; see also Australian Institute of Health and Welfare, 2012).

In explaining the increase in mentally ill people entering prisons it is commonly observed that the deinstitutionalisation movement of the 1960s and failure of governments to adequately support people with mental illness and intellectual disabilities, coupled with heightened risk aversion in the community, has meant that many are ultimately left to be 'managed' in the criminal justice system (Priebe et al., 2005). At the same time prison overcrowding, a major issue across Europe and much of the world, increases health problems in prisons, including the risk of mental health issues, and the use of psychoactive substances in their management (WHO, 2012).[2]

Why this issue matters

The increasing incarceration of mentally ill people in the prison system has serious consequences for prison management, for criminal justice policy, and for the rights and health of this group of prison detainees. Specific issues include access to medical services, balancing rights with treatment and safety issues; use of segregation, seclusion and disciplinary proceedings as management tools; and resource allocation for psychiatric facilities inside and outside prisons.

Access to treatment, and balancing rights with treatment and safety issues

The right of people in prisons to access to medical services is clearly stated in numerous international and regional documents. The UN International Covenant on Economic, Social and Culture Rights (ICESCR) (United Nations, 1966) Article 12(1) expressly recognises the 'right of everyone to the enjoyment of the highest attainable standard of physical and mental health.' This right is to be equivalent to that of non-detainees in that community. The UN Basic Principles for the Treatment of Prisoners Principle 9 encapsulates this principle of equivalence: 'Prisoners shall have access to the health services available in the country without discrimination on the grounds of their legal situation' (United Nations, 1990). More detailed requirements appear in the UN Standard Minimum Rules for the Treatment of Prisoners, including the availability of qualified medical staff, close links between prison services and

---

[2] WHO notes that overcrowding is particularly egregious in the central and eastern European countries along with much higher rates of imprisonment in the 'newly independent states'. See further eg *Dybeka v Albania* (2007); *Badila v Romania* (2011).

community health provision, and the transfer of sick prisoners to specialised institutions (articles 22 and 82) (United Nations, 1955).

This gives rise to a number of questions: who provides the medical services? Should this be the prisons service, or contracted providers, or the outside providers of health services (state or private sector)? For example, the World Health Organisation recently recommended that prison health services should generally be provided by Ministries of Health and not prisons departments. It includes questions about the standard of medical care provided in the prison, access to specialists, and access to medication, bearing in mind the principle of equivalence.

It also includes all the infrastructure that has to go around a person's medical care when they have no control over their environment: maintaining accurate and up to date records; communicating relevant information to relevant people in an environment which has vast amounts of churn (of both prisoners and staff), and linking people in to community providers as they prepare to leave.

A crucial dilemma for prison management dealing with mentally ill detainees will be balancing autonomy rights with treatment (whether or not voluntary), and with safety, of the detainee, of other detainees, and of staff. The right of equal access to high quality services may also be challenging, as a positive obligation on governments. But at a minimum, prisoners – like all members of the community – must be protected from cruel or degrading treatment. All major human rights instruments prohibit cruel, inhuman and degrading treatment and punishment (including for prisoners).[3]

The aim of containing difficult behavior may however compete with these rights. People may be placed in segregation in harsh conditions to manage disruptive behavior (discussed further below). They may be restrained physically; they may also be provided with

---

[3] ICCPR Articles 7 and 10; European Convention on Human Rights (ECHR) Article 3. Equivalent provisions apply in Australia (Victoria and the ACT), New Zealand, and under the American and African Conventions.

medications which aim to manage their behavior by keeping them in a sedated state. A forensic psychiatric nurse wrote recently of the particular challenges of having to use force to restrain a patient:

> One of the biggest conflicts of interest I have is restraining a patient from hurting themselves or others. I personally struggle with the fact that I am here to build relationships with patients and help treat and support them yet may also be called upon to restrain them if they become violent (Bello, 2011).

Prisoners cannot, however, be treated involuntarily in prison. The UK Mental Health Act 1983, for example, provides for involuntary treatment – itself a breach of rights, and therefore carefully regulated and monitored – only in recognised hospitals. Prisons do not fall into this category, and prisoners must be transferred to a NHS hospital or other secure facility if they require such treatment.[4]

Use of segregation, seclusion and disciplinary proceedings as management tools

Segregation, seclusion and disciplinary proceedings are increasingly used as management tools for difficult and disruptive mentally ill prisoners and prisoners with behavioural difficulties, as their numbers grow in increasingly overcrowded prisons. The UN Standard Minimum rules recognise the fundamentally harmful character of prison – as punishment – and require prisons to minimise further suffering through disciplinary actions, providing in

---

[4] Litigation in this area has usually focussed on *failures* to provide medical care (or any care); the priority placed on voluntary treatment in *Renolde v France* (2008), and consequent failure to check that medication was in fact being consumed, was criticised by the ECHR when it left a prisoner to relapse into psychosis and subsequent take his own life. On the other hand, an offender on a community treatment order in Australia argued he was subjected to cruel, inhuman or degrading treatment when required to follow a regime of antilibidinal medication which was producing osteoporosis The court concluded that a medically approved regime would very rarely be found to be 'cruel, inhuman or degrading': *09-085* [2009] VMHRB.

article 57 'the prison system shall not, except as incidental to justifiable segregation or the maintenance of discipline, aggravate the suffering inherent in such a [detention] situation.'

Nonetheless prison management will be faced with challenges to the 'good order' of the prison from mentally ill (and intellectually disabled, and brain damaged) prisoners and are likely to turn to disciplinary processes and segregation to maintain control. The Centre for Mental Health also notes that prisoners with serious mental health problems are placed in segregation units, because 'ordinary location' is considered to be too stressful (Centre for Mental Health, 2011: 5).

In addition to the potential breach of rights, the use of segregation and solitary confinement at the same time clearly risks creating, or aggravating, mental illness. English prisons holding mentally ill inmates in close supervision centres (CSC) run on 'highly punitive' lines to manage disruptive inmates were recently criticised. Lord Ramsbotham, a former Chief Inspector of Prisons for England and Wales, was quoted as saying that 'it had been clear for a long time that CSCs are holding people who should not be there'.

> If you are holding people suffering mental health problems, then they should be held in conditions similar to those in secure mental health hospitals. This is clearly not the case [at Woodhill] (Allison, 2011).

Many US prisons use Behaviour Management Program (BMP) regimes which correctional staff define as 'therapeutic' or offering incentives to good behavior (i.e. to stop experiencing the extreme deprivation), but which prisoners (and anyone looking at the BMP) experience as punitive. These punitive 'management' regimes are imposed in response to 'misbehaviour' – even where that misbehavior (non conformity to rules) arises from emotional or mental distress (Toch, 2008).

Successful litigation under the cruel and unusual punishment provisions of the Eighth Amendment to the US Constitution involved a challenge to repeated use of extreme segregation for a mentally ill prisoner, in response to his attempts to commit suicide in prison. As the judge noted:

> ... prison officials chose to label Walker as a bad person rather than treat the mental health problems that were apparent to inmates and staff (Toch, 2008: 395).

The extreme segregation included long periods of time in isolation, sleeping on a concrete floor, in filthy conditions, and often be left naked and cold. A psychiatric expert witness told the court in *Walker*'s case:

> If it's a security program, I think it's just cruel and inhumane. If it's a treatment, it is ethically wrong ... (*Walker v Montana* 2003: para. 66)

Resources

The issue underlying many of these challenges, however, will often be poor resourcing for (a) prisons and (b) mentally ill people. Underlying the failure to properly resource will be a lack of political will to spend money in these sectors. There are always funding issues with prisons: prisons are politically problematic, especially in a significantly punitive political climate. Privatisation has been one response to the cost of running prisons but brings its own problems – including the privatisation of health service provision.

Major reforms were recommended in the UK in the 2009 Bradley report, but it is unclear how many of these have been implemented. However, a joint announcement by the Justice and Health Ministers in March 2011 promised £3 million 'to be spent creating up to a further 40 diversion sites for adults and £2 million for up to a further 60 sites for young people', to be a national service by 2014 (Travis, 2011).

The defence in much human rights litigation in this area is that it is simply too expensive to bring old and inadequate prison infrastructure up to standard. Certainly many newer members of the Council of Europe – especially in Eastern Europe – are having difficulties with this issue. The current (northern) financial crisis will only deepen these problems. The courts reject this defence in principle. However the ultimate issue in most litigation in this area is that there is no money – or no will to allocate money – to improving prison conditions.

Drivers for change, in Europe and more widely

Solutions will need to address:

- How mentally ill people come to offend and enter the criminal justice system, and the availability of earlier intervention

- Alternative forms of disposition minimising use of prisons

- How prisoners become mentally ill in prisons, and the nature and quality of imprisonment

- Provision of mental health services in prisons

- Provision of secure hospital services instead of prison placement, and

- Continuing support and services when the person leaves prison (see Bradley, 2009).

In this chapter I want to identify at least three ways in which change may be mobilised in some of these areas. These are (a) litigation raising rights issues, (b) mental health-focussed reforms; and (c) monitoring for protection of rights.

Rights-focused litigation

One important source of rights-focused litigation is the prohibition under the European Convention, and its international equivalent the ICCPR, on cruel, inhuman or degrading treatment or punishment, and the requirement that people held in detention are held humanely. The European Prison Rules and UN Standard Minimum Rules elaborate the requirements.

These conventions are not self-executing – they have to be enforced by litigation, or through the reports of monitoring bodies (discussed further below). There is a substantial body of case law now about the application of the European Convention on Human Rights (adopted by the UK in its *Human Rights Act* 1998) in this context.

In cases alleging that prison conditions and/or a poor level of medical care provided constitute cruel, inhuman or degrading treatment or punishment, the European Court of Human Rights has made it clear that, whilst Article 3 enshrines 'fundamental values' and an absolute prohibition, its application in the prison context is not breached by suffering which is simply the 'inevitable' result of legitimate punishment. The ill-treatment has to reach a 'minimum level of severity' to fall within Article 3.

Whether Article 3 has been breached is 'in the nature of things, relative' and 'depends on all the circumstances of the case, such as the duration of the treatment, its physical and mental effects and, in some cases, the sex, age and state of health of the victim.' (*Dybeku v Albania*, 2007 [36]). At the same time, there is no need to prove a positive intention to humiliate or debase: crowded and unsanitary conditions of detention have been held to breach Article 3 without evidence of any malevolent intent (e.g. *Badila v Romania* 2011 [79]).

The tests applied in a particular case where the applicant's health is at issue are '(a) the medical condition of the prisoner; (b) the adequacy of the medical assistance and care provided in detention, and (c) the advisability of maintaining the detention measure in view of the state of health of an applicant.' (*Dybeku* [42]; *Slawomir* 2009 [88]) As an example, in 2007 a prisoner suffering from paranoid schizophrenia, who received very limited psychiatric support and was generally held with other healthy prisoners in overcrowded conditions in Albanian prisons, was found to have suffered inhuman and degrading treatment in *Dybeku v Albania* (2007).

In another case, a Polish prisoner suffering from epilepsy, schizophrenia and other mental disorders brought a complaint under Article 3 after being held in various locations in overcrowded cells, without adequate psychiatric care, arguing that he should have been held in a psychiatric institution (*Slawomir v Poland*, 2009). The Court concluded that the conditions in which Slawomir had been held 'would not be considered appropriate for any person deprived of his liberty, still less for someone like the applicant with a history of mental disorder and in need of a specialised treatment' (*Slawomir*, 2009 [95]). It held that there had been a breach of Article 3. In deciding that the conditions breached the Convention, the Court observed:

> Undeniably, detained persons who suffer from a mental disorder are more susceptible to the feeling of inferiority and powerlessness. Because of that an increased vigilance is called for in reviewing whether the Convention has been complied with (*Slawomir*, 2009 [96]).

Whilst emphasising that Article 3 did not automatically require the release or transfer of a detainee to a civil hospital where they were suffering an illness that was difficult to treat, the Court observed that it does require the state to ensure that prisoners are held in conditions in which 'given the practical demands of imprisonment, their health and well-being are adequately secured.' (*Slawomir*, 2009 [86]).

The State in *Dybeku* argued that the conditions of detention in Albania should be benchmarked against other Council of Europe member states who were similarly in the process of reform, and that they 'should be assessed with reference to the economic situation of the State and the standard of living of the country.' (*Dybeku*, 2007 [33]). The Court rejected the arguments based on either cost generally or country relativity:

> The Court does not underestimate the significance of the financial difficulties referred to by the Government ...

However, it observes that many of the shortcomings outlined above could have been remedied even in the absence
of considerable financial means. In any event, a lack of resources cannot in principle justify detention conditions
which are so poor as to reach the threshold of severity for
Article 3 to apply (*Dybeku*, 2007 [50]).

In *Renolde v France* (2008) a prisoner suffering from acute psychosis had been disciplined for an assault and placed in solitary
confinement as punishment for a 45 day 'sentence'. He had been
provided with medications for his psychosis but had not been
supervised in taking the medications. He did not take the medications, complained often of hallucinations and distress, and ultimately hanged himself. His sister brought an application under
Article 2 of the European Convention (the obligation to protect
life) as well as Article 3. The Court found both Articles to have
been breached. It observed that when deciding whether treatment
or punishment breaches Article 3, in the case of mentally ill people, the Court has to:

> ... take into consideration their vulnerability and their in-
> ability, in some cases, to complain coherently or at all about
> how they are being affected by any particular treatment
> (*Renolde*, 2008 [120]).

The tension between treating a mentally ill prisoner as a patient, and the reality of the prison setting, was highlighted in the
additional (concurring) judgment written by one of the judges.
The judge specifically criticised the statement by the doctor responsible for the in-prison medical service that staff would not
verify whether a patient took the prescribed medications as this
was 'contrary to the principle of trust which underlies the therapeutic alliance in a hospital environment' (*Renolde*, 2008 [34]).
Judge Villiger commented:

> While such trust might be an important element of a rela-
> tionship between a medical doctor and a responsible and

206

mature patient, I fail to see how such trust can at all be established with a vulnerable person such as the applicant's brother, who in addition had already attempted to commit suicide.

Whilst there have been a number of successful cases, remedies from these findings in favour of the prisoner applicants have been limited. The courts have generally only urged improvements in facilities, and on occasions awarded a small sum of financial compensation. It has been left to the State to implement (or not) the recommend changes. In *Slawomir* the court observed that

> ... it is primarily for the State concerned to choose the means to be used in its domestic legal order in order to discharge its legal obligation under ... the Convention, provided that such means are compatible with the conclusions set out in the Court's judgment. [In this case] the Court considers that the respondent State must secure, at the earliest possible date, the adequate conditions of the applicant's detention in an establishment capable of providing him with the necessary psychiatric treatment and constant medical supervision (*Slawomir*, 2009 [107][108]).

Two US cases offer interesting alternative approaches to remedies for litigants. In 2010 the US Supreme Court confirmed (by a majority of 5:4) the decision of a Federal judicial panel to order that approximately 34,000 prisoners to be released from Californian prisons as a remedy for deplorable conditions of overcrowding breaching constitutional guarantees.[5] This represented the imposition of a population cap of 137.5% of prison capacity.

The Supreme Court hearing followed many years of interim hearings in cases filed on behalf of prisoners with 'serious mental disorders' who could not obtain adequate care and whose 'unbearable conditions result[ed] in a substantial suicide rate', and on be-

---

[5]*Brown v Plata* 131 S.Ct 1910 (2011). The three-judge panel was convened under the special provisions of the Prison Litigation Reform Act 1995.

half of prisoners with 'serious medical conditions' who could not obtain necessary treatment. (Strutin, 2012: 1325).

An order for prisoner release – population reduction – was seen as the only option in view of the system-wide overcrowding and clear incapacity or unwillingness of the State of California (already in financial difficulties) to implement the necessary reforms. In fact no prisoners were ultimately released: new legislation was immediately passed moving non-violent, minor offenders from state to local (county funded) jails. These reportedly have their own overcrowding problems (Strutin, 2012: 1340).

However it appears that a more indirect impact of *Brown v Plata* has been legislative and judicial moves to reduce the use of imprisonment, or at least the length of prison terms (Strutin, 2012: 1342). Some suggest, on the other hand, that the drivers to reduce levels of imprisonment have simply been financial: that the current financial problems across at least the northern hemisphere are pushing governments to reduce the high daily cost of imprisonment.

In a second example – more useful to the individual litigant - the Supreme Court of Montana in *Walker v Montana* (2003) held that Walker's constitutional rights had been breached – and ordered direct monitoring by the court of reforms to the system in the relevant prison

> We [require the prison] to conform the operations of its administrative segregation units to the requirements of this Opinion and to report, in writing to [the] court within 180 days as to the actions taken. The District Court may, thereafter, order inspections or further remediation as in that court's discretion is necessary under the circumstances (paras. 83-84).

Mental health-focused reforms

The quality and level of mental health services in prisons has been the subject of many reports and reforms in the UK. In 1996

Lord Ramsbotham, then Chief Inspector of Prisons for England and Wales, published a discussion paper, 'Patient or Prisoner'. Beginning with the statement of the principle of equivalence – that 'Prisoners are entitled to the same level of health care as that provided in society at large' – he recommended that prison health care should become the responsibility of the National Health Service to ensure that this entitlement was fulfilled (HM Inspectorate of Prisons for England and Wales, 1996). This recommendation was implemented effectively by 2006 with the establishment of regionally based 'in-reach' teams.

Lord Ramsbotham also called for improvements in the speed with which seriously mentally ill patients were transferred from prisons to NHS hospitals or regional secure units. In 2009 Lord Bradley revisited the issue of delay in transferring people from the prisons system to hospital, and recommended a 14-day maximum waiting target. He identified various obstacles, including communication breakdowns across the system, lack of bed availability and security issues, but also 'different attitudes and perceptions of prison and hospital staff towards mental illness and offenders' (Bradley, 2009: 105).

The then Chief Inspector of Prisons commented in her Annual Report in 2010 that the Bradley review had not yet led to major changes in mental healthcare in prisons, noting 'particular concerns about the lack of primary mental health services, and of daycare provision for those less able to cope on the wings' (HM Chief Inspector of Prisons for England and Wales, 2010: 29). In 2011, following the release of the Green Paper, *Breaking the Cycle* (2010) the Government announced that they had allocated £5m 'to put into 100 'diversion sites' across England and Wales as part of their plan to create a national liaison and diversion service by 2014' (Travis, 2011).

Other drivers for reforms in Europe include the WHO and European monitoring bodies. The European Committee for the Prevention of Torture (CPT), the monitoring body established under the European Convention for the Prevention of Torture, notes in its Reports its successes in achieving reform but also, on occasions, that its recommendations from previous visits have not been adopted (as discussed further below).

A recent WHO proposal addresses the issue of where prison health care should be located. It proposed in 2010 that general healthcare in prisons should routinely be the responsibility of domestic Ministries of Health rather than the prisons ministry (Hayton et al., 2010). Whilst noting that the capacity of Health ministries to provide high standard care should also be monitored, its report observes that health care is already provided through the general health system in Norway, France, some Australian states, and the UK. Factors which they highlight as having driven this change in a range of countries included human rights – e.g. the requirement under Article 12 of the ICESCR that prisoners are entitled to 'the highest attainable standard of physical and mental health' – and related concerns about the poor standard of prison healthcare, particularly for people with mental illnesses.

Monitoring for protection of rights

There are at least three levels of monitoring that may be useful here: international, national, and local or civil society.

International agencies. UN and Council of Europe monitoring bodies carry out visits to places of detention, and make reports and liaise with States to achieve reforms. At the Council of Europe level the monitoring body is the CPT. Since 2006 countries have also been ratifying the Optional Protocol to the UN Convention Against Torture (OPCAT). This requires signatories both to develop domestic National Preventive Mechanisms (NPMs) and to provide access for the UN Subcommittee for the Prevention of Torture (SPT) to make announced and unannounced visits to places of detention. International non-government agencies such as Amnesty International and the International Red Cross Red

Crescent Societies also do important monitoring and reform work on conditions in detention.

The UN and European monitoring bodies can do no more than bring issues to the attention of the State and encourage their adoption. They only release their reports with the consent of the State; many state reports are not released. In recent human rights litigation the European Court of Human Rights has noted unfulfilled CPT recommendations when assessing the conditions in dispute. For example in the case of *Dybeku* (2007) noted earlier, the court cited the CPT report of 2006 stating that 'Material conditions of detention were appalling in all the pre-trial detention facilities visited' (*Dybeku*, 2007 [21]). The CPT report of 2006 expressed frustration that its earlier report had not been implemented, stating that its later visit 'demonstrated that not a single of the specific recommendations repeatedly made in this respect by the CPT in previous visit reports had been implemented in practice, despite the explicit assurances given to the contrary by the Albanian authorities' (CPT, 2006: par. 23).

In the 2011 case of *Badila v Romania* the court quoted the CPT's 2008 report, in which the CPT 'declared itself gravely concerned by the fact that a lack of beds remained a constant problem ... and that this had remained the case since its first visit to Romania in 1999' (CPT, 2008: par. 70). Resistance to external monitoring was also noted (for example) in the report of the Hungarian Helsinki Committee and the Mental Disability Advocacy Center on Criminal Psychiatric Detention in Hungary (2004).

National human rights institutions

Most countries have bodies such as human rights commissions and ombudsman offices, which have jurisdiction over prisons and other places of detention. Some receive individual complaints; some also have power to make announced and unannounced inspections. France, for example, has had a National Commission of Security Ethics (CNDS), and created the office of the *Contrôleur général des lieux de privation de liberté* following the ratification of OPCAT.[6]

In England and Wales HM Inspectorate of Prisons has been a proactive monitor of prison conditions for many years. Reports are published, and the office is influential at least in publicising failures to protect the dignity and rights of people in detention. The Prisons and Probation Ombudsman also receive complaints from prisoners, and can report on individual and systemic problems in the system.

In 2009, after ratifying the Optional Protocol to the UN Convention Against Torture (OPCAT), the UK established a National Preventive Mechanism (NPM) consisting of 18 existing bodies which visit and inspect places of detention, co-ordinated by the Inspectorate of Prisons as the 'head' NPM. The group includes agencies with oversight both of prisons and of hospitals and mental health care, such as the Prison Independent Monitoring Boards, Inspectorate of Constabulary, Care Quality Commissions, Mental Welfare Commission for Scotland, and Scottish Human Rights Commission. National Preventive Mechanisms are required to have statutory powers and to be granted free access for their visits, and signatory States must agree to publish their reports.

Many European countries also encourage the disclosure of information, including information about conditions in detention, with whistleblower protection legislation, the most comprehensive of which include the UK Public Interest Disclosure Act 1998 (PIDA) and the Norwegian *Act relating to working environment, working hours and employment protection*. All Australian states (and many in the US) have whistleblower protection legislation. In Australia whistleblower disclosure has led to important public inquiries into conditions, for example, in juvenile detention (Om-

---

[6] These agencies may subsequently have been disestablished: International Observatory of Prisons – French section (OIP) 2010.

budsman Victoria, 2010). The Council of Europe recommended in 2010 that all member states develop comprehensive legislation (Council of Europe, 2010).

Local agencies and representatives of civil society

Given space limitations, I will mention the prison monitoring bodies; many other localised visiting groups also exist to act as 'the eyes of the community' in places of detention. Civilian prison monitoring is carried out in various European countries, such as the Prisons Monitoring Boards in Turkey, and the Independent Monitoring Boards (IMBs) and Visiting Committees in the UK. The UK IMBs are located at individual prisons. Members visit prisoners and staff and identify and follow up complaints. They also present public reports on their concerns. In their report in 2012 summarising key issues of concern to IMBs through 2011, the National Council of the IMBs emphasised that the 'issue of healthcare and particularly mental health, were repeatedly raised and of long-term concern' (National Council of the Independent Monitoring Boards, 2012: 3).

Conclusion

The problems of incarcerating the mentally ill are only too clear. All of the evidence indicates that the numbers (and proportion) of offenders with mental illnesses and disabilities will continue to increase. Increasing numbers will enter the prisons, and therefore add to the numbers of people for whom prison itself creates or exacerbates existing mental illness.

In addition to the individual human damage caused, prison management will also become more challenging, with increasing numbers of prisoners who are difficult to manage, difficult to communicate with, and at greater risk of harm to themselves and others.

The solutions are less clear. In this chapter I have outlined three possible drivers for change: human rights litigation, governmental and regional reforms, and monitoring. All have limitations, and all confront often hostile public opinion, together with political pressures to reduce expenditure within the criminal justice system. This is however too important an issue to ignore.

Bibliography

Allison, E. (2011) 'High-security prison unit criticised for holding mentally ill inmates', *The Guardian*, 25 October. Available from http://www.guardian.co.uk/society/2011/oct/25/high-security-prison-mental-illness [12 August 2012].

Australian Institute of Health and Welfare. (2012) *The mental health of prison entrants in Australia 2010.* Bulletin no. 104. Cat. no. AUS 158. Canberra: AIHW.

Bello, T. (2011) 'Mentally ill offenders: Our fear of introducing them back into society'. *The Independent Blogs*, 15 September. Available from http://blogs.independent.co.uk/2011/09/15/mentally-ill-offenders-our-fear-of-introducing-them-back-into-society/ [10 August 2012].

Bradley, K. (2009) *The Bradley Report: Lord Bradley's Review of People with Mental Health Problems or Learning Disabilities in the Criminal Justice System.* London: Central Office of Information.

Centre for Mental Health. (2011) *Briefing 39: Mental health care and the criminal justice system.* London: Centre for Mental Health.

Council of Europe. (2012) *Council of Europe anti-torture Committee publishes report on France and response of the French Government.* Available at: http://www.cpt.coe.int/documents/fra/2012-04-19-eng.htm (Accessed 16 August 2012)

Council of Europe. (2010) *Resolution 1729 (2010) Protection of 'whistle-blowers'.* Available at: http://assembly.coe.int/main.asp?link=/documents/adoptedtext/ta10/eres1729.htm (Accessed 12 August 2012).

CPT (2008) *Report to the Government of Romania on the visit to Romania by the European Committee for the Prevention of Torture and Inhuman or Degrading Treatment or Punishment (CPT) from 8 to 19 June 2006.* Strasbourg: CPT.

CPT (2006) *Report to the Albanian Governmment on the visit to Albania carried out by the European Committee for the Prevention of Torture and Inhuman or Degrading Treatment or Punishment (CPT) from 28 to 31 March 2006.* Strasbourg: CPT.

Edgar, K. and Rickford, D. (2009) *Too little too late: an independent review of unmet mental health need in prison.* Available at: http://www. prisonreformtrust.org.uk/ProjectsResearch/Mentalhealth/Toolittletoolate (16 August 2012).

Fellner, J. (2006) 'A Corrections Quandary: Mental Illness and Prison Rules'. *Harvard Civil Rights-Civil Liberties Law Review*, 41: 391-412.

Hayton, P., Gatherer, A. and Fraser, A. (2010) *Patient or Prisoner: Does it matter which Government Ministry is responsible for the health of prisoners?* Available at: http://www.euro.who.int/__data/assets/pdf_ file/0014/126410/e94423.pdf (16 August 2012).

HM Chief Inspector of Prisons for England and Wales. (2010) *Annual Report 2008-09*. London: The Stationery Office.

HM Inspectorate of Prisons for England and Wales. (1996) *Patient or Prisoner?* London: Home Office.

Hungarian Helsinki Committee and the Mental Disability Advocacy Center. (2004) *Prisoners or Patients: Criminal Psychiatric Detention in Hungary.* Available at: http://www.mdac.info/sites/mdac.info/files/ English_Prisoners%20or%20Patients.pdf (10 August 2012).

National Council of the Independent Monitoring Boards. (2012) *Issues of Concern: Major Issues Raised in Annual Reports to the Secretary of State.* Available at: http://www.justice.gov.uk/downloads/about/imb/imb-issues-concern.pdf (12 August 2012).

Ombudsman Victoria. (2010) *Whistleblowers Protection Act 2001:Investigation into conditions at the Melbourne Youth Justice Precinct.* Victoria: Victorian Government Printer.

Priebe, S., Badesconyi, A., Fioritti, A., Hansson, L., Reinhold, K., Torres-Gonzales, F., Turner, T. and Wiersma, D. (2005) 'Reinstitutionalisation in mental health care: comparison of data on service provision from six European countries'. *BMJ*, 330: 123–6.

Strutin, K. (2012) 'The Realignment of Incarcerative Punishment: Sentencing Reform and the Conditions of Confinement' *William Mitchell Law Review*, 38(4): 1313-1374.

Toch, H. (2008) 'Punitiveness as 'Behaviour Management'. *Criminal Justice and Behaviour*, 35(3): 388-397.

Travis, A. (2011) '£5m scheme to divert mentally ill offenders from prison' *The Guardian*, March 28. Available from http://www.guardian.co.uk/ society/2011/mar/28/divert-mentally-ill-offenders-prison (10 August 2012).

United Nations. (1990) Basic Principles for the Treatment of Prisoners. Available at: http://www.un.org/documents/ga/res/45/a45r111.htm (Accessed 20 February 2014).

United Nations. (1966) *International Covenant on Economic, Social and Cultural Rights*. New York: United Nations. Available at:

http://www.ohchr.org/EN/ProfessionalInterest/Pages/CESCR.aspx (19 February 2014).

United Nations. (1955) *Standard Minimum Rules for the Treatment of Prisoners*. Geneva: United Nations.

World Health Organisation. (2012) *Prisons and Health: Facts and Figures*. Available at: http://www.euro.who.int/en/what-we-do/health-topics/health-determinants/prisons-and-health/facts-and-figures (10 August 2012).

13

The Electronic Monitoring of Offenders in the European Penal Imaginary

Mike Nellis

Introduction

Electronic monitoring (EM) is the use of remote surveillance technologies to pinpoint the locations and/or movements of offenders and/or defendants. It was first used in Europe a quarter century ago, and has become an established – although by no means ubiquitous or dominant – feature of the continent's collective 'penal imaginary', its imagined and projected sense of what it is possible, necessary and legitimate to do with a range of offenders and defendants (Mayer et al., 2003; Nellis et al., 2012). The 'imaginary' remains mosaic-like in the sense that there are still significant differences between countries in both penal priorities and practices, but a pan-European vocabulary for discussing EM has emerged under the auspices of the Conference Permanente Europeene de la Probation (CEP), and more recently the Council of Europe, specifically its Council for Penological Co-operation (2014), which has issued an ethical 'Recommendation' to guide member states' thinking on EM. There are now Europe-wide networks of academics, sentencers, policymakers and probation practitioners, as well as commercial operators and human rights lawyers, who routinely engage in conversations about EM's mundane operations, as well as its potential and dangers, although whether either of these latter factors are fully understood is a moot point. Nonetheless, for the foreseeable future a range of EM technologies will undoubtedly figure in European debates about penal policy and in the broader – and vital – re-imagining of the purpose and nature of imprisonment. The precise technical forms and legal and policy frameworks in which it will be used in different countries, and the scale on which it will develop, are less easy to predict.

Defining Europe at its broadest, EM was used (or at least legislated for) in 2011 in Andorra, Austria, Belgium, Croatia, Cyprus, Czech Republic, Denmark, Estonia, Finland, France, Georgia, Germany, Iceland, Italy, Luxembourg, Netherlands, Norway, Poland, Portugal, Romania, Spain, Catalonia, Sweden, Switzerland, England and Wales, Northern Ireland and Scotland (27 countries). It is not used in Armenia, Azerbaijan, Bosnia-Herzgovina, Greece, Ireland (although it has been piloted), Latvia, Lithuania, Malta, Moldova, Monaco, San Marino, Slovenia and Turkey (13 countries – although this is changing) (Aebi and Marguet, 2012). Radio frequency (RF) EM still remains the commonest technology, (using landline and cellphone networks to enforce curfews or house arrest), but GPS (Global Positioning System) satellite tracking (which, once augmented by cellphone networks, enables the creation and monitoring of exclusion zones as well as anytime-everywhere pinpointing) is increasingly used. Voice verification and remote alcohol monitoring are being experimented with in a few countries. EM is embedded in different legal and administrative modalities for bail, sentencing, and/or post-release and in divergent discourses of 'public protection', 'victim protection' and 'reducing reoffending'. In Sweden, Finland and the Netherlands EM technology has been used to monitor inmates inside open or semi-secure prisons as well as a form of community supervision; whether these constitute 'prisons of the future' remains moot (Kenis et al., 2010).

While EM may be established in Europe, it remains controversial: few user-countries are without some sceptics, even outright opponents, coming from both left and right. In some degree it remains a focus of political and professional debate precisely because the ethical, political and administrative issues it raises as a surveillance technology seem intuitively different in kind from those pertaining to existing community measures and sanctions, many with roots in longstanding humanitarian and public service institutions, and bolstered now by human rights principles. Over 25 years, however, attitudes towards EM have become less sceptical. Initial uncertainties, exaggerated hopes and dystopian anxieties have, especially in the countries which pioneered it, been ameliorated by professional experience and reliable academic research, to the point where there is a strong enough penal constituency in many countries to sustain and legitimate its existence. Across Europe there is a younger generation of politicians, criminal justice professionals and administrators who have never known a world without the availability of EM, and for whom, if penal modernisation is desired, it is always a possible option. Among those wedded to the traditional probation ideals of care, rehabilitation and re-integration, and among those who fear the emergence of 'surveillance societies' more broadly, doubts still linger as to whether it is desirable to invest further resources in EM, particularly in newer technologies, if this, in the longer term, precipitates political dis-investment in an ethic of care.

The need to reduce prison overcrowding, or to toughen existing forms of community supervision or to create entirely new forms of supervision, especially for high risk offenders, figure prominently across the continent in *policy-based* explanations of why EM has been adopted in particular situations. There is, as yet, however, no *sociologically* compelling way to account for the advent and expansion of EM in Europe, or even, for that matter, in particular national jurisdictions: techno-corrections have, in general, been under-theorised. Mainstream theories of penal change have neglected EM and treated it as a somewhat marginal phenomena, arguably under-estimating its appeal and yielding only little guidance as to what its future forms and trajectories might be. At the very least some insights may have been gained from Manuel Castells conception of 'the network society' (2000), because the very existence and availability of EM (unlike say, probation or community service) derives from, indeed depends on, the local availability of a vast 'mega-technical system' of digital information and communication technology – mobile phone networks, the internet, GPS satellites. This infrastructure emerged independently to service neoliberalism (and to some extent American militarism) and to consolidate globalisation, and transcends any specific penal concerns but, crucially, it has afforded late modern governments a multitude of opportunities for e-governance, and in particular, a versatile and potentially significant penal resource. Information and communication technology has facilitated the creation of new surveillance architectures and new permutations of penal discourse, and brought new commercial players into the penal field, often with defence, security or telecommunications backgrounds (Jones, 2006). Over and above anxieties about surveillance technology, the depth and scale of private sector involvement, the sense that EM may have an affinity with neoliberal rationalities (particularly marketisation and rational choice theories of offender motivation), further fuels controversy about it (Paterson, 2007).

Imagining EM in science fiction and futurology

EM was an American invention which, by the time it arrived in Europe (via England and Wales) in the late 1980s and early 1990s, was already becoming an easily implemented, mundane operation, stripped of the futurist (utopian and dystopian) rhetoric with which its early champions and critics alike had infused it. Long before EM actually became an experimental, notionally rehabilitative, technology in the hands of behavioural psychologists Ralph and Robert Schwitzgebel (later Gable) at Harvard University in the

1960s approximations to it – the notion that the locations of convicted criminals could and should be pinpointed and/or tracked had been imagined by science fiction writers and futurologists. The Schwitzgebel's themselves admitted the influence of a science fiction story (about a wearable device, 'the tickler', which seemingly helps people to organise their day) by Fritz Leiber (1962) on their early conception of it (Schwitzgebel and Schwitzgebel, 1973: 151). It was invariably the remote tracking of people's movements rather than 'presence monitoring' in a single location that was being imagined, although in Kuttner and Moore's short story 'Two Handed Engine' (1956) a silent robot was both stationed outside a convicted murderers home while he was indoors, as well as following him everywhere whenever he left it, constantly reporting his whereabouts to the authorities, and stigmatising him in the eyes of passers-by. Robert Sheckley's (1953) much anthologised short story 'Watchbird' posited a technology more akin to unmanned aerial vehicles ('drones') than tagging or tracking via a wearable device, but its idea of a targeted, individualised, pre-emptive approach to crime prevention – the remote mind wave-reading watchbirds can detect and zap a person on the verge of committing acts of violence – shared the pinpointing principle with what was later to be called 'electronic monitoring'. Larry Niven's (1972) hovering 'copseyes' were similar devices, safeguarding strolling women from creeps and predators, although unlike Sheckley he approved of incapacitative zapping. Anthony and Magroff's (1968) *The Ring* – a wearable device wired into the offender's nervous system (a quasi-implant) may have been an extrapolation of Schwitzgebel's actual experiments, insofar as it worked by conditioning-out bad behaviour, and inflicting pain if aggression was contemplated. The authors obliquely commended this fictional form of 'disciplinary probation' as 'the best solution to the problem [of reoffending] in the history of penology' (Anthony and Magroff, 1968: 58).

The Schwitzgebels were Skinnerian behaviourists who disagreed that punishment was an effective means of changing offenders' behaviour; preferring encouragement, approval and reward for successful compliance with rules as a better way of eliciting law-abiding behaviour. They confidently anticipated significant reductions in the use of imprisonment if their technology was adopted (Schwitzgebel et al., 1964). Others believed that 'the development of [computerised] systems for telemetering information from sensors implanted in or on the body will soon make possible the observation and control of human behaviour without actual physical contact' – including remote stimulation of the brain (Ingraham and Smith, 1972: 35). They conceived of this as a quasi-medical treatment modality rather than punishment, but its totalitarian connotations were obvious not only to influential leftist critics like Nancy Mitford (1973) (who saw the more innocuous 'Schwitzgebel machine' in the same terms), but more widely, and such cachet as these measures once had was erased during the mid-nineteen seventies backlash against behaviourism, and the broader decline of the rehabilitative ideal.

Computer scientist Joseph Meyer's (1971) proposal for a terrestrial 'transponder (not satellite-based) surveillance system' was explicitly about deterrence, not treatment, and somewhat more attuned to the emerging political mood. He envisaged a nationwide network of computerised transceivers attached to buildings which would monitor in real-time unique radio-frequency signals from transponders on the wrists of 25 million convicted criminals. Even in 1971 he considered it technically feasible to programme individualised curfew and territorial restrictions into the system, and for some transceivers to trigger a sonic alarm if an offender approached it. The actual form of EM developed a decade later for Albuquerque-based Judge Jack Love was used in the punitive vein Meyer anticipated to enforce curfews and daytime home detention, although it had no capacity for tracking. Short range radio-frequency (RF) based technology, using an ankle tag and a home monitoring unit linked to the telephone system, initially became the defining modality of EM, which spread steadily from the US to Canada, Australia, England and Wales, Sweden and the Netherlands. In England and Wales, Tom Stacey's Offenders' Tag Association (founded 1981) also promoted a terrestrially-based tracking system rather than curfews, while settling for what the available RF technology could do at the time (Stacey, 2006).

Tracking remained, however, the imagined ideal of EM. Although science fiction writers had anticipated orbiting observation and communication satellites before the Russians launched Sputnik in 1957, the navigation and location monitoring potential of GPS, devised by the American military (and secret until the 1970s), seems neither to have been anticipated nor extrapolated upon by science fiction, nor to have exited the imaginations of futurologists, and certainly not seen to have correctional applications. The offender in the one well-known tracking story from the 1970s has 'undergone the implantation of a Telltale, the miniaturised broadcaster which always betrayed his location to the computers of the telemachine complex', but it was unspecified if signals from satellites enabled this (Bunn, 1974: 185). Even in 1991, when Colorado probation officer Max Winkler proposed a shift from 'first generation' EM house arrest to a better, 'second generation' of tracking technology (and a better still, in his view, 'third generation' involving tracking, implants and remote zapping), he thought in terms of the burgeoning mobile telephony system rather than GPS as the basis of it. Winkler (1991) (who was not the only probation officer to toy with tracking at this time) called the proposed approach 'walking prisons', although the term begs the question of whether a trope grounded in the notion of 'confinement' is an apt or accurate way to characterise the type of disciplinary regime created by EM, or of projecting how it actually feels to experience this type of punishment. Against a backcloth of much improved pinpointing and smaller, wearable GPS equipment, a number of commercial defence contractors, casting around for new markets in the aftermath of the post-Cold War peace dividend, and stimulated by probation interest, soon recognised the correctional potential of 'tracking'. The first pilots took place in the US in the late 1990s, and then spread elsewhere, as RF technology had done before it.

To a significant extent, the development of EM has been haunted by its precursors in science fiction, not least because a Spider-man comic strip (in which a villain locks an armband radio transmitter to the superhero, primed to explode if removed without a special key) became part of the legend of its origins. Jack Love randomly gave the strip, among other papers, to Michael Goss when he asked him if 'electronic monitoring' was possible, but its significance has been exaggerated (Burrell and Gable, 2008). Like many twentieth century innovations, EM has often been glibly described as 'science fiction come true', but not always in a good way. Its imagined dystopian potential has coloured much debate about it, and it has been prone to thin-end-of-the-wedge criticism, aimed not so much at the practical forms it currently takes (which may be just-to-say acceptable) but at the more dangerous forms it might – or will – take in the future. Meanwhile, I will describe the mundane ways in which policymakers and practitioners in Europe have sought to imagine and deploy EM, rationalising it in much the same way as traditional alternatives or post-release measures, as something which enables the person to remain in (or return to) the community, accessible to work, able to support his or her family, benefit from positive community ties – all of which are indeed ruptured when imprisonment is imposed.

Implementing EM in Western Europe

England and Wales, Sweden and the Netherlands were the first European countries to show serious interest in EM, in the mid-1990s, and although they shared a rhetorical commitment to 'modernising' criminal justice, adapting to perceived new challenges, they were to implement it in rather different ways. England and Wales pioneered it in a 1989-90 EM bail-pilot at a time when a right-wing government was pushing the probation service away from its social work base towards becoming an agency of 'punishment in the community', openly threatening its replacement with voluntary or private sector organisations if it did not comply. EM technology, delivered by a private company, was used to threaten probation interests, intensifying the latter's hostility towards it, who branded it an unwelcome 'American' import and hyped up its Orwellian implications. It nonetheless became a nationally available stand-alone sentence, and an early release from prison scheme, which were mostly unintegrated with social work, in 1999.

Both Sweden and the Netherlands had already established national EM-curfew schemes (in 1996) by this time, embedding them within their probation services and integrating them with social work, rather than following the English stand-alone model. This reflected the strength of their indigenous social democratic and liberal traditions, but also their fear that the English approach, by polarising probation and EM, risked losing the benefits that EM could bring to probation. The Swedes always spoke of '*intensive supervision with* electronic monitoring' (ISEM), and sought to ensure its use as an alternative to short custodial sentences. The ISEM regime required offenders to be involved in employment or education, to participate in offending behaviour programmes, and to submit to house arrest at all other times.

Unlike the British government, the Swedish and Dutch governments both sought to overcome the resistance to EM from traditional probation officers by winning their support for it rather than setting it up as a rival form of supervision. Commercial providers were used only to supply equipment and technical back-up to publicly-funded agencies. In England, the probation service acquiesced in the existence of three private sector providers, believing that if EM failed (as many officers hoped it would), nothing would reflect badly on them – but it also gave them the perfect excuse to ignore EM and avoid debate on its merits. Probation attitudes to the technology, if not its commercial delivery, became more emollient, as a younger generation of officers, more used to tech-gadgets, adapted to the times. Sweden, the Netherlands and England and Wales came to represent distinct models of EM service delivery, and all three were often consulted by other European countries who considered using EM.

Uniquely among western European countries with well-established probation services, the Federal Republic of Germany never established RF EM as a nationally available measure, and at the root of that has been a different way of imagining what it represents. Individual regions (*land*) have had the discretion to implement it since 2000, but only Hesse has sustained it. In essence, even in the 1990s and subsequently, state-surveilled home detention retained a totalitarian taint in Germany, as something redolent of the Stasi, whose mass surveillance in the former East Germany always showed a high degree of technological ingenuity. Social work academics also pressed the argument – *contra* Sweden's efforts to blend EM with social work – that the very nature of EM was simply incompatible with the inherently dialogical, relational nature of social work (Lindenberg, 2003), and, to a lesser extent, EM was held at bay by a right wing constituency who disdained its limited punitiveness. The Hesse scheme, adapting the Swedish intensive supervision model, focused on those whose lifestyles would not otherwise be sufficiently stable for them to gain benefit from a rehabilitative community sanction, has been successful in terms of completion and reducing recidivism, although its critics contend that this could have been achieved by different, better, non-technological means (Jessen, 2009). Paradoxically perhaps, given the deep cultural resistance to RF EM in Germany, the Federal government did adopt GPS satellite tracking in 2012 as a nationwide measure following a ruling by the European Court of Human Rights (ECHR) that forbade the extended imprisonment of still risky sex offenders beyond the end of their original sentence, and required their release.

Neither Italy nor Greece have well established probation services, or traditions of using community penalties systematically. Italy legislated to use EM in 2003 as a means of enforcing an existing house arrest measure at the pre-trial stage, under the control of the police and the Ministry of the Interior. Hardly any orders have been made (fourteen up to 2013). EM is not apparently liked by the judiciary, nor by the police, whose traditional enforcement of house arrest sentences by random home visits is seemingly threatened by EM. This failure to implement EM occurred despite Italy having had seriously overcrowded prisons for some time, and resorting to an emergency early release programme in October 2012. Memories of fascism seem not to have been a factor.

Greece, like Germany, has traditionally shown antipathy towards surveillance technologies generally, certainly public space CCTV, even including speed cameras, associating them with its years of dictatorship (Samatas, 2004). In 2013 RF EM-house arrest was mooted as a possible cheaper alternative to prison, partly because of the country's dire economic situation, but also – cynics have suggested – because the politicians incriminated in the recent financial crises will prefer to serve time at home rather than in prison. The use of EM in Portugal, on the other hand, which also had a history of dictatorship, seems not to have been tainted by cultural memories from that era, although the form of pre-trial EM-bail that Portuguese judges consider acceptable requires full 24 hour house arrest (with discretionary authorised absences for family crises, hospitalisation etc), sometimes for periods of up to a year or more (but usually less). This is not the preferred model in western Europe, which tends to restrict EM-home confinement to part of the day, allowing offenders and defendants 'free-time' to demonstrate that they are engaging in rehabilitative and re-integrative activities and, as crucially, to take the pressure off other members of a household with whom the offender is confined.

In Eastern Europe, where EM spread in the twenty-first century in conjunction with democratising initiatives, some Balkans and the Baltic states, which had previously used house arrest as a penal measure enforced by the police, have also considered that a '24 hour lockdown' model of EM is defensible, and actually consistent with human rights simply because the prison conditions in which the person would otherwise be serving time are often appalling. Morgerstern (2009) cites evidence from Estonia which suggests that EM was not in fact needed to bring about the conditional early release from prison that it was claimed to have facilitated. This raises an important question: under what conditions do governments come to imagine that technological innovation (as opposed to reconfigurations of humanistic measures) is a plausible and legitimate solution to perceived social or administrative problems, a publicly understood signifier of penal progress?

Spain is interesting in this respect. The modernising socialist government which came to power in 2005 introduced a range of legal and social measures to combat the long-neglected problem of domestic violence, including, for the first time in Europe, the use of GPS tracking as a means of enforcing restraining orders, to keep perpetrators and victims apart. Both offender and victim wear a tracking device, enabling real-time detection of any approach by the offender to the victim, whether at their home, workplace or in public space; any violation results in alerts being communicated to both parties, and the police. Politically, the insertion of sophisticated technology into arrangements for belatedly dealing with domestic violence signalled not only strong governmental commitment to overdue modernisation (and notionally to feminism), but also the seriousness and determination with which the issue was being addressed (Gonzalez, 2009). Sweden, Portugal and France have all emulated this use of GPS tracking, on a small scale, although countries with less to prove in challenging domestic violence have not felt as pressured to adopt EM in this context, at least up to now.

To sum up, EM is now used in some shape or form in almost thirty countries in Western and Eastern Europe. No one jurisdiction uses all the available technologies, legal options or pro-grammes – and nowhere uses it on a vast scale. However, there is no doubt of EMs versatility: it can be constructed as a solution (or part-solution) to a wide range of perceived penal problems. What some countries have found acceptable others have found unaccep-table, e.g. using EM on juveniles. Some countries have not used it at all, and a full account of why and how EM is permeating Euro-pean penal practice (or not) must be as attentive to the 'resisters' as well as 'accommodators'. These facts alone militate against any kind of simple 'technological determinist' account of EM's devel-opments and lend themselves much more to a 'social construc-tivist' account. The very varied scale and pace of EM's expansion suggests that differences of culture and tradition, and of contem-porary political configurations, have shaped the legal and admin-istrative forms in which the technology is set. On the other hand, whatever the differences, EM has been adopted in some degree in a lot of jurisdictions in a distinct twenty-five year period, suggest-ing that some consistent influences have been at work, as well as a consistent cultural and political receptivity to its general appeal.

Theorising EM as a socio-technical innovation

The reason why it has thus far been difficult to give a compelling theoretical explanation for EM's development may derive from the sociologically inadequate way in which its nature has been described. Commonplace terms like 'home detention', 'home con-finement', 'prison without bars', 'prison without inmates', even 'vir-tual prison' connote images of sequestration and affinities with traditional forms of penal restraint. EM can replicate these forms, but it does so telemetrically, acting at a distance, using radio waves and optic fibres more than bricks and mortar, and it does not ul-timately incapacitate in the way that the locks, bolts and bars of prison do. The fact that even the most basic forms of RF EM re-quire a nationwide electronic infrastructure is often underplayed in discussions of its adoption, and it is here that the concept of a 'penal imaginary' as the *sole* framework in which decisions about the use of EM must be supplemented with the concept of a 'socio-technical imaginary', defined as 'imagined forms of social life and social order that center on the development and fulfilment of innovative scientific and/or technological projects' (Jasanoff et al., 2009: 1). Despite extensive transnational co-ordination of techno-scientific research, countries still vary in their aspirations and capacities for technological innovation, and in the spheres of life in which they prioritise its application, but few elites in Europe have been immune to the allure of the high-tech corporate futurism that defines 'modern' in contemporary capitalism, with its relentless emphasis on speed, cool and the aesthetics of efficiency. It is at the intersection of socio-technical and penal imaginaries, and in the melding of the hitherto separate policy networks that create and sustain e-governance, that the forms and trajectories of EM are being determined.

Portraying EM as too akin to *existing* community measures obscures its distinct, technical character as a form of remote, real-time surveillance which makes possible what William Mitchell (1999) has called 'economies of presence' (notionally cost-effective mixes of 'actual' and 'virtual' contact with offenders), and enables the unprecedentedly meticulous monitoring of mobility and location of thousands of people on a vast national scale, from just one or two monitoring centres. Those monitored must themselves respond to the partly automated demands of the system (precise curfew times, texted warnings of lateness and proximity to the perimeter of an exclusion zone), as well as personal contact with monitoring officers, and engage in 'regulated self-regulation' (Crawford, 2003) to demonstrate their compliance with the regime. Traditional community alternatives, whatever their more humanistic merits, cannot replicate this modality of enforcement, least of all its approximation to sustained (and with GPS, incessant) 'real-time' oversight (a key selling point over probation in EM-company advertisements). Although EM has primarily been used (where it has not simply net-widened) as an alternative to short custodial sentences – of under a year, often much less – there is no clear data in Europe on the length of time people are spending on EM as a post-release measure. Anecdotes suggest that while parolees may well be on it for several years, the vast majority experience it for only short, though maybe intermittent, periods.

There is no straightforward way of answering what the optimum period of EM is (in terms of bearability for individuals and families), because its 'punitivity' can be eased or accentuated by varying its intensity over time, graduating the daily curfew hours, reducing the number of requirements it is combined with and relaxing the severity of enforcement. Evidence from offenders themselves suggest they do find EM punitive, mentally demanding, and stressful on them and their families (Vanhaelemeesch and Vander Beken, 2013). Some do emphasise a sense of confinement, others a sense of being watched, and not all prefer it to imprisonment. Some have nonetheless welcomed the degree of accountability it imposes on them to demonstrate compliance and desistance (Hucklesby, 2008; 2009).

Adopting a socio-technical perspective on EM's development, as opposed to a more narrowly penal one, arguably makes it easier to understand and contextualise EM as one among many emergent forms of surveillance, and to grasp that its future trajectories may be shaped as much by attitudes to technology as by attitudes to punishment. EM's champions have often been ambivalent about formally calling it 'surveillance' precisely because, in Anglophone countries, the term has sinister connotations and easily evokes the spectre of Orwell's Big Brother – something which liberal critics of EM have understandably exploited to the full. Even when decisions to use EM are taken within traditional (penal) policy communities, the normalisation of surveillance practices in other fields of security (CCTV, DNA databases, interception of electronic communications, no-fly lists), gives it a political and cultural legitimacy as a specifically penal measure that it may not otherwise have gained, or gained as quickly. Mathiesen (2013) has documented the emergence of a transnational 'surveillance state' apparatus in late twentieth century Europe, borne of concerns about organised crime, migration, asylum seeking and, after 9/11, in 2001, terrorism. He does not specifically address EM, but with such vast state/ commercial investment in other surveillance practices, lingering qualms about monitoring the whereabouts of ordinary criminals are easily dispelled. In a world in which ordinary citizens utilise unobtrusive pinpointing technologies (mobile phones), and barely register the digital trails and traces left by their credit cards and social media, caring little for the loss of locational privacy that this entails, the case for pinpointing the locations of harmful people in real-time seems unproblematic and nondescript; it is not easily depicted as ethically problematic, or even draconian.

Notwithstanding the existence of some 'populist punitive' constituencies in most European countries, which oppose the use of EM because it is insufficiently punitive, and which have in some jurisdictions impeded EM's expansion, the understanding of EM as something with 'technological momentum' precisely because it is part of an ever more pervasive electronic infrastructure does support the liberal case for fearing it. Liberal critics rightly fret that the humanistic values and practices traditionally associated with probation (challenges to offenders' attitudes and behaviour as well as care and support) will sooner or later be eclipsed by impersonal surveillance technology (why will governments continue to pay for both if surveillance proves 'good enough', and cheap, on its own?) without making much difference to the overall use of imprisonment. A crude 'technological determinism' – if it can be done it will be done – coupled with a mistrust of governments under pressure to reduce penal costs, and tempted by corporate promises of efficient control, has often underpinned these anxieties, but it is not entirely without foundation, especially if appealing new forms of EM become available.

In his recent satirical dystopian novel, Dave Eggers (2013: 420-422) has plausibly imagined what near-future forms of 'electronic monitoring' might look like, at least in affluent parts of the US (or Europe). He depicts a vast American tech company – The Circle – which has superseded Facebook, Google, Apple and Microsoft, incorporating and extending all their capacities for real-time search, data-gathering and communication, and accentuating their aspirations, not least continuous technical innovation and diversification into new products which are commensurate with its corporate credo of 'all that happens must be known'. One such extends the idea of Neighbourhood Watch into an environment saturated by ubiquitous computing, in which every home can digitally monitor all local residents as colour-coded avatars whose fingerprints, retinas, phones and body profile are all known to the system. Visiting strangers would show up in a different colour, until someone local vouches for them, or not. Registered ex-offenders would then show up in another colour, and a response would be mobilised. What makes this 'next step' seem plausible is the ease with which it could be customised from available infrastructures and data – its core logic comes from existing community notification of sex offender schemes, and it trades on well-established, socially generated fears, but its allure comes from an already viable and taken-for-granted digital communications architecture, and the commercial futurist ethos which projects unquestioned confidence in technology to create perfect security.

Conclusion

The social, economic and political environment in which contemporary penal policy is made changed irrevocably in the last quarter century. The socio-technological milieu in which all life in the twenty-first century West is lived cannot be wished away, and by degrees is re-calibrating the European penal imaginary. The affordances which make EM possible must simply be taken for granted, and allowed to play a part in re-imagining better forms of penality, while simultaneously serving as a warning of dangerous possibilities (on which, see Toombs, 1995). From Portugal, Nuno Caiado (2012) rightly makes the point that EM technology is not so significant that it can transform penal practice in its own right, but not so insignificant that it could not be used to create new and better forms of alternative to custody. Caiado invites thorough deliberation on its potential – not exaggerating it, but not trivialising or marginalising it either. Serendipitously, this formulation neatly blends the tension between 'technological determinism' and 'social constructivism', recognising that the material drivers of EM are politically irresistible, but insisting that fully informed professionals still have leeway to shape the policy and practice frameworks in which it is used. The European record on EM so far confirms that this has been so, but Jacques Ellul's (1964) fear that *la technique* (a hegemonic mix of managerial and technical praxis) remains to be reckoned with: he considered a 'police state' a near inevitability once meticulous means of surveilling citizens behaviour became feasible. Among more recent Catholic social theorists, Paul Virilio (1997) has engaged with the implications of digital technology but shares Ellul's pessimism about the cultural and political direction in which it is taking us. Whether EM can remain, or fully become, what the late Ivan Illich (1973) called a 'tool for conviviality', a modest technology fully subordinated to larger humanistic and democratic ideals, serving in this instance to help re-imagine the scale on which imprisonment is used, remains a daunting penal challenge.

Bibliography

Aebi, M. F. and Marguet, Y. (2012) *SPACE II: Council of Europe Annual Penal Statistics: persons serving non-custodial sanctions.* Strasbourg: Council of Europe.

Anthony, P. and Magroff, R. E. (1968) *The Ring.* New York: Tor Books.

Bunn, C. (1974) 'And Keep Us from Our Castles'. In: Olander, J. D. and Greenberg, M. H. eds' *Criminal Justice through Science Fiction.* New York: New Viewpoints.

Burrell, W. and Gable, R. (2008) 'From B F Skinner to Spiderman to Martha Stewart: the past, present and future of electronic monitoring of offenders'. *Journal of Offender Rehabilitation* 46(3/4): 101-118.

Caiado, N. (2012) 'The Third Way: an agenda for electronic monitoring in the next decade'. *Journal of Offender Monitoring* 24(1) 5-10.

Castells, M. (2000) *The Rise of the Network Society. 2nd edition.* Oxford: Blackwell.

Crawford, A. (2003) 'Contractual Governance of Deviant Behaviour'. *Journal of Law and Society*, 30(4): 479-505.

Council for Penological Co-operation (2014) *Recommendation on Electronic Monitoring.* Strasbourg: Council of Europe.

Eggers, D. (2013) *The Circle.* New York: Knopf.

Ellul, J. (1964) *The Technological Society.* New York: Knopf.

Gonzalez, A. V. (2009) *La Transformation de la Regulacion Mediante Las Practicas de Monitorizacion Electronica.* PhD Thesis. Universitat Autonoma Barcelona.

Hucklesby, A. (2009) 'Understanding Offender's Compliance: A case study of electronically monitored curfew orders'. *Journal of Law and Society*, 36(2): 248-71.

Hucklesby, A. (2008) 'Vehicles of Desistance? The impact of electronically monitored curfew orders'. *Criminology and Criminal Justice*, 8: 51-71.

Illich, I. (1973) *Tools for Conviviality.* London: Fontana.

Ingraham, B. L. and Smith, G. S. (1972) 'The Use of Electronics in the Observation and Control of Human Behavior and its Possible Use in Rehabilitation and Parole'. *Issues in Criminology*, 7(2): 35-53.

Jasanoff, S., Kim, S. H. and Sperling, S. (2009) *Sociotechnical Imaginaries and Science and Technology Policy: a cross national comparison.* A Research Proposal. Cambridge, Mass: Harvard University.

Jessen, D. (2009) *The Implementation of Electronic Monitoring in Germany.* A Research Proposal. Max Planck Institute for Foreign and International Criminal Law.

Jones, R. (2006) "Architecture", criminal justice and control'. In: Armstrong, S. and McAra, L. eds. *Perspectives on Punishment: the contours of control.* Oxford: Oxford University Press.

Kenis, P., Kruyen, P. M., Baaijens, J. and Barneveld, P. (2010) 'The Prison of the Future? An Evaluation of an Innovative Prison Design in the Netherlands'. *The Prison Journal*, 90(3): 313-330.

Kuttner, H. and Moore, C. E. (1955) 'Two Handed Engine'. *The Magazine of Fantasy and Science Fiction* 9(2): 3-23.

Leiber, F. (1962) 'The Creature from Cleveland Depths'. *Galaxy*, 21(2): 2-25.

Lindenberg, M. (2003) 'From Social Work to Control Work: An observation on electronic monitoring and its impact on social work'. In: Mayer, M., Haverkamp, R. and Levy, R. eds. *Will Electronic Monitoring Have a Future in Europe?* Freiberg: Max Planck Institute.

Mayer, M., Haverkamp, R. and Levy, R. (2003) *Will Electronic Monitoring Have a Future in Europe?* Freiberg: Max Planck Instute.

Meyer, J. A. (1971) 'Crime Deterrent Transponder System'. *Aerospace and Electronic Systems*, 7(1): 2-22.

Mitchell, W. J. (1999) *E-topia.* Cambridge, Mass: The MIT Press.

Mitford, N. (1973) *Kind and Unusual Punishment: The prison business.* New York: Knopf.

Mathiesen, T. (2013) *Towards a Surveillant Society.* Winchester: Waterside press.

Morgerstern, C. (2009) 'European Initiatives for Harmonisation and Minimum Standards in the Field of Community Sanctions and Measures'. *European Journal of Probation*, 1(2): 128-141.

Niven, L. (1972) 'Cloak of Anarchy'. *Analog*, March: 74-92.

Nellis, M., Beyens, K. and Kaminski, D. (2012) *Electronically Monitored Punishment: international and critical Perspectives.* London: Routledge.

Paterson, C. (2007) 'Commercial Crime Control and the Electronic Monitoring of Offenders in England and Wales'. *Social Justice*, 34(3-4): 98-110.

Samatas, M. (2004) *Surveillance in Greece: From Anticommunist to Consumer Surveillance.* New York: Pella.

Stacey, T. (2006) 'Electronic Tagging of Offenders: A global view'. *International Review of Law, Computers and Technology*, 20(1): 117-121.

Toombs, M. (1995) 'Monitoring and Controlling Criminal Offenders Using the Satellite Global Positioning System Coupled to Surgically Implanted Transponders; is it viable?' *Criminal Justice Policy Review*, 7(3-4): 341-346.

Schwitzgebel, R. L. and Schwitzgebel, R. K. eds. (1973) *Psychotechnology: Electronic control of mind and behaviour*. New York: Holt, Rinehart and Winston.

Schwitzgebel, R. L., Schwitzgebel, R. K., Pahnke, W. N. and Sprech Hurd, W. (1964) 'A Programme of Research in Behavioral Electronics'. *Behavioral Science*, 9(3): 233-238.

Sheckley, R. (1953) 'Watchbird'. *Galaxy Science Fiction*, February: 74-95.

Vanhaelemeesch, D. and Vander Beken, T. (2012) 'Electronic Monitoring: Convict's experiences in Belgium'. In: Cools, M., de Ruyver, B., Easton, M., Pauwels, L., Ponsaers, P., Vande Walle, G., Vander Beken, T., Vander Laenen, F., Verhage, A., Vermeulen, G., Vynckier, G. eds. *Social Conflicts, Citizens and Policing*. Antwerp: Government of Security Research Paper Series (GofS) Series 6.

Virilio, P. (1997) *Open Sky*. London: Verso.

Winkler, M. (1991) 'Walking Prisons: the developing technology of electronic controls'. *The Futurist*, July-August: 34-36.

14

Prison Education across Europe: Policy, Practice, Politics

Anne Costelloe and Kevin Warner

Introduction

The provision of some form of education for those held in prison has been a common feature of the modern penitentiary since its inception. In Europe today, virtually all countries have education available in at least some of their prisons, although there is great variety in what is provided. This chapter identifies and examines two of the root causes of this variation, firstly, different understandings of the aims of, and possibilities afforded by, education in prison, and secondly, the fact that the type of education provided in different countries mirrors the attitude to people held in prison in that country. It is argued that the way prison education is conceived and how the person in prison is perceived are two sides of the same coin.

The chapter begins by outlining, in broad-brush fashion, some of the main approaches to prison education in Europe, contrasting in particular those based on an adult and community education perspective with those which adopt employment-focused or offence-focused approaches. It is held that learning grounded in an adult education philosophy offers a far richer and more authentic form of education. Such education can facilitate changes in a learner's perception, attitudes, and worldview that are more likely to be truly transformative and lasting. The second part of

238

the chapter is an analysis of different concepts of the imprisoned person. It explores how the more negative or restrictive of these concepts hollow out and curtail the kind of education offered.

An illustration of how the perception of men or women held in prison shapes the education offered may be seen in comparing two 2005 publications, from the Norwegian and British governments. Norway's White Paper on education in prison, *Another Spring* (Norway Ministry of Education and Research, 2005), takes a wider and more holistic view of the prisoner's needs than a Green Paper on the same subject in England, *Reducing Re-offending Through Skills and Employment* (England and Wales, Ministry of Education and Skills, 2005). What comes across most strongly in the Norwegian document is that the person in prison is primarily a *citizen*, entitled as such to *rights* to education. However, in the English document, he or she is primarily an *offender* and the concern is with 'outcomes', the primary one being to stop or reduce re-offending, a far narrower perspective. Regarding the person in prison as a citizen or member of society reflects a 'penal welfare' or characteristic Council of Europe way-of-thinking; seeing him or her mainly as an offender is a narrower perspective more in keeping with the 'culture of control' or 'the new punitiveness' (Garland, 2001; Pratt et al., 2005).

Approaches to prison education

Seeing the person in prison as a citizen, a member of society, is central to Council of Europe penal policy in general and prison education policy in particular. The Council's policy on prison education is set out most fully in *Education in Prison* (1990), and this is endorsed strongly in the *European Prison Rules* (Council of Europe, 2006). Imprisoned men and women are regarded as entitled to a form of adult education that those in the community outside should have available to them.[1] The Council of Europe sees adult education as 'a fundamental factor of equality of educational opportunity and cultural democracy', and sees it as promoting 'the development of the active role and critical attitudes of women and men, as parents, producers, consumers, users of the mass media, citizens and members of their community' (Council of Europe, 1990: 17-18).

This wide view of the role of adult education is emphasised also in the most recent European Union Council policy statement on lifelong learning:

> In the period up to 2020, the primary goal of European co-operation should be to support the further development of education and training systems in the Member States which are aimed at ensuring: (a) the personal, social and professional fulfilment of all citizens; (b) sustainable economic prosperity and employability, whilst promoting democratic values, social cohesion, active citizenship, and intercultural dialogue (European Union Council, 2009: 1).

Returning to the Council of Europe's kindred policy, adult education is 'seen to be about participating and experiencing rather than about the passive absorption of knowledge and skills; it is a means by which people explore and discover personal and group identity' (Council of Europe, 1990: 18). Thus, a key recommendation in *Education in Prison* is that all prisoners should have access to a wide curriculum, the aim being 'to develop the whole person bearing in mind his or her social, economic and cultural context' (Council of Europe, 1990: 8). The approach here is very clearly to see the person in prison as a full citizen and as a 'whole person'.

---

[1] Various other international bodies uphold the right to education, including the European Convention for the Protection of Human Rights and Fundamental Freedoms, the Charter of Fundamental Rights enforced through the Lisbon Treaty, and the United Nations General Assembly (see Conclusion below). The 4th International UNESCO Conference on Adult Education declared the 'right to learn', which included 'the right to read and write ... to question and analyse ... to imagine and create ... to develop individual and collective skills'.

However, developments in prison education in some countries suggest a distinct retreat from that holistic perception.

In Council of Europe policy, prison education is understood to have a further role, in addition to those just described – that of counteracting the negative impact of the institution, limiting 'the damage done to men and women through imprisonment' (1990: 15). All these important functions lie behind the Council's assertion that 'education shall have no less a status than work within the prison regime and prisoners shall not be disadvantaged financially or otherwise by taking part in education' (2006: 28.4).

While such policy on prison education is clear, provision (and the philosophy behind that provision) varies considerably across countries. In places, comprehensive programmes of education that are well-resourced and based on Council of Europe principles are offered to all in prison, while elsewhere there are only patchy offerings of weak and narrow forms of learning.

The different approaches to education in prison evident across Europe can be categorised in three broad typologies (see European Commission, 2011). First, provision is embedded in a traditional and wide mainstream secondary school curriculum, but oriented towards the interests and needs of adults. Second, training programmes are focused more on employability than traditional education and are almost exclusively centred on basic skills and vocational training. Third, programmes are offence-focused and provide courses influenced directly by the prison context (elaborated in more detail below). Of course, combinations of these elements exist, with countries giving different weightings to the different types of education. It is important to note here that, while each of the above is essentially different, they are viewed by some as being interchangeable, and are often all lumped together under the label of 'education'. Such variance in provision and philosophy continues even while individual countries remain signed up to well-defined Council of Europe and European Union principles and policies.

Understanding the difference between education and training is crucial. In essence, training is the learning of a skill, learning how to do something, and is focused on employability. Education, on the other hand, is concerned with understanding, and with the values generated from that understanding, and is focused ultimately on developing the capacity for critical reflection. Training tends to be measured by what you can do when you have completed it, education is measured by what you know and your ability to apply and analyse that knowledge. This is why we contend that much of the employment-focused 'education' provided in some countries does not constitute education as it is understood generally in the field of adult education, or indeed 'prison education' as understood by the Council of Europe.

A crucial quality of the adult education approach is that it is an end in itself, not just a means to an end as is the case with employment-focused and offence-focused courses. The essence of adult education is that it facilitates the learner in developing as a 'whole person bearing in mind his or her social, economic and cultural context'. In this process, adult education promotes significant creative and critical thinking (see Brookfield, 1987), the development of which can lead to profound and lasting change in a person's conscientisation, worldview and direction. This perspective transformation (see Mezirow, 2000) entails three significant dimensions – psychological, convictional and behavioural – which lead to and mirror three incremental changes in the learner. These are changes in understanding of the self, changes in belief systems, and changes in behaviour (see also Clark, 1993). Its potential for prisoner education is the same as in the community outside and lies in the learner's capacity to transform perceptions of self and others. It is these perceptions that determine the way people act.

To illustrate this further, it is useful to analyse various approaches to adult literacy learning in Europe. Once again, even the labels used tell us much about the attitudes held, and while to the non-educationalist the distinction may seem subtle, they are telling. For example, in England, literacy learning is referred to as basic or functional skills and its relevance for prison education is closely aligned to employability and up-skilling the prisoner. Basic skills is synonymous with the concept of functional literacy. This concept sees literacy to be a cogitative skill, the ability to read and write. It is a skill that can be taught just like learning to drive and nothing more.

In Ireland, with its emphasis on the adult education approach, the conceptualisation of literacy is based in the ideal of critical literacy. This view of literacy considers it to be intellectual transformation. It is more than the simple acquisition of a skill. Instead, through the process of learning that skill, the learner's cognitive and intellectual development is enhanced and transformed. Proponents would suggest that 'reading is understanding the world, writing is reshaping it' (Hughes and Spark, n.d.). In this way, literacy is seen as an empowering and powerful tool used to reshape our lives and the world in which we live. We contend that adult education in general (and accordingly prison education grounded in the adult education tradition) operates in much the same manner and is of similar fundamental importance (see Bailey, 2004).[2]

The curtailment of prison education

Limitations to the education offered to those in prison arise, in particular, when they are *not* perceived as citizens, members of society, or as whole persons. When men and women in prison are represented merely as 'offenders', or seen mainly in relation to the labour market, or demonised, or thought of as 'other', then a full and appropriate form of education will tend not to be offered to them. The term 'offender' is particularly offensive, being both one-

---

[2] Inez Bailey states: 'Adult education can make a major contribution both in meeting the skill requirements of a rapidly changing workforce, as well as improving social cohesion and equity in the emergence of a broadly inclusive and proactive civil society. The inclusion of a philosophy of literacy as broader than just workforce development distinguishes literacy in Ireland from the market-driven rhetoric that is dominant in U.K. and U.S. policy in this area.' (2004: 198).

dimensional and negative, as if there were no other aspects to their lives and personalities (Costelloe and Warner, 2008).

A 'culture of control' and a 'new punitiveness' are seen to dominate penal policy in English-speaking countries of late. Such thinking and attitude gives us a very different picture of those in prison to their positive characterisation by the Council of Europe. Punitive thinking holds diminished and very negative views of the person in prison. Consequently, even where education is offered, there will be a tendency among authorities holding such views to restrict this provision in a number of ways, notwithstanding the urgings of the European institutions. Four examples of such limiting or distorting are given below. It should be noted, however, that in many places several of these restrictive attitudes may operate together.

The 'criminogenic' curtailment

If the person in prison is seen and thought of only as a criminal or 'offender', this can lead to a concentration on 'programmes' that claim to 'address offending behaviour', to the neglect of learning that facilitates personal development in a wider and deeper sense. This may mean a narrowing of educational aims, curriculum, activities and methods. It may also mean programmes being offered, not to all prisoners, but only to some groups who are 'targeted' as likely prospects for a reduction in re-offending.

The classical example of the abandonment of 'liberal' education in prison in favour of offence-focused programmes comes from British Columbia in Canada in the early 1990s. Federal authorities stopped funding highly successful 'humanities' courses that had been provided in prisons for some 20 years by Simon Fraser University. Instead, the authorities wanted an education that concentrated on 'criminogenic factors' through programmes such as cognitive skills, anger management and addiction. Ironically, subsequent research funded by the Canadian Correctional Service itself indicated the humanities courses had, in addition to their general educational benefits, been much more effective in reducing recidivism, the supposed objective of the new courses (Duguid, 1997; 2000).

Yet, Canadian offence-focused 'programmes' have been exported and have had significant influence in parts of Europe, often displacing more conventional education, particularly in Britain, Netherlands and the Nordic countries. Clearly, what happened in Canada amounted to a narrowing of perspective whereby the person in prison came to be seen mainly as an 'offender', rather than as a 'whole person' with all the strengths and weaknesses, relationships, experiences and potential, hopes and fears, that being a 'whole person' implies. Consequently, opportunities for people to develop via a fuller education were lost.

The curtailment to 'the undeserving'

If people in prison are regarded in a very negative way, perhaps as 'career criminals', or (as an Irish Justice Minister once described those in his care) as 'thugs and scumbags', then there will seem little point in offering them quality education. For education is about drawing out talent, ability, potential and creativity. If one is blind to such positive qualities in people, then one will not be inclined to support genuine education for them.

For most of the last two or three decades, adult education was a strong feature of the prison system in Ireland, with a high level of teaching resources funded by the Department (i.e. Ministry) of Education, good funding for other aspects from the Department of Justice, and strong support generally from prison authorities. For many years, more than half of all prisoners participated in education, about half of these on a very intensive basis. Facilities varied from prison to prison, but for many years virtually all prisoners had access to education if they wished, and a wide range of learning opportunities was available, with especially strong activity in basic education, university education and the creative arts.

Much of this provision remains, due in particular to the ring-fenced allocation of teachers from the Department of Education. However, the support of prison authorities for prison education has been less evident in recent years. Most aspects of Irish Prison Service finance for education were cut in half between 2008 and 2010, appropriate facilities for education are now often not provided when new prison accommodation is built, and for hundreds of prisoners locked up for 22 or 23 hours each day access to education is clearly impossible.

Without doubt, a crucial factor in this undermining of education in Irish prisons is the more negative perception of the prisoner held by those running the system ever since the emergence of a 'punitive turn' in Ireland in the late-1990s. Both the administrative and political leadership, at least until recently, routinely described the entire populations of particular prisons, or of the prison system as a whole, in terms that depict them *all* as dangerous, violent and a threat to the public. Such imagery is not supported by the evidence, but is, of course, reinforced by similar discourse in part of the media (Warner, 2011). Very recently, there have been some indications of less blinkered and less punitive attitudes, but for several years many of those running the prison system saw little sense in supporting developmental activity like education for people who they could not envisage developing. This attitude applied especially to costly courses like university education, and what were seen as frivolous activities such as the creative arts. In 2008, 141 men and women studied at university level in Irish prisons, through the Open University and the National College of Art and Design. By 2013, that number was reduced to 49 (Deputy Lynch asks Minister Shatter, 2013).

The 'employability' curtailment

Another way in which 'the whole person' in prison is reduced to just one aspect of his or her personality is when the focus of support is restricted primarily to vocational training, the apparent idea being to help them get jobs upon release (see Downes, 2011).[3] Even this narrowed aim is often only a pretence, and the reality in many prisons is that the 'training' offered does not correspond to labour market requirements, the 'working day' is far shorter, and digital exclusion means that a vital requirement for most jobs in the community is prohibited. A UK Home Office study (Harper and Chitty, 2005) of basic skills provision in prisons concluded that most prisoners who found employment post-release were returning to a previous job or had obtained work through family or friends. Furthermore, when those prisoners who re-offended were asked about possible factors that could have caused this, their most common responses related to drink or drugs, and lack of money. Fewer linked their offending to problems with employment, obviously their difficulties were more complex and deep-seated (see also Schuller, 2009).

Clearly, many in prison need the opportunity to develop in a range of ways, beyond training for a specific job, if they are to overcome difficulties and give themselves a better chance of obtaining *and retaining* employment. Yet a concentration on training for work fits easily with having a diminished view of the man or woman in prison. It also fits with attitudes in welfare policy which see work, especially hard manual work, as an appropriate punishment generally for the poor and marginalised who are seen as lazy and feckless. A concentration on work and training for work is widespread in European prisons, and notably so in Eastern Europe and England.

---

[3] The following comment on the English Green Paper (which was referred to in the Introduction above) in a recent EU report questions this overemphasis on employability: 'While a national strategic approach to access to lifelong learning in prison is to be welcomed in this English example, it nevertheless remains a concern regarding the subordination to the goal of employment of other legitimate goals of lifelong learning – such as active citizenship, social cohesion and personal fulfilment. An EU Commission conception of access to lifelong learning operates with a broader lens and includes all citizens, and therefore encompasses prisoners and prison education within its ambit and relevance' (Downes, 2011: slide 72).

This outlook is evident in England in the words of Lord Filkin, Minister for Offender Education, who said: 'The sole priority of education is to get offenders into work – anything else is a means, not an end' (OCR, 2005). Consequently, important elements of education are ignored or reduced. For example, there has been a serious undermining of the arts in English prisons, and Paul Clements speaks of 'the reduction of opportunity in prison to engage with the arts, replaced by an instrumental agenda concerning basic, key and cognitive skills.' (2004: 169).

Regarding work as a punishment is common to many social policies in Britain, and is clearly bound in to negative stereotyping of those at the sharp end of such policies. In August 2011, Travis writing in *The Guardian* reported: 'Unemployed offenders face a full week of unpaid work, including the possibility of hard manual labour, under plans to toughen community penalties as an alternative to prison.' In the same edition, a commentator depicts the thinking of the political leadership in relation to those receiving social welfare thus:

> ... that there is a degenerate rump at the bottom of society, and no point getting hot and bothered about any apparently harsh or intrusive treatment meted out to them. They are, after all, nothing like the rest of us (Harris, 2011).

The curtailment by measurement

Another form of curtailment of education in prison is one which arises in education generally beyond the prison walls, although its common source may be seen in 'managerialism', a feature David Garland (2001) identifies in penal policy and which he classifies as one of the 'indices' of the culture of control. Bureaucratic attitudes, whether in prison systems or in the wider world, can give rise to *curtailment by measurement,* where the focus of education provision is on 'making the measurable important, rather than making the important measurable' – and so, the box-tickers in head offices devise impractical forms for the practitioners to complete.

The associated emphasis on cost-effectiveness is a worrying trend for many prison educators, as they are aware that the outcomes of complex educational processes can be very challenging to measure and frequently fall beyond the scope of economic analysis. Given the complexity of the learning process, and because learning is not confined to the prison classroom, it is almost impossible in reality to single out and identify for certain outcomes that can be attributed to specific educational initiatives or processes. Moreover, the lack of clarity as to what comprises education in the prison context can make it even more difficult to establish which activity it is that makes a difference or is most effective. Furthermore, by concentrating on returns to the state rather than gains by the individual learner, only part of the picture is drawn. Regardless of such significant issues, 'difficult to measure' (but highly valuable) interventions are in danger of being side-lined in favour of less complex, 'easier to measure' ones.

In this way, some of the most important progressions that can take place through education, and those that are particularly important in a prison context, can be marginalised. This deeper learning is not recognised and consequently not valued, at least in the eyes of the bureaucracy, as it is not very amenable to measurement. Such progressions include becoming aware of new potential within oneself, finding new interests, growing in self-confidence and self-esteem, and growing in understanding, in particular in social and civic awareness.

Managerialism also tends to hamper one of the defining characteristics of adult education, the distinctive methodology of adult learning and teaching. For example, adult education methods traditionally respect the life experience of the learner, and see this experience as a valuable resource in the learning process. The starting point is always 'what you know rather than what you don't know'. Adult educators also tend to be trusting of the judgement of the learner, and accept that he or she should have a substantial say in what is studied, how it is studied and how learning is assessed.

Such methods are difficult to square with a form of education that focuses narrowly on the restricted range of skills or knowledge stipulated by bureaucracy. Even more critically, such adult education methods are hardly reconcilable with the various negative ways of thinking about people in prison.

Conclusion

In 1990, the UN General Assembly adopted the 'Basic Principles for the Treatment of Prisoners', which outline the need to treat prisoners with respect and recognise their rights and freedoms as set out in the Universal Declaration of Human Rights. They included specific reference to the right of prisoners to take part in 'cultural activities and education aimed at the full development of the human personality' (United Nations, 1990). This suggests the same kind of wide curriculum and broadly-aimed education outlined by the Council of Europe; and in speaking of the 'full development of the human personality' it echoes the Council of Europe concept of 'the whole person'.

However, in many locations in Europe, the education offered to people in prison has been reduced and hollowed out by a retreat from a wide concept of education, and by a failure to recognise the full personality of the imprisoned person. The curtailment of education and the diminished view of the prisoner are closely-related issues. Education in prison in much of Europe is often far less than it can be, as a result of two related over-simplifications: rather than seeing 'the whole person' in the prisoner, we see only the criminal; and rather than offer adult education in all its challenging richness, we offer only a limited range of 'skills'.

The late K. J. Lang, the long-serving Director General of the prison system in Finland, had a deep sense of those in his prisons as people– the lives they lived, their backgrounds, their personalities, their needs. Remarkably, for someone in his position, he identified their greatest need as being to improve their self-confidence. He said, 'Therefore, all our efforts when organising correctional services should be analysed as to their ability to support, uphold and redress the self-esteem of the prisoner' (Lang, 1993: 9). The kind of education methods and activities that would flow from such a perspective (not to speak of the different penal policy) would be radically different from those, for example, which merely think of 'addressing offender behaviour' or of 'getting offenders into work'. Neither the people in prison, nor the learning opportunities offered to them, should be so crudely simplified or reduced.

Bibliography

Bailey, I. (2004) 'Overview of the Adult Literacy System in Ireland and Current Issues in its Implementation'. In: Comings, J., Garner, B. and Smith, C. eds. *The Annual Review of Adult Learning and Literacy, Volume 6.* (Harvard: NCSALL, National Center for the Study of Adult Learning and Literacy).

Brookfield, S. D. (1987) *Developing Critical Thinkers: Challenging Adults to Explore Alternative Ways of Thinking and Acting.* San Francisco: Jossey-Bass.

Clark, M. C. (1993) 'Transformational Learning'. In: Merriman, S. B. ed. *The new update on adult learning theory. New Directions for Adult and Continuing Education, No. 57.* San Francisco: Jossey-Bass.

Clements, P. (2004) 'The Rehabilitative Role of Arts Education in Prison: Accommodation or Enlightenment?' *Jade,* 23(2): 169-178.

Costelloe, A. and Warner, K. (2008) 'Beyond Offending Behaviour: The Wider Perspectives of Adult Education and the European Prison Rules'. In: Wright, R. ed. *In the Borderlands: Learning to Teach in Prisons and Alternative Settings, 3rd edition.* San Bernardino: California State University.

Council of Europe (1990) *Education in Prison. Recommendation No. R (89) 12 adopted by the Committee of Ministers of the Council of Europe on 13 October 1989.* Strasbourg: Council of Europe.

Council of Europe (2006) *European Prison Rules.* Strasbourg: Council of Europe.

Deputy Lynch asks Minister Shatter. (2013) 30 May, 805(3): q. 203, PQ 26328/13.

Downes P. (2011) *A Systems Level Focus on Access to Education for Traditionally Marginalised Groups in Europe: Comparing Strategies, Policy and Practice in Twelve European Countries. Comparative Report: LL2010.* Brussels: Education and Culture DG. Available at: http://lll2010. tlu.ee/meetings/final-conference-on-lll2010-results-leuven-7-8th-of-february-2011/lll2010-leuven-conference-presentations/comparative-sp5-presentation-leuven-feb-2011.pdf/view (Accessed 31 January 2014).

Duguid, S. (1997) 'Cognitive Dissidents Bite the Dust – the Demise of University Education in Canada's Prisons'. *Journal of Correctional Education,* 48(2): 56-68.

Duguid, S. (2000) *Can Prisons Work: The Prisoner as Object and Subject in Modern Corrections.* Toronto: University of Toronto Press.

England and Wales. Ministry of Education and Skills (2005) *Reducing Re-Offending Through Skills and Employment.* Norwich: The Stationery Office. Available at: http://www.unlock.org.uk/userfiles/file/employment/Reducingreoffendingskillsandemployment.pdf (Accessed 29 January 2014).

European Commission (2011) *Prison education and training in Europe – a review and commentary of existing literature, analysis and evaluation.* Brussels: Education and Culture DG.

European Union Council (2009) *Council conclusions of 12 May 2009 on a strategic framework for European cooperation in education and training 'ET 2020', EU Council (2009/C 119/02).* Strasbourg: Publications Office of the European Union.

Garland D. (2001) *The Culture of Control: Crime and Social Order in Contemporary Society.* Oxford: University Press.

Harper, G. and Chitty, C. (eds.). (2005) *The impact of corrections on re-offending: a review of 'what works'.* London: Home Office Research, Development and Statistics Directorate.

Harris, J. (2011) 'Working for peanuts – a new recipe for the likes of them'. *The Guardian,* 24 August.

Hughes, R. J. and Spark, R. (n.d.) *What is Critical Literacy?* Available at: http://www.wordtrack.com.au/lit/crit.html (Accessed 29 January 2014).

Lang, K. (1993) What kind of prisoners do we meet in the 1990s?, *Report from 'Beyond the Walls', conference of European Prison Education Association.* Sigtuna, Sweden, 14-17 June.

Mezirow, J. (2000) 'Learning to Think Like and Adult: Core Concepts of Transformation'. In: Mezirow, J. et al. eds. *Learning as Transformation: Critical Perspectives on a Theory in Progress*. San Francisco: Jossey-Bass.

Norway. Ministry of Education and Research (2005) *Education and Training in the Correctional Services: 'Another Spring'. Short Version of the Report to the Storting (2004-2005)*. Oslo: Ministry of Education and Research. Available at: http://www.epea.org/uploads/media/AnotherSpring_Norway_.pdf (Accessed 29 January 2014).

OCR (2005) *Offender Learning and Skills News*, February.

Pratt J., Brown, M., Brown, D., Hallsworth, S. and Morrison, W. (2005) *The New Punitiveness: Trends, theories, perspectives*. Cullompton: Willan Publishing.

Schuller, T. (2009) *Crime and Lifelong Learning*. Leicester: National Institute for Adult and Continuing Learning.

Travis, A. (2011) 'Jobless offenders face tougher work in the Community'. *The Guardian*, 24 August.

United Nations. (1990). *General Assembly: A/RES/45/111*. Available at: http://www.un.org/documents/ga/res/45/a45r111.htm (Accessed 29 January 2014).

Warner K. (2011) 'Valued members of society? Social inclusiveness in the characterisation of prisoners in Ireland, Denmark, Finland and Norway'. *Administration*, 59(1): 87-109.

15

Speaking the Truth to Power: *Parrhesia,* Critical Inquiry and Education in Prisons

Aislinn O'Donnell and Jonathan Cummins

'That's a slave's life – to be forbidden to speak one's mind' (Jocasta speaking to Polyneices in Euripides' *The Phoenician Woman.*)

'The man who exercises power is wise only insofar as there exists someone who can use *parrhesia* to criticise him, thereby putting some limit to his power, to his command' (Foucault, 2001: 29).

Introduction

This chapter reflects upon the question of education in one contemporary institution: the prison. Its setting is the Republic of Ireland, but these reflections should also be of interest for anyone thinking about education more broadly. Unusually for a piece of writing about education in prison, it argues that a central principle guiding any approach to education that claims to involve critical inquiry must be to create a space for *parrhesia* or 'fearless speech' for all participants. We explain why this is of particular importance in the prison. *Parrhesia* is described as 'speaking one's mind', 'speaking truth to power' or 'truth-telling'. This latter sense should not be understood in a confessional or legal sense; rather it involves the kind of examination of self by self that was promoted by the Ancient Greeks and which came to form part of a lineage that extends from the Pre-Socratics to Early Christians. We examine the significance of different exercises of *parrhesia* – personal, institutional and political – for the person in prison, as human being and as citizen. We also wish to acknowledge that those working within institutions may also feel and be silenced, but this chapter will not reflect on *parrhesia* in relation to their experiences.

As Bruce Arnold (2009) and others have argued, the Republic of Ireland is yet to come to terms with the troubling and brutal legacy of its institutions, including the forced detention of thousands of men, women and children in psychiatric institutions and industrial and reformatory schools. Many of the men and women in our prisons today have been affected directly or indirectly by this history. It is important to bear this in mind when reflecting upon contemporary practices of imprisonment if we want to think critically about our present. What seems commonplace or acceptable practice at one moment of time can appear monstrous to later generations, and legacies of abuse, trauma and conflict persist trans-generationally.

Even with knowledge and acknowledgement of this, it may still feel discomfiting to examine contemporary institutions with a critical eye. Indeed, for many of the general public, little of substance is, or can be, known of the history and *modus operandi* of our institutions. Nor is there a great deal of appetite to understand rather than to judge, for which the media bear considerable responsibility. It remains near impossible to hear the testimony or voice of the prisoner in the public domain without caricature or censure. It is difficult for researchers to gain access to closed institutions, or for those inside to feel that they can speak without censure. To help us to reflect upon our institutions and our practices therein we suggest adopting an approach that has been called 'critical freedom'. This asks that we look at our present as though through the eyes of a stranger, suspending our ready-made preconceptions about how things are, or even how they ought to be. This practice constitutes an integral dimension of teaching in philosophy and art at third level. Indeed, perhaps this is needed if imprisonment is to be re-imagined.

The lived experience of incarceration

The Jesuit Centre for Faith and Justice Report, *The Irish Prison System: Vision, Values, Reality* (2012), underscores the conviction, also articulated in the *Whitaker Report*, that imprisonment itself is the punishment and no further punishment should be inflicted upon the prisoner (Committee of Inquiry into the Penal System, 1985). Both reports acknowledge that unfortunately far from serving as institutions to humanise, as all institutions should, prisons damage people. 'Depth' of imprisonment is a significant contributory factor in determining the quality of life of the person in prison. It is, without doubt, important to ensure that prisoners have rights, such as access to families, appropriate living conditions, sufficient time out of the cell, just as it is important that the European and Irish Prison Rules as well as the recommendations of the Committee for the Prevention of Torture are implemented, but improvements in these areas alone may not be sufficient. Reports, like the Council of Europe's (CoE) 1990 Report, *Education in Prison*, (1990) draw the reader's attention to factors that can help a prisoner cope with his or her sentence. One of these is education, and the CoE argues that the ethos of adult education in the prison ought to be continuous with provision outside.

To understand the significance of imprisonment for a human being we must begin with the quality and nature of his or her lived experience. Being in prison means 'doing time'. We all understand what it means to experience different qualities of lived experience. Illness, boredom, loneliness, joy, laughter, anxiety, despair, and fear change the texture and atmosphere of a situation and a life. If we spend but a short time reflecting on imprisonment, we will quickly understand how living under a regime of near total surveillance, often locked up for between 17 and 23 hours a day, in stressful conditions, possibly dealing with addiction or violence, can quickly corrode the identity and deepen the isolation of the prisoner. We ought to become even more concerned when we hear stories of people who are no longer disturbed by these conditions so habituated are they to this life, sometimes having spent much of their lives since childhood in institutions. Habituation aside, any person on a moderate to long sentence will find that institutionalisation is inevitable.

Our imagination in respect of the prison tends to be limited, in part because of the partisanship of much of the media and in part because we live in a culture saturated with images of violence, criminality and prisons. It is also limited because the image of this institution has been constituted through polarised discourses at considerable variance with one another. One position views the sole function and purpose of the prison to be punishment, and even vengeance, whilst another position, often termed liberal, locates it as a site for potential personal redemption and/or rehabilitation, including preparation to re-enter the social and civic spheres. The role of education is thus deeply ambiguous: sometimes its very existence is sharply contested; sometimes its primary function is to act in the service of other objectives, such as reducing recidivism; at other times it is presented as a vital tool for rehabilitation or personal development. It has become increasingly rare to hear arguments in the public domain that support the adult educational ethos that underpins the CoE report.

The situation is further complicated when education is itself instrumentalised by some prisoners who perceive it (often correctly) to be part of a broader network of control to which they should subject themselves in order to secure a more favourable outcome before a parole board or a judge. In such cases what may appear to be *parrhesia* may be just a form of flattery. Vansieleghem notes, 'The flatterer is someone who, when speaking, works to enhance the superior's sense of power in order to get what he wants from him. In making use of the superior's superiority in this way, he also reinforces it' (2011: 329). Still others may resist education if they view participation as an extension of a broader socialising and correctional agenda that includes, for example, life skills courses, anger management, or personal development courses[1], or if it is seen to be part of a system and society they view (often correctly) as unjust.[2]

In a set of meditations written for O'Donnell's philosophy class, one man who was in prison wrote:

> A long stay in prison, as you may well think, is not good for a variety of reasons: health, financial, mental and many more. However, you can maintain your health and perhaps even become healthier, and you can just about maintain relationships outside. Your biggest fear is keeping your sanity, your mental health and not letting your personality change too much for the worse because of what you are going through. Institutionalism will sneak up on you after years of incarceration. This cannot be avoided. It happens, and you have to be aware of it sneaking up on you, trying to take over you and change you. At the end of each day, have a think about what happened during that day and analyse your actions. If you are careful and aware, you fend off the institutionalism, boredom and lethargic feelings.

He then offers some advice to the novice prisoner:

> You now have a lot of free time on your hands so use it wisely. Education, the gym or a combination of all that is on offer in prisons today. Make no mistake. You are in a war, a war to keep your sanity, dignity and self-respect whilst all those around you succumb to drugs, depression and suicide.

The severity of this man's analysis of the effect of imprisonment should not be underestimated. The *Whitaker Report* powerfully communicated what it meant to be imprisoned. Many of its find-

---

[1] See Costello and Warner, 2003. Also see Duguid, 2000.

[2] See Bayliss, 2003. In this essay, Bayliss questions the implications of expectations that prison education will increase chances for employment and reduce recidivism. He also raises a series of criticisms of curricula centred on core or basic skills and the cognitive-behavioural agenda in prisons.

ings are resonant with imprisonment today whilst few of its recommendations were heeded:

> The ordinary citizen, with his own home, free to come and go as he pleases, able to choose his company and pastimes finds it difficult to visualise the lot of the prisoner, confined within a forbidding perimeter and bleak environment, shut up alone in a cell for sixteen hours of every day, his movement restricted at every turn by locks and bars, his daily regime one of utter predictability and barely tolerable monotony, deprived of access to a toilet at night, under constant observation and thus enjoying no privacy, his correspondence censored, his visits regulated and supervised, no time in private with loved ones, and in the case of a 'subversive', not only frequent strip searching but never an embrace of even a handshake from a wife or child (A relaxation was approved in March 1985 for Portlaoise prisoners). Such deprivations and constraints are not all a prisoner suffers: they are usually accompanied by social stigmatisation for life, a lowering of dignity and self-esteem, reinforcement of feelings of inadequacy, diminished scope for the exercise of moral responsibility, loss of self-confidence, depression, a stronger inclination towards the criminal subculture and towards institutionalisation and, in many cases, irretrievable breakdown in family life and relationships (Committee of Inquiry into the Penal System,1985: 38).

Another man writes:

> This isn't home. This is never home. Nothing good will come from here. It's evil and crawls up and down the blood of everyone here. Trauma and pain exist here in laughter. That isn't right. It's scary. If you have ever wondered what a snail feels like after being hit with a sledge-hammer. Come to prison to plan your future.

> 'What will you do today?' 'Eh, the same thing as every day...'. And it's not being glib. If I don't do the same thing at the same time every day my mental health declines and I will then become physically incapacitated in an environment

so hostile and fluid that soon friend and foe imagines your death as an escape.

Parrhesia, Flattery or Silence?

When reading these observations and accounts, one might be tempted to abandon oneself to hopelessness. This is the full reality of life in prison for many men and women. Yet, such testimonies also constitute an example of a form of *parrhesia* that has emerged from philosophy classes. Truth is being spoken to power in their address. As citizens, perhaps we should begin to ask, since these are *our* prisons, what is our responsibility, if any, to those who inhabit them? Do we have a responsibility to understand *our* institutions? Should being in prison mean that one should be silenced? Most prisons not only strive to ensure that the voice of the prisoner is not heard in the public domain, but also serve to foreclose opportunities for self-determination, critical analysis or speaking freely within the walls for prisoners. (The commitment to a collective identity and to a set of beliefs and values of 'political prisoners' – usually Republican prisoners in the context of the Republic of Ireland – can lend itself to a different experience from that of other prisoners.) However, broadly speaking, for many prisoners there is little support for genuine self-reflection, critical thought or even social critique, as they try to figure out what is required of them by the system, or simply ignore the system, including education. The belief that the regime has no interest in fostering the thinking of prisoners was succinctly voiced in a conversation with one man in O'Donnell's philosophy class:

'They don't want you to think, they want to think for you.'

'Who is "they"?'

'All of them. The system.'

As Bayliss also argues, the difficulty of coping with imprisonment is compounded by the variety of ways, rightly or wrongly, that prisoners feel compelled to 'play the system' to ensure release or transfer (2003). Courses offered for personal transformation or development, when tied to models of assessment that report to the regime, or which focus on ascertaining whether one has made the appropriate choices and/or is fit for release or transfer, tend to have the consequence of focusing the prisoner's attention on ensuring that they say what is expected of them.[3] The lack of opportunity for truthfulness or honesty because of fears of sanction is not specific to the institution of the prison, but it becomes intensified given the depth of imprisonment experienced in many prisons, and the real consequences of failure to meet standards, in particular for life sentenced prisoners.

One challenge for the educator, as distinct from the professional employed to further the rehabilitative agenda of the prison regime, involves finding an approach that ensures that the aims of education neither become subordinated to systemic objectives, nor become mobilised to produce 'acceptable' identity formation. Not only do such approaches betray the commitment an educator should have to the integrity of the practice of education, they will be resisted by prisoners. The following observations were written by men who were in prison. They communicate the suspicion of any form of education that is bound to a socialising agenda or to the agenda of the State. The first man writes:

> Like the others who decided to attend the class I was curious enough to turn up, but I also suspected that like so many enterprises within the prison it might be just another way of introducing some sociological indoctrination via a simplified and childishly moralistic reduction of genuine philosophy. Prisoners generally expect to be patronised. Because most prisoners are from a similar social background, there is a tendency to assume that they have uniform values, dispositions and interests. It is also very convenient for the evangelist or proselytiser to overlook individuality in order to accommodate the sweeping generalisations of their prejudicial assertions.

---

[3] Falshaw et al., 2003.

The second writes even more critically of approaches to adult education solely aimed at attaining national accreditation from the Further Education and Training Awards Council (FETAC).

> Death has convinced teachers that Education (like life) has an inevitable end, and that end in prison seems to be in and around a FETAC Level 4. The first thing I noticed in prison was how the most 'disciplined, revolutionary scholars' refused to partake in the education provided by the prison. ... I resist all attempts at gentle reform through mind-altering FETAC level 5. Teachers don't care and neither should they because we don't depend upon them for learning. We have learned that a prison education requires a broken spirit.

It is important for the man or woman in prison to find spaces that encourage autonomy, expression, disagreement, and self-determination. If this is transformative in someone's life, this needs to be on the student's terms, just as is the case in any educational setting. Such spaces need to welcome critique, analysis, humour and justifiable anger if the exercise of critical inquiry and reflection is to be encouraged amongst all parties, including the teacher. This points to a further difficulty with much of the rhetoric of policy-makers, stakeholders and even academics in respect of education in prison. When the rationale for educational provision is couched in the language of social inclusion, skills, or employability – all of which are valuable in many respects – it reduces education to a means for attaining objectives that are oriented to life *outside* the prison, rather than looking to a process and practice of education that is responsive to the significance of doing time and what it means to be *inside*. It serves to make the prison responsible for 'fixing' complex political and social problems by deflecting attention from our responsibilities, as citizens, to address deep-rooted social inequality and injustice, such as inter-generational drug abuse and/or poverty, abuse, social exclusion, and prejudice. We should be instead asking with the student above, what will enable a man or woman to finish his or her sentence without succumbing to drugs, suicide, depression or insanity? By focusing on some of the ways in which the space of education can afford the opportunity for *parrhesia* for people in prison, we take a deliberate distance from the traditional discourses of reform and rehabilitation that have often framed discussions of imprisonment and the role of education therein.

A slave's life

> In the political field we saw that there was a need for *parrhesiastes* who could speak the truth about political institutions and decisions, and the problem there was knowing how to recognise such a truth teller (Foucault, 2001: 93).

Acknowledging that institutions, such as prisons, are *our* institutions can constitute a first step to re-imagining them and the practices that epitomise them. When psychiatrist and founder of La Borde Clinic in France, Jean Oury, claims that psychiatric institutions themselves are ill, he asks that prejudices, clichés and assumptions be swept away *(balayer)* and that other kinds of relationships or bridges *(pontonnier)* be built (2005). These two images of sweeping and creating bridges offer a powerful image for the conditions for critical thinking and critical inquiry in any educational setting. In Oury's view, it is fundamental to the healthy functioning of any institution, that an atmosphere is created that ensure that people feel permitted to express themselves freely without fear. This also means that they must be listened to, whether this be in an educational setting, within an institution or within the broader public domain.

This chapter began with the words of Jocasta as she asks for *parrhesia*. 'That's a slave's life – to be forbidden to speak one's mind.' When someone asks if they can exercise *parrhesia*, she speaks from a position of lesser power so she voices the concern that if she speaks freely, she will be punished. Another possibility is that because of the way in which a person has been constituted, for example, as prisoner, that she will not be heard. Erving Goffman's landmark book *Asylums* reveals the multitude of ways in which merely being labelled insane in an institutional setting means that even if one speaks, one won't be heard (1961). This is because it has already been decided that one is incapable of intelligent or truthful speech or action. In a discussion of Goffman's text that took place in O'Donnell's philosophy class, one of the men immediately related the experience of labelling to his experience. He laughed and said that it is just like the prison – no matter what you are saying, you will be ignored; you will be invisible.

The first condition for *parrhesia* is that you should be able to speak without fear. A second condition for *parrhesia* is that when you speak truthfully, or speak your mind, that you will also listened to as a subject – a fellow human being and citizen – rather than as an object – a case or specimen. The following transcription of a dialogue from Frederick Wiseman's 1967 documentary film, *Titicut Follies*, underscores the way in which a professional can fail to *hear* the person, who, in this case, was a patient/inmate in Massachusett's Correctional Facility, or Institution for the Criminally Insane, Bridgewater (Titicut Follies, 1967). It took a further twenty-three years before the general public in the US was permitted to see this film which documented the ordinary life of patients and staff in the institution using an approach called direct observation. (Incidentally, only 15% of men had been convicted of any crime.) Whilst the authorities had originally given full permission for the filming, and had even apparently been quite happy with the result as they saw it as an opportunity to make the case for further funding, they quickly withdrew their support when audiences voiced their outrage.

The following is an excerpt of dialogue from a staff meeting with a patient, Vladimir.

> '*Well, Vladimir, as I have promised you before, if I see enough improvement in you...*'

> 'But how can I improve if I am getting worse. I am trying to tell you, day by day, I am getting worse because of the circumstances, because of the situation. Now you tell me that until you see an improvement. Each time I am getting worse.

Obviously it is the treatment I am getting or the situation or the place or the patients or the inmates. I do not know which. All I want is to go back to the prison where I belong. I was supposed to only come down here for observation. What observation did I get? You call me up a couple of times, you say take some medication. Medication for the mind? You are supposed to take medication if you have some bodily injury. Not for the mind. My mind is fit. I am obviously logical. I know what I am talking about. ... This place is doing me harm. I come in here. Every time I come in here, you tell me I look crazy. If you don't like my face, that's another story. But that has nothing to do with my mental stability. I have an emotional problem now. Yes. That I did not have. ...

There is one thing a patient does need if they have a mental problem, an emotional problem, and that is quiet. Yet I am thrown in with over a hundred of them and all they do is walk around, yell, the television is blaring, and that is doing my mind harm ...

Back at the other place I have all the facilities to improve myself. I have the gym. I have the school. I have all kinds of uh, anything I want.

Obviously I do not need group therapy. I need peace and quiet. This place is disturbing to me. It is harming me. I am losing weight. Everything that is happening to me is bad.

If you leave me here, that means that *you* want me to get harmed which is an absolute fact. That's plain logic. And that proves that I am sane.'

'*Well.* (Smiles and leans forward.) *That's interesting logic..*'

'It's absolutely perfect. ... Obviously you intend me harm.'

Shortly, the doctor says thank you and the patient is removed.

A conversation ensues between the professionals at the staff meeting.

'*He argues in a perfect paranoid pattern. If you accept the basic premise, then the rest of it is logical. But the basic premise is not true.*'

Vladimir's basic premise is that he is being damaged by his experience of the institution, a premise that the staff fail to take seriously when they pathologise his words. This example operates as a prompt to reflect upon how our prisons operate in practice and to ask what opportunities exist for *parrhesia* within our institutions? What kind of relationships do prisoners feel they have with officers, psychologists, probation officers, governors, teachers or social workers? What difference does this absence or presence of *parrhesia* make to the experience of education within the prison? Do our institutions promote a culture of truth-telling amongst all their stakeholders? One man in prison wrote:

> A teacher in a prison is confronted daily with the corrupt and brutal excesses of a hidden state and yet in all their teaching they have failed to expose this hidden world of wrong.

What kind of responsibility do employees in institutional settings have to reflect critically and speak about what they witness? What opportunity and support is afforded to them to do so? Again, we might remember once more upon the history of institutional life in the Irish context and the ways that people, as Simon Wiesenthal and Primo Levi tell us, chose and choose not to see and not to perceive.

A test of our institutions, of democracy and of our society is whether or not there exists a culture that supports 'speaking the truth to power'. Certainly, historically, this would seem not to have been the case and we have witnessed the consequences of this with the suppression of the reports such as the critical report by Father Moore (1962) which has only been partially published, and the subsequent publication of a series of reports from the Kennedy Report (1970) to the Ryan Report (2009) and the Ferns Report (2005) which provide a devastating critique of the industrial school and reformatory system. Michel Foucault thinks that those in power ought to welcome *parrhesia*. He writes:

> The man who exercises power is wise only insofar as there exists someone who can use *parrhesia* to criticise him, thereby putting some limit to his power, to his command (Foucalt, 2001: 29).

Jocasta thinks that one might as well be a slave if one is forbidden to speak one's mind which Foucault explains when he writes:

> But something else is also implied, *viz,* that if you do not have the right of free speech, you are unable to exercise any kind of power and thus you are in the same situation as a slave (Foucalt, 2001: 29).

This is a considerable challenge, in particular for those who claim that the rehabilitative regime of a prison is a preparation for citizenship, an idea that receives ambivalent responses from the Department of Justice and the Irish Prison Service: the most recent Mission Statement of the Irish Prison Service states that it supports 'their endeavouring to live law abiding and purposeful lives as valued members of society' (which presumably means that prisoners are not yet valued members of society). Ought those who have been consigned to the most contemporary form of exile be permitted to exercise *parrhesia*? Let us return once more to the lived experience of someone in prison.

Parrhesia and practice

It might seem peculiar to draw so heavily upon an obscure philosophical concept like *parrhesia* when writing about education in the prison. However, the testimonies, analyses and observations offered above will hopefully have given some sense of why a space in which one can speak one's mind can be so important to someone within a prison environment. Speaking directly and frankly is a risk. The literature and philosophy of the Greeks tell us that when those without power wish to speak, they had to ask 'Can I use *parrhesia*?', and if this request were granted, they would then be protected from retribution or sanction. Having to ask to use *parrhesia* draws into relief the asymmetry of power relations in society.

Education is no exception, in particular when prisoners have had poor experiences of school. In order to foster the kind of criticality that is needed to do philosophy or make art, people must feel that they can speak freely.

Writing of political *parrhesia*, Foucault addresses the question that some educators will raise: Do not students need instruction or education in order to become capable of being *parrhesiastes*? Some will object to prisoners being permitted to use *parrhesia*. Ought they not be schooled, instructed, taught, rehabilitated and reformed as indeed a number of key documents indicate they should. It is perhaps, in part, a fear that one will only encounter, what he describes as 'ignorant outspokenness' that has motivated the silencing of the voice of the prisoner within the institution and outside. He outlines the central difficulty that *parrhesia* raises: 'the problem is one of recognising who is capable of speaking the truth within the limits of an institutional system where everyone is equally entitled to give his own opinion.' Democracy by itself is not able to determine who has the specific qualities which enable him to speak the truth (and thus should possess the right to tell the truth) (Foucalt, 2001: 73). So he asks:

> The first concerns the question: who is entitled to use *parrhesia*? Is it enough simply to accept *parrhesia* as a civil right such that any and every citizen can speak in the assembly if and when he wishes? Or should *parrhesia* be exclusively granted to some citizens only, according to their social status or personal virtues? (Foucalt, 2001: 72)

He finally states:

> The second aspect of the crisis concerning the function of *parrhesia* has to do with the relation of *parrhesia* to *mathesis*, to knowledge and education – which means that *parrhesia* in and of itself is no longer considered adequate to disclose the truth. The *parrhesiastes*' relation to truth can no longer simply be established by pure frankness or sheer courage, for the relation now requires education or, more generally, some sort of personal training (Foucalt, 2001: 73).

That one solely gains *mathesis* (wisdom) through formal education or training seems unlikely to us, but *parrhesia* does tend to involve undertaking some form of education or training (*askesis*). Historically, such examples of *askesis* included writing, meditation, reflection or walking, but they could equally involve film-making or philosophical analysis. We suggest that the material for making art-work, including film, or for doing philosophy must have some connection to a person's experience for it to be meaningful for them and for them to engage with it critically. For instance, it is difficult to engage with concepts of 'justice', 'equality', 'desire', or 'knowledge' unless one understands what is at stake and why it matters. To make a case or argument and to offer reasons requires that one anticipate and reflect upon and welcome possible objections and perspectives. This is part of the practice of doing philosophy or art. Rather than instruction, the student has to come to feel that he or she can speak freely, without fear. One disposition that is cultivated through this practice is truthfulness (rather than the claim to having the truth) as she struggles to understand and articulate what she thinks. Foucault writes in *The Hermeneutics of the Subject* that what is at stake in *parrhesia* is 'the frankness, freedom, and openness that leads one to say what one has to say, as one wishes to say it, when one wishes to say it, and in the form one thinks one is necessary in saying it' (Foucalt, 2005: 372). One must be able to exercise *parrhesia* if one is to engage in philosophical thought or to make an art-work that is critical and/or expressive.

However, arguably, it is not just the capacity to *be* a *parrhesiastes*, in the political sense, that is of interest to us but the experience of exercising *parrhesia* within an institution that, as a rule, is rigidly authoritarian and repressive. Creating an atmosphere of criticality and dissent that is challenging, personally and politically, and that can provoke thought, involves trust, truthfulness and fearless speech. Anyone serious about exploring ideas and images in film-making or philosophy must constantly question and examine his or her assumptions, beliefs and values and be open to having those beliefs, ideas and their own work challenged. Moreover, in prison, as outside, for some, experiencing and exercising *parrhesia* has a more intimate value, shifting the existential texture of a life and allowing for a different kind of relation to the self and others. In *Fearless Speech*, Foucault calls this personal *parrhesia*, saying that this is an exercise of destroying self-delusion, not only having the courage to tell the truth to others but also to disclose the truth about yourself. Again, to confront this truth about yourself requires *askesis* (education or training). Although this has superficial affinities with discourses of rehabilitation or even cognitive-behavioural therapy it has a deeper ethico-political resonance for Foucault, and is a way of living to which most of us fail to accede.

One man from Cummins' class describes what making film collaboratively meant to him:

> You know the conversations we had in the cell. Sometimes you can have them one on one or there will be an audience of another man and you will speak to another man like you would never speak to another human being, your wife or anyone. And having that conversation, and see for that 15 or 20 minutes in a cell, just touching that sweet-spot with someone emotionally, coming through prison, the loss, what is happening outside and that conversation you are having and then it (clicks) you turn a switch and you are getting locked up and this that and the other and from that going onto, in front of the camera. It is that springboard that gives you that opportunity to sit there, you are on in two minutes. I need to put this down, I need to put this down.

Working at third or fourth level with students in art colleges or in philosophy departments requires an approach that encourages self-determination and decision-making on the part of students. An instructional or didactic methodology is eschewed in favour or a more open-ended and unpredictable, albeit rigorous, approach that supports the student in locating his or her interests and in framing a project. The approach adopted for philosophy seminars in the prison involves students and teachers co-determining and co-developing a curriculum that allows for points of interest to emerge organically and through negotiation and dialogue. By voicing his or her doubts and questions, the teacher can transform the relations of authority that many students have come to expect from their experience of more traditional forms of education, allowing for the process of education to become an act of mutual enquiry, thus facilitating trust. When one is a researcher or practitioner as well as a teacher, it is important to be honest and share one's practice, in particular the research that emerges from thinking from the context of the prison. Since classes take an exploratory, research-oriented rather than instructional format, this cultivates the commitment to co-inquiry and demands careful attentiveness to openness and honesty.

Pursuing the practice of philosophy or art, be it collectively in a seminar or group or in a tutorial format requires disciplined rigour and thoughtfulness, criticality and responsiveness. Such capacities, attitudes and dispositions contribute to responsible *parrhesia* because these are virtues intrinsic to the practice of thinking through film and through ideas and concepts. Manifesting one's position in the form of film or writing, or even speaking, involves, in some sense, being as a *parrhesiastes* if one has taken one's practice seriously. Art and philosophy are often subversive in form and content, and may even be explicitly anti-authority but this contestation tends to be staged without violence. They can offer alternative ways to express opposition to the status quo and an individual's place in the world and its institutions, even creating physical and imagined places where the world and self can be constructed, deconstructed and reflected upon.

So, if prisons are to be re-imagined, then whose voices will be heard? What role does education have to play in the practice of *parrhesia*? If we are to re-imagine our institutions, can we create a civic culture that welcomes *parrhesia* even from within the walls of the prison?

Bibliography

Arnold, B. (2009) *The Irish Gulag: How the State Betrayed its Innocent Children*. Dublin: Gill and MacMillan.

Bayliss, P. (2003) 'Learning behind Bars: Time to Liberate Prison Education', *Studies in the Education of Adults*, 35(2): 157-172.

Committee of Inquiry into the Penal System. (1985) *Report of the Committee of Inquiry into the Penal System* (Whitaker Report). Dublin: Stationery Office.

Costello, A and Warner, K. (2003) 'Beyond 'Offending Behaviour': The Wider Perspectives of Adult Education and the European Prison Rules', *9th EPEA International Conference on Prison Education*. Langesund, Norway, 14-18 June.

Council of Europe. (1990) *Education in Prison*. Strasbourg: Council of Europe.

Duguid, S. (2000) *Can Prisons Work? The Prisoner as Object and Subject in Modern Corrections*. Toronto: University of Toronto Press.

Falshaw L., Friendship, C., Travers, R. and Nugent, F. (2003) 'Searching for 'What Works': An Evaluation of Cognitive Skills Programmes', *Home Office. Online Findings*. Available at: www.homeoffice.gov.uk/rds/pdfs2/r206.pdf (Accessed 20 July 2012).

Foucault, M. (2005) *The Hermeneutics of the Subject*. New York: Picador.

Foucault, M. (2001) *Fearless Speech*. Los Angeles: Semiotext(e).

Goffman, E. (1961) *Asylums: Essays on the Social Situation of Mental Patients and Other Inmates*. New York: Anchor Books.

Jesuit Centre for Faith and Justice. (2012) *The Irish Prison System: Vision, Values, Reality*. Dublin: Jesuit Centre for Faith and Justice.

Oury, J. (2005) *Le Collectif: Le Séminaire de Sainte Anne*. Nimes: Champ Social.

Titicut Follies (1967) Frederick Wiseman [DVD]. Massachusetts: Zipporah Films.

Vansieleghem, N. (2011) 'Philosophy with Children as an Exercise in Parrhesia: An Account of a Philosophical Experiment with Children in Cambodia'. *Journal of Philosophy of Education*, 45(2): 321-37.